The Cold War

Mike Sewell

Tutor in History, Cambridge University
*Institute of Continuing Education and
Fellow of Selwyn College*

CAMBRIDGE
UNIVERSITY PRESS

CAMBRIDGE UNIVERSITY PRESS

Cambridge, New York, Melbourne, Madrid, Cape Town, Singapore, São Paulo

Cambridge University Press
The Edinburgh Building, Cambridge CB2 8RU, UK

www.cambridge.org
Information on this title: www.cambridge.org/9780521798082

First published 2002
7th printing 2007

Printed in the United Kingdom at the University Press, Cambridge

A catalogue record for this publication is available from the British Library

ISBN 978-0-521-79808-2 paperback

ACKNOWLEDGEMENTS

Cover, © Bettmann/CORBIS; 40, www.nsa.gov; 44, 84, 105, 131, Popperfoto;
65, Dwight D. Eisenhower Library, Department of Defense Subseries, box 4,
JCS (10); 100, AKG London.

The cover photograph shows President Nixon welcoming the Soviet leader
Leonid Brezhnev at the White House on 18 June 1973.

Contents

Contents

Abbreviations

ABM	Anti-Ballistic Missile
CCP	Chinese Communist Party
CMEA	Council on Mutual Economic Assistance or Comecon
CPSU	Communist Party of the Soviet Union (Bolshevik)
CSCE	Conference on Security and Cooperation in Europe
DDR	Deutsche Demokratische Republik (former East Germany; also GDR German Democratic Republic)
EDC	European Defence Community
FRG	Federal Republic of Germany (former West Germany)
IMF	International Monetary Fund
INF	Intermediate Nuclear Forces
KPD	German Communist Party (see SED)
MBFR	Mutual and Balanced Force Reductions
MFN	Most Favoured Nation
MIRV	Multiple, Independently-targeted Re-entry Vehicle
NATO	North Atlantic Treaty Organisation
NSA	National Security Agency
OAS	Organisation of American States
OSS	Office of Strategic Services (the secret US warfare organisation, abolished by Truman after the end of the Second World War)
PRC	People's Republic of China (its army is referred to as the PLA)
SALT	Strategic Arms Limitation Treaty
SAM	Surface-to-Air Missile
SDI	Strategic Defense Initiative or 'Star Wars'
SEATO	South East Asia Treaty Organisation
SED	East German union of left-wing parties. (The successor to the KPD was created in a more or less forced merger with the SPD (Social Democrats) to form the Socialist Unity Party)
START	Strategic Arms Reduction Treaty
UNO	United Nations Organisation

Introduction

In the 1830s, the French writer Alexis de Tocqueville predicted, in a way that mingled ideals, political systems and geopolitics, that Russia and the USA would dominate world affairs:

> All other peoples seem to have nearly reached their natural limits . . . [The American] relies on personal interest and gives free scope to the unguided strength and common sense of individuals. The [Russian] in a sense . . . concentrates the whole power of society in a single man. One has freedom as the principal means of action; the other has servitude.[1]

The superpower confrontation (that came to be known as the Cold War) in the decades after the Second World War manifested all these traits and more. This book is an attempt to describe its course and the main themes that emerge from its history.

The Cold War was a bundle of contradictions. The arms race involved the real risk of annihilation of the human race. Fear of nuclear holocaust meant that stability was prized, even when this meant effectively co-operating with ideological rivals in managing dangerous situations. One leading historian of the confrontation has described it as the 'long peace', pointing to the stability of the Cold War international system and the absence of great power wars.[2] At the same time, regional conflicts around the developing world were exacerbated (in fact, some were created) by the Cold War and massive loss of life ensued. The confrontation was ideological and military, yet it ended when politics and economics in the Soviet bloc dictated a new course. The end of the Cold War saw Europeans breathe more freely, yet the disorder of the subsequent years has blighted Europe as well as other continents. The Cold War has ended, yet its legacies remain, including minefields in Mozambique, Angola and Cambodia that kill and maim thousands, rotting nuclear submarines in Russian ports, US confrontation with Cuba, Russian sensitivity and antagonism to NATO, instability in Afghanistan[3] and uneasy efforts to ease confrontation in Korea.

The end has prompted re-evaluations of the beginnings. The collapse of the Cold War in eastern and central Europe[4] pointed the focus of scholarship about its origins back towards Soviet policy there. A US policy maker who was intimately involved in these events offered an evaluation that perhaps narrows the focus too much but reminds us of lasting US perceptions:

> The Cold War was not, in its essence, a set of misunderstandings, mistakes, and miscalculations. It was the product of Soviet conduct, above all Soviet

domination of Eastern Europe and the forward deployment of more than half a million Soviet troops in the heart of Europe. The Cold War began in, and because of, Eastern Europe.[5]

This focus has been all the more marked because the end of the Cold War also saw the release of documentation from archives in that region, as well as some in Moscow, that allowed scholars for the first time to write truly multi-archival, international histories. In the 1990s, for example, Hungarian, Czech and other former Warsaw Pact archives were used to produce full accounts of the Hungarian Rising of 1956 and the Warsaw Pact intervention in Czechoslovakia in 1968. This book aims to synthesise conclusions derived from the new Cold War scholarship. Such is the flood of work that it can only suggest some of its depth and offer a glimpse of its richness.

Historians and sources

Limited availability of sources constrains all historians: we don't know what we can't know. For students of contemporary history there are additional problems. We don't know what we are not permitted to know. We are sometimes deliberately misled and we are sometimes so close to events that we don't know the significance of what we know. Significance can change in the light of new events. If, as it is reported, the Chinese statesman Zhou Enlai felt that it was still too soon to comment on the significance of the French Revolution, what hope is there for contemporary historians?

What we think we know and how we interpret it will be altered by time and events. New material will continue to emerge that will force reinterpretations. The Cold War might still yield secrets in the way 1970s disclosures about Ultra[6] transformed historians' understanding of the Second World War. There is an aspect of Cold War studies that makes them especially prone to such revelations: during the Cold War, and to an extent to this day, the history of the confrontation has been written using essentially Western sources. Our knowledge of the details of Western policy making and politics remains deeper on many issues than for the Soviet side, where sources on most controversies have been much scantier and less reliable.[7] For years Milovan Djilas's[8] recollections were the best source available to Western scholars about Stalin. Khrushchev's memoirs and defectors' accounts gave a partial view in more ways than one. In the last decade important material has emerged. Its declassification, however, has not always been the result of an open process and its provenance is sometimes doubtful. Availability of sources is still a problem, despite the efforts of bodies such as the Cold War International History Project.[9] Much material remains inaccessible, especially in Moscow, Belgrade and Beijing, and there is much that awaits declassification in Western capitals. Many conclusions are, therefore, provisional.

If Cold War historians are prisoners of their sources, so they are the hostages of contemporary politics. The Cold War involved a battle for the past into which historians were drawn. (There was a joke about the Soviet system that said it was the first society in which the future was scientifically certain whereas the past continually changed.) In Cold War studies debates about the past have reflected competing visions of the future as well as the circumstances of the time. Some work, such as patriotic or ideological histories whose conclusions were obvious from their premises, was undertaken as much to influence opinion on contemporary matters as to study the past objectively. Scholars' investigations can reflect their views on contemporary affairs. Richard Pipes' Russian history textbooks, Isaac Deutscher's biography of Stalin and William Appleman Williams' vision of an aggressive and expansionist USA reveal as much of the authors' contemporary concerns as of their historical researches.

The two sides in the Cold War went out of their way to influence history and to mould perceptions of events in the light most favourable to them. This trend included attempts at plausible deniability for covert operations, propaganda efforts, forgeries and attempts to influence intellectuals and opinion shapers.

Attempts to assert control of societies in the present led to attempts to control interpretation of the past. Not until the very end of the USSR did the authorities in Moscow permit historians to publish the truth about the secret protocols of the Molotov–Ribbentrop Pact of 1939 or the April 1940 massacre of Polish officers on Stalin's orders.[10] British governments refused to acknowledge the peacetime existence of the security services, let alone their role in such matters as the overthrow of Mossadeq in Iran or plots to assassinate Nasser of Egypt. For decades, Italians knew little or nothing of the role played by the CIA in their crucial 1948 elections. The CIA was somehow behind any political perturbation in the developing world. The KGB was allegedly responsible for the European peace movements of the 1980s. In such a climate myths proliferated (and still do: some continue to believe that Americans are being held captive in Vietnam years after the end of the war there). The combination of governmental secrecy and active measures of disinformation remains a serious problem for the historian.[11] A member of the CIA's historical division recently undertook research into the CIA's operations against the Arbenz government in Guatemala in the 1950s. He found that recommended reading for the CIA's training courses had included historical work reliant on sources that were part of a CIA-backed 'Psyops'[12] campaign of rumour and falsehood. The Cold War produced history in more ways than one.[13]

Access to previously closed sources has facilitated major reinterpretations of some old controversies and revealed how far the availability of sources and contemporary politics affected historians' perceptions. The debate, based on US and South Korean material, about whether there had been a chance to avert the Korean War has been altered thanks to material that describes the Stalin–Mao–Kim Il Sung triangle of decision making. Their reaction to Dean Acheson's pronouncement of an offshore security perimeter, for example, can be evaluated more confidently than ever before.[14] The debate about whether the West lost a chance to split the communist world before the 1960s has been transformed by new sources that reveal how unhesitating Mao was in his 'lean to the left' after 1949.[15] We are now in a position where such book titles as We now know are not without justification.[16]

The history of the early Cold War shows how views have developed. The initial scholarship outside the Soviet bloc, where analysis was subordinated to party doctrine and all information was tightly controlled, relied heavily on the public record as presented by Western leaders. The power politics/realist interpretation of world affairs that emerged from the Second World War was the dominant analytical framework for both policy makers and scholars. The political assumption that dealing with one totalitarian despot was much like dealing with another found its scholarly counterpart in the literature on totalitarianism. Both based their thinking on the 'lessons' of the 1930s.[17] The orthodox view was steadfastly 'realist', based on ideas about the primacy of power politics.

By the 1960s, and with a continued reliance on Western sources only, a mirror image emerged, itself the product of Cold War politics. Analyses of the origins of the Cold War were 'revised' by a generation of historians who took Williams' ideas and applied them in the midst of the ferment over the war in Vietnam. The revisionist image of a defensive, passive USSR and an aggressive USA stood old notions on their head as it depicted domestic politics, a search for markets or raw materials, and the demands of advanced capitalism as driving US policy.[18] For both sides only US sources were available in any depth and even many of these documents were inaccessible. Contact with Soviet scholars was near to non-existent. Indeed, the USSR had no institute for the study of the USA until the détente era. All this led to overconcentration on US actions and a schematic image of the USSR. The USA's role as the key agent of developments was emphasised by apologists and critics whose sources reflected a Washington-based viewpoint. As European archival material became more accessible in the 1970s the role played by third parties came to be appreciated more fully.[19] Newly released US government documents, new developments in the Cold War itself and scholarly criticism eroded the revisionist critique. By the 1980s scholars were writing new, post-revisionist syntheses on Cold War origins.[20] Since *glasnost*,[21] materials released from former Warsaw Pact sources have tended to support some older 'orthodox' analyses against revisionist accounts that were based on exclusively Western sources.[22]

Release of documents by governments remains carefully controlled. When President Yeltsin sought to make gestures of reconciliation towards Hungary and South Korea by partial releases of documents about 1956 and 1949–53 respectively, controversy ensued because of their alleged incompleteness. Commentators detected the influence of domestic and international political agendas.

These developments are not unique to Cold War history. Interpretations of contemporary history run through stages that are the product of both the collective imagination of the generation that experienced it and the availability of material. Journalism is characteristic of the immediate aftermath of events. This can appear in newspapers, periodicals such as *Foreign Affairs* or books. Halberstam's treatment of US policy towards Vietnam is a good example, as are recent works by Oberdorfer or Beschloss and Talbott on the end of the Cold War.[23] They rely heavily on interviews and privileged access to key individuals and they tell the first version of a story from a contemporary perspective.

Memoirists, biographers and commentators produce the next wave of scholarship. Examples include books written by 'Camelot' insiders in the years after Kennedy's assassination or memoirs by figures such as Anatoly Dobrynin, the Soviet ambassador in Washington from 1962 to the mid 1980s, Mikhail Gorbachev or successive US presidents. A longer perspective informs these works and they may be based on some documentary sources. They also tend to be partisan and self-justificatory or remain engaged in old controversies.[24]

The next turn of the cycle is that more primary sources become available and perspectives change. Passions cool, self-justification becomes less of a preoccupation and the passage of time allows new perspectives to emerge. Works such as Garthoff's on the last two decades of the Cold War or Garton Ash's on the German/European question from the 1960s to the 1990s fall into this category.[25] Some works result from collaboration between the subject/author and a professional historian.[26] US scholars have pioneered a new approach, known as 'critical oral history'. This brings participants from all sides together with scholars and journalists to revisit events. Such occasions produce surprise revelations as well as new perspectives.[27]

This more mature scholarship allows greater confidence that we do indeed now know better what happened. Our understanding of the Cuban Missile Crisis, for example, has grown enormously in recent years. We have known since 1990 that there were tactical nuclear weapons on the island. We know better what Castro's and Khrushchev's motives and priorities were. We have a fuller appreciation of Kennedy's key role in US decision making. The early memoirs tended to oversimplify, to pay off old debts or scores, to be too focused on the USA and to portray the crisis decision making as much neater and simpler than was really the case. Since the late 1990s historians have returned to some extent to the original heroic account of Kennedy's actions in the crisis of October 1962, based on transcripts of White House discussions during the crisis. They have also seen more clearly how his actions and rhetoric in the previous two years exacerbated Soviet and Cuban insecurities to the point where they pursued the missile deployment.[28]

Retrospective determinism

Beyond archival revelations, Cold War history is confronted by what Garton Ash, following the eminent philosopher Henri Bergson, has termed 'the illusions of retrospective determinism'.[29] The concept refers to the dangers of reading outcomes too readily into intentions and emphasises the need to avoid assuming that the course taken by events was the most obvious or that which would lead to the best possible outcome. It is difficult now to avoid noticing the roots of the USSR's collapse throughout Soviet history. Analysis of events in East Germany in 1953, Hungary in 1956, Czechoslovakia in 1968 or Poland in 1979–82 can slip easily into assumptions that they were rehearsals for 1989.

When Gorbachev's reforms encouraged debate among historians and Soviet archives began to yield some of their secrets, Soviet scholars turned their attention to the issue of whether Stalin's rejection of the Marshall Plan had been an error. The focus of such interest reflected a different sort of retrospective determinism, no less invidious than that just discussed. It is of a piece with US historiography's Vietnam-era fixation with whether or not there was a 'US empire' bred of inherent capitalist expansionism. Present-day concerns dictate research agendas. In contemporary history this may, to some extent, be inevitable but the history produced can be flawed.

Certain ideas and actions that, with hindsight, seem mistaken or foolish should be taken seriously. Many in the 1950s assumed that a nuclear superpower war was inevitable. Many in the 1970s wrote of the détente era as the end of the Cold War. After the Helsinki Accords of 1975 there was a body of literature on the stability of the Cold War functioning as a system of international relations. Garton Ash points out how the perceived advantages and disadvantages of Brandt's *Ostpolitik* and the Helsinki process have been re-evaluated in recent years. He writes insightfully of how perceptions at the time differed from what we now consider the most significant aspects of those processes. He also suggests that reunification had a major impact on politicians' memories of their past views and utterances. A similar point is raised by Frances Fitzgerald's work on SDI.[30] She questions post Cold War claims by Reagan administration personnel that they deliberately and presciently forced the USSR to spend itself to collapse.[31] The short-sightedness of contemporary opinion and the tendency of politicians to self-serving reinterpretation of events exacerbate the problem for contemporary historians of avoiding the pitfalls of assuming one's present to be an end point rather than a way station.

History matters

A key theme of this book is that history was profoundly important in shaping Cold warriors' perceptions of their present, moulding their attitudes and priorities and, thus, limiting policy options. John F. Kennedy recommended Barbara Tuchman's *The guns of August* to policy makers to remind them of the dangers of blundering into war, which he perceived had happened in 1914. During October 1962 ExComm[32] was restrained from a surprise attack on Cuba partly because of memories of Pearl Harbor. From the time of George Kennan's interpretation of Soviet conduct in his Long Telegram of 1946 (which was hugely influential on the US government) and, more publicly, after he published an article in *Foreign Affairs* in 1947, historical analogy shaped the superpowers' understanding of their adversaries. While views differ on whether there is a 'Vietnam syndrome' that limits or prevents US military intervention overseas, memories of that conflict affected the *conduct* of US operations in Africa, the Middle East and Central America.

For Stalin, memories of Western backing for the Whites in the civil war was a crucial reference point. Andrei Gromyko recalls Stalin telling advisers at the Potsdam conference in 1945 that the Anglo-Americans wished to throttle the USSR, just as Churchill had tried to do at its birth.[33] Soviet leaders long remained conscious of such memories as they sought recognition of their status and borders, and to avoid encirclement. One historian has described Khrushchev's attitudes during the Berlin Crisis of 1958–62 as 'a cocoon of pre-1941 fears'.[34] The other great influence on Soviet leaders was the Second World War. Writing in the 1980s about Franco-German *rapprochement*, Gromyko commented, 'Have the French really forgotten so soon?'[35] Only at the very end of the Cold War did Soviet leaders overcome historic fears of Germany and accept a reunited German state.

The tendency to draw historical lessons was not confined to the White House and Kremlin. Each political culture derived lessons from its own past. To Chinese and Vietnamese leaders the memory of humiliations by European powers was a crucial formative experience. To British and French statesmen the lessons of appeasement were different from those drawn from the same period by Gromyko or Stalin. The French were obsessively concerned about the threat posed by a rearmed Germany and additionally worried that such a state might repeat the Rapallo *rapprochement* with the USSR.[36] For those reasons keeping Germany divided seemed attractive. To post-1945 German politicians the past held a variety of different lessons. For Poles the new frontiers of 1945 were a constant reminder of their historic animosity with Germany and possible revanchism.[37] The past mattered to the peoples of eastern-central Europe who reclaimed their history at the Cold War's end. Memory, experience, a sense of historical grievance or status and perceptions of the operation of historical forces all shaped the attitudes of Cold War leaders.

As such 'lessons' were assimilated by policy makers, they became unspoken assumptions that informed the interpretations of events and people. Even nuclear deterrence was an exercise in such reasoning. No-one would know whether deterrence worked until it didn't. Until then it was presumed – from the absence of actions that it was intended to prevent – that it had. To US leaders the perceived value of toughness along the lines of the 'Munich analogy'[38] became self-reinforcing as events over Iran in 1946, Cuba in 1962 and Egypt in 1973 were read as triumphs against a foe who, history taught and experience repeated, respected force.[39]

Some analogies were more flawed than others. The USSR had learned to live with US missiles in Turkey, so Khrushchev assumed that the Americans would learn to tolerate Soviet missiles in Cuba. Because the USSR had never deployed such weapons outside its borders the Kennedy administration discounted evidence that it might be doing so. US assumptions about Vietnam were informed by lessons from Munich and British counter-insurgency in Malaya, while French experience in Indochina was rejected. As May and Neustadt have argued, the key is to select the right analogy even if it is 'bothersome'.[40]

Recurrent limits and influences

History and its lessons did not stand alone in shaping the Cold War. Other noteworthy themes will recur throughout this work. Perceptions and, more generally, misperceptions were fundamental in shaping Cold War behaviour.

USA and its allies

USSR and its allies

Pacific Ocean

CANADA

USA

GUATEMALA

GR

PANAMA

CUBA

DOMINICAN
REPUBLIC

PUERTO RICO

HOLLAND–
BELGIUM–

Atlantic Ocean

Leaders of the USSR perceived
themselves 'surrounded' by the West
and its allies. In the late 1940s and the
1950s the USA developed a global
system of alliances. The map shows the
pattern of alliances in the mid 1950s.

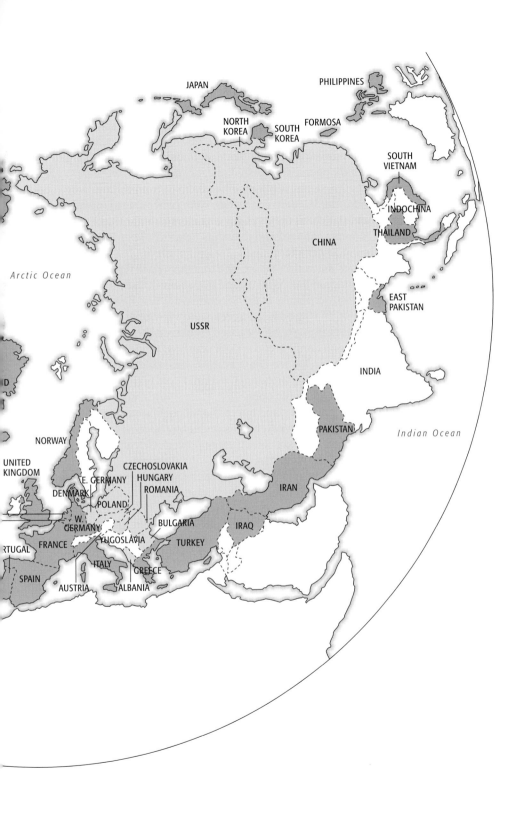

JAPAN

PHILIPPINES

NORTH
KOREA

SOUTH
KOREA

FORMOSA

SOUTH
VIETNAM

INDOCHINA

THAILAND

CHINA

EAST
PAKISTAN

Arctic Ocean

USSR

INDIA

PAKISTAN

Indian Ocean

NORWAY

IRAN

UNITED
KINGDOM

CZECHOSLOVAKIA

HUNGARY

ROMANIA

E. GERMANY

DENMARK

POLAND

W.
GERMANY

BULGARIA

IRAQ

TURKEY

RTUGAL

FRANCE

YUGOSLAVIA

ITALY

GREECE

SPAIN

AUSTRIA

ALBANIA

D

Ideas about one's country's security and how to promote it produced policies that made others more insecure. Notions of credibility, deterrence, status, prestige and saving face all played a key part in a confrontation whose global nature exaggerated the importance of being seen to be winning.

More than ever we appreciate that from the time of the Marshall Plan to *perestroika* and *glasnost* the Cold War was an economic as well as a political competition. Both superpowers built huge stocks of arms and gave lavish aid to their allies, while also seeking to compete in domestic growth and welfare. In so doing, both strained their systems. Ideology drove them to compete and drove them to aid their friends. The Western economies were better able to provide guns and economic assistance, as their system was more adaptable to technological and economic changes and they thus came to be perceived as more successful than the Soviet alternative.

Both sides placed limits on confrontation, and this theme will repeatedly emerge. From an early stage in the Cold War the threat of warfare on a scale that would dwarf even the destructiveness of the Second World War had an impact on superpower behaviour. During both the Korean and Vietnam wars there was a reluctance to take steps that might have caused escalation towards nuclear confrontation. The costs and dangers of the Cold War bred tendencies to co-existence that modified and limited confrontation. Real Cold War figures had long internalised Q's advice to that archetypal fictional Cold warrior, James Bond, always to keep an escape route open.

Other themes will recur. Domestic and international politics interacted in a two-way process in all countries. Weaker allies frequently became tails that wagged the dog in their manipulation of their more powerful friends. This leverage of the weak limited the simple bipolarity of the Cold War and meant that the superpowers never operated in a world that was totally dominated by them and their policies. Countries other than the superpowers influenced the Geneva conferences of 1954 and 1955[41] or the Berlin Crisis of 1958–62. Their leaders (such as Adenauer, Ulbricht and Macmillan) played independent roles and often manipulated, as well as followed, their patrons.

The Cold War was not just a geopolitical contest for power between two states. It involved other actors, it had a strong ideological component and it affected the daily lives of millions of people. Leaders' belief systems played a major part in limiting and defining options. Their personalities mattered hugely, perhaps more in the communist states than in the Western democracies. Domestic political and economic considerations also played a major role in all powers' calculations. In all states there was a strong influence from vested interests and from bureaucratic politicians. In the one-party states there were ideological and other factions. In the liberal states partisan politics constantly influenced foreign policy. As we are only beginning to appreciate, the history of secret intelligence communities must also be integrated into the diplomatic and military histories.

In the USSR and other communist states another theme recurred. Their leaders persistently manifested a strong desire to secure recognition of their status as equals of the capitalist powers. A leading Soviet expert on the USA called this 'revolutionary inferiority syndrome'.[42] This affected Soviet diplomacy from the interwar years all the way to the end of the Cold War. This is evident in works such as Chuev's excerpts from his conversations with Molotov or from Andrei Gromyko's memoirs. It was clearly in evidence in the Soviet leaders of the 1940s and 1950s. Khrushchev's son remembered his father's response to being invited to the USA: 'Who would have guessed, twenty years ago, that the most powerful capitalist country would invite a Communist to visit? This is incredible. Today they have to take us into account. It's our strength that led to this.'[43] The touchiness was also clear in Chinese relations with both superpowers. In East Germany diplomatic recognition of the state's permanence, as of the post-1945 borders, was a key feature even as West German policy traded qualified recognition for 'buying free' dissidents and economic links that rendered the DDR dependent on the West.

Buffeted by these often conflicting pressures, the people implementing the foreign policies of the superpowers were often inconsistent. They could and did change their minds and pursue contradictory policies in pursuit of multiple ends. Their actions frequently had unintended consequences and their inability to read the motives and behaviour of outsiders to their systems led them to acts that brought about the very behaviour in their opponents that they had sought to prevent. Short- and long-term motives and gains could conflict.

All this means that any effort to render the Cold War too simple is doomed to failure. It had no single cause, no single driving force and no single factor that brought it to an end. We do not yet know enough about it to offer more than a tentative suggestion about its significance. The study of the Cold War is only just beginning to be a matter of international research in which we know enough about most major participants to write international history. This book tries to do justice to its complexities and contradictions, while also telling the story of the fifty years war[44] that shaped our world.

Notes and references

1 A. de Tocqueville, *Democracy in America*, tr. G. Lawrence, New York, 1988, pp. 412–13.

2 J. L. Gaddis, *The long peace*, Oxford, 1987, pp. 215–45.

3 In the war on the Taleban regime in Afghanistan in 2001, the USA used former Soviet territory as a base of operations against groups it had backed against the USSR in the 1980s. The situation in Afghanistan in the years after 1991 was the outcome of Cold War interventions intersecting with local rivalries.

4 Poles, Czechs and Hungarians consider themselves central, not eastern, Europeans, therefore Warsaw, Prague, Budapest and Berlin may be said to be in eastern-central Europe while Bucharest, Minsk and Kiev are in eastern Europe.

5 R. Hutchings, *American diplomacy and the end of the Cold War*, Baltimore, 1997, p. 36.

6 Ultra was the codename for the Allied effort to decrypt German codes and remained secret until 1975.

7 Some issues of the period since détente, notably concerning Germany, Poland,

Czechoslovakia and Hungary, reverse this pattern because of lustration policies regarding the documentary records of the fallen regimes.

8 Milovan Djilas, *Conversations with Stalin*, London, 1963. He was a leading Stalinist in Yugoslavia who eventually broke with Tito and published his memoirs in the West.

9 Cold War International History Project [henceforth CWIHP] material is available online at http://cwihp.si.edu

10 M. Vulfsons, *Nationality Latvian? No Jewish. Cards on the table*, Riga, 1998, pp. 79–85, 104–15, recounts his efforts to force a reluctant Gorbachev to openness about 1939. P. and A. Sudoplatov, *Special tasks. The memoirs of an unwanted witness – a Soviet spymaster*, tr. J. L. and L. P. Schechter, London, 1994.

11 See C. Andrew and O. Gordievsky, *Instructions from the centre*, London, 1993, pp. 47–52, 140–55, 190–201, on KGB disinformation, or 'active measures', in the 1980s.

12 'Psyops', or Psychological Operations campaign, spread disinformation and propaganda and aimed to destabilise the enemy while boosting morale at home.

13 N. Cullather, *Secret history. The CIA's classified account of its operations in Guatemala, 1952–1954*, Stanford, 1999, p. xii.

14 For example, K. Weathersby, 'To attack or not to attack?', *CWIHP Bulletin*, no. 5 (1995); also S. Goncharov, J. Lewis and Xue Litai, *Uncertain partners: Stalin, Mao and the Korean War*, Stanford, 1993, pp. 101–04, 254–56.

15 W. I. Cohen et al, 'Rethinking the lost chance in China', *Diplomatic History*, vol. 21 (1997).

16 J. L. Gaddis, *We now know. Rethinking Cold War history*, Oxford, 1997. See also reviews by R. Ned Lebow, 'We still don't know', *Diplomatic History*, vol. 22 (1998); and M. Leffler, 'The Cold War: what do "we now know"?', *American Historical Review*, vol. 103 (1999).

17 See, for example, G. Kennan, *American diplomacy*, Chicago, 1951; or Hannah Arendt, *The burden of our time*, London, 1951, on totalitarianism.

18 Compare A. M. Schlesinger, 'Origins of the Cold War', *Foreign Affairs*, vol. 46 (1967); and Barton J. Bernstein, 'America in war and peace', in his *Towards a new past*, New York, 1967. The flavour of the controversies was caught by Norman Graebner, 'Cold War origins and the continuing debate', *Journal of Conflict Resolution*, vol. 13 (1969). See also M. Leffler, 'The interpretive wars over the Cold War, 1945–60', in G. Martel, *American foreign relations reconsidered*, London, 1994.

19 For example, P. Boyle, 'The British Foreign Office view of Soviet–American relations, 1945–46', *Diplomatic History*, vol. 3 (1979); or D. C. Watt, 'Introduction', in A. Iriye and Y. Nagai (eds.), *The origins of the Cold War in Asia*, New York, 1977, p. 14, for his comments on pluralist interpretations. The first wave of such scholarship was synthesised in D. Reynolds, 'The origins of the Cold War: the European dimension', *Historical Journal*, vol. 28 (1985).

20 J. L. Gaddis, 'The emerging post-revisionist synthesis on the origins of the Cold War', *Diplomatic History*, vol. 7 (1983).

21 *Glasnost* (openness) was one of Gorbachev's reform policies after 1985. It was intended to stimulate debate and criticism within the system and to help create *perestroika* (restructuring).

22 J. Halsam et al, 'Soviet archives: recent revelations and Cold War historiography', *Diplomatic History*, vol. 21 (1997). For a perceptive appraisal of recent scholarship, see O. A. Westad, 'The new international history of the Cold War', *Diplomatic History*, vol. 24 (2000).

23 D. Halberstam, *The best and the brightest*, New York, 1969; D. Oberdorfer, *From the Cold War to a new era: the United States and the Soviet Union, 1983–1991*, 2nd edn, Baltimore, 1998; *The turn*, 2nd edn, London, 1992; and M. Beschloss and S. Talbott, *At the highest levels: the inside story of the end of the Cold War*, London, 1993.

24 A. Dobrynin, *In confidence. Moscow's ambassador to America' six Cold War presidents*, New York 1995. Schlesinger, *A thousand days. John F. Kennedy in the White House*, London, 1967. R. Hilsman, *To move a nation*, Garden City, N. Y., 1967. Memoirs such as M. S. Gorbachev, *Memoirs*, London, 1995; R. Nixon, *RN: the memoirs of Richard Nixon*, London, 1978; H. Kissinger, *Years of upheaval*, London, 1982; *The White House years*, London, 1979; *Diplomacy*, New York, 1994; A. Gromyko, *Memories*, tr. H. Shukman, London, 1989; and F. Chuev, *Molotov remembers. Inside Kremlin politics*, ed. A. Resis, Chicago, 1993, all present more problems but remain important sources.

25 R. Garthoff, *Détente and confrontation: American–Soviet relations from Nixon to Reagan*, revised edn, Washington, DC, 1994; *The great transition: American–Soviet relations at the end of the Cold War*, Washington, DC, 1994; and T. Garton Ash, *In Europe's name: Germany and the divided continent*, London, 1993.

26 Recent examples include R. S. McNamara with B. VanDeMark, *In retrospect. The tragedy and lessons of Vietnam*, vintage edn, New York, 1995; McNamara, J. Blight, R. Brigham, T. Biersteker, Colonel H. Schandler, *Argument without end. In search of answers to the Vietnam tragedy*, New York, 1999; R. R. Bowie and R. H. Immerman, *Waging peace. How Eisenhower shaped an enduring Cold War strategy*, Oxford, 1998; and R. Bissell and J. E. Lewis, *Reflections of a Cold warrior: from Yalta to the Bay of Pigs*, New Haven, 1996. Henry Stimson and McGeorge Bundy, *On active service in peace and war*, New York, 1947, was an early example.

27 J. G. Blight, B. J. Allyn and D. A. Welch (eds.), *Cuba on the brink. Castro, the Missile Crisis and the Soviet collapse*, New York, 1993, pp. 6, 10.

28 Key early works include R. Kennedy, *Thirteen days*, London, 1969; and G. Allison, *Essence of decision*, Boston, 1971. New perspectives include A. Fursenko and T. Naftali, *'One hell of a gamble': the secret history of the Cuban Missile Crisis*, London, 1997; V. Zubok and C. Pleshakov, *Inside the Kremlin's Cold War. From Stalin to Khrushchev*, Cambridge, Mass., 1996, ch. 8; R. Ned Lebow and J. Gross Stein, *We all lost the Cold War*, Princeton, 1994, chs. 2–6. The critical oral histories include J. G. Blight, B. J. Allyn and D. A. Welch (eds.), 'Back to the brink: proceedings of the Moscow conference on the Cuban Missile Crisis', *CSIA Occasional Paper*, no. 9, Latham, Md., 1992; J. G. Blight and D. A. Welch (eds.), *On the brink: Americans and Soviets reexamine the Cuban Missile Crisis*, New York, 1990; and Blight et al, *Cuba on the brink*. New sources include E. May and P. Zelikow, *The Kennedy tapes: inside the White House during the Cuban Missile Crisis*, Cambridge, Mass., 1997; and *Foreign Relations of the United States* [henceforth FRUS], 1961–63, vol. IX, 'Cuba', Washington, DC, 1996.

29 T. Garton Ash, 'Ten years after', *New York Review of Books*, 18 November 1999.

30 The idea behind SDI was that a massively complex array of satellites, early warning systems, anti-ballistic missiles and lasers might be able to protect against nuclear missile attack. Proponents of the system advocated a space shield (hence the allusive popular shorthand of 'Star Wars'). Critics maintained that it would not protect against terrorist attacks, Cruise missiles, conventional bombers or submarine launched missiles and that it could only ever be developed at enormous cost, while counter-measures would be cheaper and easier to produce. They suggested that it was little more than an expensive way of procuring a localised 'point defence' system that might protect missile silos and in so doing would destabilise deterrence.

31 F. Fitzgerald, *Way out there in the blue. Reagan, Star Wars and the end of the Cold War*, New York, 2000; and L-E. Nelson, 'Fantasia', *New York Review of Books*, 11 May 2000.

32 ExComm, or the Executive Committee of the National Security Council, was convened by Kennedy to deal with the crisis.

33 Gromyko, *Memories*, p. 111. Andrei Gromyko was the Soviet foreign minister from 1957 to 1986. He had previously served as ambassador in Washington (1943–45), to the UNO (1946–52) and in London (1952–53) and had held top posts in Moscow.

34 V. Zubok, 'Khrushchev and the Berlin Crisis (1958–1962)', *CWIHP Working Paper*, no. 6 (1993), p. 8, following Walter Lippmann's contemporary views.

35 Gromyko, *Memories*, p. 191.

36 In 1922 the USSR and Germany, then both pariah states, had secretly come together to conclude the Rapallo Treaty, in which they agreed to co-operate on military and economic matters.

37 General Jaruzelski interview, *Cold War*, programme 1, Turner/BBC, 1998.

38 The 'Munich analogy' summarises the line of thought that Chamberlain's appeasement of Hitler at Munich in 1938 only encouraged Hitler to increase his demands. Therefore, the 'lesson' was that dictators should be resisted rather than appeased.

39 In Iran in 1946 the USSR appeared to Truman to bow to US pressure to back down from supporting a revolution against the Shah and from keeping its wartime forces in the country. Egypt in 1973 refers to the Yom Kippur Crisis when Kissinger thought that it was his tough stance that prevented the USSR from intervening to aid its ally against Israel.

40 Yuen Foong Khang, *Analogies at war: Korea, Munich, Dien Bien Phu and the Vietnam decisions of 1965*, Princeton, 1992; and E. May and R. Neustadt, *Thinking in time*, New York, 1986, especially ch. 5.

41 J. Cable, *The Geneva conference of 1954 on Indochina*, 2nd edn, London, 2000, stresses British influence in a Cold War summit. Z. Karabell, *Architects of intervention. The United States, the third world and the Cold War, 1946–1962*, Baton Rouge, La., 1999; and M. Light (ed.), *Troubled friendships. Moscow's third world ventures*, London, 1993, both stress peripheral influences on the superpowers. See also T. Smith, 'A pericentric framework for the study of the Cold War', *Diplomatic History*, vol. 24 (2000).

42 G. Arbatov, *The system: an insider's life in Soviet politics*, New York, 1993, pp. 169, 189. See also Dobrynin, *In confidence*, p. 104, for how a test ban treaty was seen in Moscow as 'another confirmation of the Soviet Union's place as a superpower alongside the United States'.

43 S. Khrushchev, *Khrushchev on Khrushchev. An insider's account of the man and his era*, tr. W. Taubman, London, 1990, p. 356.

44 R. Crockatt, *The fifty years war*, London, 1995.

Origins of the Cold War to 1946

1917–20	Russian Revolution and Civil War
1922	*April:* Rapallo Treaty between Germany and USSR
1933	*November:* USA recognises USSR
1934–39	Stalin pursues collective security policies
1939	*23 August:* Molotov–Ribbentrop Pact
	September: Second World War breaks out in Europe, USSR expands to the west
	November: USSR goes to war with Finland
1941	*June:* Germany invades USSR
	December: Pearl Harbor bombed and USA drawn into Second World War
1943	*May:* Comintern dissolved
	November: Tehran conference
1945	*February:* Yalta conference
	May: War ends in Europe
	July: Potsdam conference
	August: USSR declares war on Japan; atomic bombs dropped; Pacific War ends
1945–46	*November to April:* Iranian Crisis
1946	*February:* Stalin makes his election speech
	March: Churchill makes his 'iron curtain' speech
	Summer: Turkish war scare; Greek Civil War
	September: Clifford Memorandum; Byrnes makes his Stuttgart speech
1947	*12 March:* Truman Doctrine speech

Unlike most 'hot' wars of the twentieth century, the Cold War did not begin at a precise date. For any given country, various moments can be identified as symbolic declarations of Cold War. The clearest, perhaps, is Mao Zedong's statement in the summer of 1949 that the new China would 'lean to one side'.

The issue of 'when?' affects those of 'why?' and 'by whom?'. Most historians see the events of the years immediately after the Second World War as crucial. They posit that the Cold War was by no means inevitable and that it was brought about by the inability of the victorious powers to come to an arrangement among themselves. Others see the same period as vital, but place the emerging confrontation between the USA and the USSR in the context of the growth of two empires.[1] In this story the USSR and the USA extended their power and their principles into the vacuum created by the collapse of Europe's traditional powers. Others suggest that the Cold War was the result of Stalin's (or the Soviet leadership's) insecurity,[2] ideology,[3] search for military security[4] or historically conditioned sense of vulnerability.[5] This list by no means exhausts the possibilities on the Soviet side. In contrast, other scholars have stressed the importance of Western motives and the West's role as the key agent of developments rather than simply reacting in response to the East's policies. The 1970s revisionists' efforts to blame the USA for the entire Cold War confrontation now seem dated.[6] Many still view the drive of US leaders for dominance (the better to achieve their vision of national security through world order and stability) as the crucial element in the power struggle.[7] Others take a similar line, arguing that domestic politics, and especially the role of lobbies, drove a corporatist polity towards confrontation.[8] Yet others emphasise the role played by the USA's commitment to democracy as a principle,[9] US concerns about strategically important regions[10] or the interaction between the USA and its European allies, who are sometimes depicted as manipulating the Americans into confrontation.[11] Yet others adopt a more international approach, with one scholar making the case for a psychological explanation for the USA's position.[12]

Roots before 1941

There is also a widespread range of possible explanations that date further back than the end of the Second World War. Many scholars trace US–Soviet or Western–Soviet rivalry back to the Russian Revolution.[13] They stress the part played by the ideological antagonism between Wilson's and Lenin's views of the future of the world as well as their different political interests in leading to conflict. In this version, bourgeois politicians such as Wilson, Lloyd George and Clemenceau made peace after the First World War in a context coloured by the Bolshevik seizure of power and by revolutions in Hungary and Germany (their temporary failure did not reassure these leaders about the stability of democracy). As well as punishing Germany for the war, the West also sought to isolate the new USSR. They chose not to moderate the harsh terms of the Treaty of Brest-Litovsk that Germany had imposed on Trotsky and the Soviet leadership in 1918 (which had involved the loss of much territory). They also intervened in support of anti-Bolshevik forces.

Interpretations of the Cold War's origins that emphasise the personalities, security interests, experiences and ideology of the Soviet leadership tend to feature such experiences prominently. They locate the roots of the Cold War in the sense of vulnerability that underlay the USSR's persistent quest for security through territory. The ideological imperative of seeking world revolution fused, in the era of civil war, with concern about subversive activities by anti-Bolshevik forces at home and led to an abiding fear of encirclement by 'imperialists' plotting communism's downfall (see map on pp. 8–9). Such fears were fed by denunciations of Bolshevism by foreign leaders, military intervention and backing for the Whites by the West in the civil war and loss of territory in the 'shame' of the Treaty of Brest-Litovsk.[14] This was strengthened by the memory of the Bolshevik regime's exclusion from the diplomacy of the 1920s. This produced, according to Nation, a pattern of oscillation between accommodation, isolation, ideological confrontation and co-existence that lasted throughout Soviet history. The Cold War was only part of this bigger pattern.[15]

Attitudes that affected behaviour after 1945 were moulded in the West too. Bondholders, White Russian exiles and anti-Bolsheviks who feared the spread of communism propagated ideas that linked domestic and foreign anti-communism and saw the USSR as a threat to domestic and international stability, prosperity and property. These ideas would later resurface. The acts and the attitudes of the major protagonists, going back at least to 1917, shaped the Cold War.

At the same time, ideological confrontation on all sides was capable of being subordinated to the state's interests. As 'socialism in one country' took hold in the USSR, the interests of revolutionary communism came to be associated with those of the Soviet state. The Comintern might have been the organisation through which international communism was co-ordinated from Moscow but, as Mao Zedong repeatedly found, local communists were not necessarily the beneficiaries. Stalin insisted that the USSR's interests came first:

> We never had any orientation towards Germany, nor have we any orientation towards Poland and France. Our orientation is towards the USSR alone. And if the interests of the USSR demand *rapprochement* with one country or another which is not interested in disturbing the peace, we adopt this course without hesitation.[16]

After the Rapallo Treaty of 1922, the USSR maintained connections with Germany. From 1933 it followed popular front alignments and anti-fascism until the Molotov–Ribbentrop Pact in August 1939. This shows how the quest for Soviet security took precedence. The pact returned territory lost in 1917 and gave Stalin a free hand in the Baltic states, Moldavia and eastern Poland. It also meant that Stalin was spared the threat of a war on two fronts at a time when he was engaged in military confrontation with the Japanese army in the Far East.

Stalin persisted with collective security for as long as he felt that he had more to fear from Japanese–German encirclement than from the prostrate economies of the Western powers. Just as the latter were becoming more amenable to his blandishments, however, he shifted his position. In the West a persistent fear of communism held back those who might have made common cause with Stalin against Hitler – Chamberlain and French leaders, for example, found it hard to decide who was the greater threat. Stalin lost patience with them in the summer of 1939; his reason for doing so is located by the historian Kennedy-Pipe in his reading of the compromises of the Munich conference of 1938 as an attempt to turn Hitler eastwards. Nation suggests that Stalin's fear of Germany, coupled with his frustration at Western negotiating tactics, led him to decide to accommodate Hitler rather than risk war against him. Stalin leant towards xenophobic advisers, who were less internationalist than foreign minister Litvinov, whom he replaced with Molotov in the spring of 1939.

The annexations of 1939–40, the war against Finland and the move into Bessarabia demonstrate continuity with Stalin's subsequent behaviour in eastern

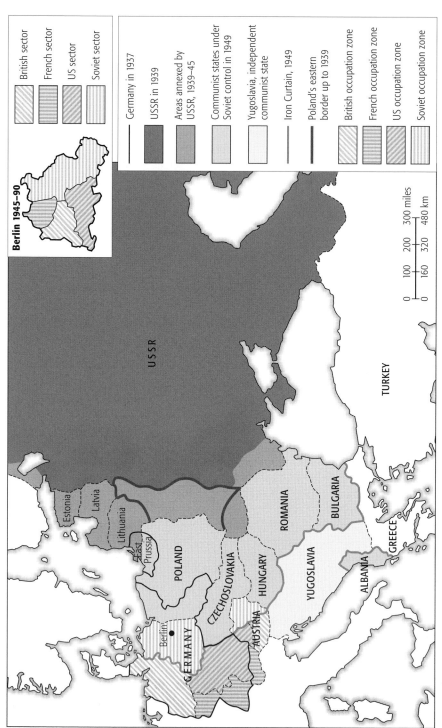

Berlin 1945–90

British sector
French sector
US sector
Soviet sector

Germany in 1937
USSR in 1939
Areas annexed by USSR, 1939–45
Communist states under Soviet control in 1949
Yugoslavia, independent communist state
Iron Curtain, 1949
Poland's eastern border up to 1939
British occupation zone
French occupation zone
US occupation zone
Soviet occupation zone

USSR

TURKEY

Estonia
Latvia
Lithuania
East Prussia
POLAND
GERMANY
Berlin
CZECHOSLOVAKIA
AUSTRIA
HUNGARY
ROMANIA
BULGARIA
YUGOSLAVIA
ALBANIA
GREECE

0   100   200   300 miles
0   160   320   480 km

Europe's borders, 1937 and 1949.

and central Europe in the mid 1940s. His major concern seems to have been to gain territory and to make the USSR bigger and more secure. Acquiring more territory was seen to provide safety, as it had traditionally done to Russian rulers.

The Second World War

With the onset of war in June 1941, Stalin (who had ignored intelligence of impending danger) sought an alliance with the Anglo-Americans. It was an alliance of convenience, not conviction, 'of desperation, not trust'.[17] Wartime priorities placed geopolitical considerations – such as the future strength of Germany, Soviet technological lag behind the Allies and the physical security of Soviet borders – ahead of ideology. Ideological mistrust and memories of Munich remained strong. This was reinforced by Stalin's suspicions that the Anglo-American strategy was to fight Hitler to the last Russian or even to countenance a compromise peace at Soviet expense. Stalin was determined that the trauma caused by the devastating invasion of 1941 must never be allowed to be repeated. Senior diplomatic advisers in the USSR planned for peace on the assumption that weakening Germany and creating a secure zone on their western border were to be the key elements of policy. Suggestions from advisers such as Litvinov that security and territory were not synonymous were rejected.[18] Nevertheless, he and others all advocated continued co-operation with Britain and the USA to maintain peace, spheres of influence in Europe and friendly anti-fascist solidarity among those states that were grateful for their liberation by the Soviets. Soviet leaders assumed that they would be able to turn Anglo-American tensions into diplomatic advantage. They also assumed that the Americans had not expanded their definition of security needs. An example of this logic can be seen in Soviet proposals at Potsdam that they be given the former Axis colonies in Africa and elsewhere. The Anglo-American solidarity in rejecting the idea came as a surprise to the Soviets.[19]

During the war, the Soviets discussed their aims with their Western allies. A British diplomat commented on a 1942 conversation with Stalin:

> When he spoke of 'minimum conditions' he meant that his government insisted on recovering the territory violated by Hitler, and they could make no concessions in this respect. Further, it was not sufficient simply to restore what existed before the war; the Soviet government must secure their North-Western and South-Western frontiers.[20]

Deals were possible, especially with the British, as is shown by the tentative agreement on percentages of influence in the Balkans in November 1944. Differences among the Allies were not simply Western–Soviet antagonisms. Soviet perceptions of Anglo-American friction were not ill-founded and were encouraged by Roosevelt's actions at the Tehran and Yalta summit conferences: on the issues of imperialism, France's future role and British influence in the Middle East, Roosevelt sided against Churchill. The US president remained confident that he could deal with Stalin on the basis of the mutual trust that had been built up during the war. When the OSS acquired a Soviet codebook, the president insisted that it be returned, uncopied, which (so far as is known) happened. The codebreakers found another way around, helped by a codebook that was seized at the end of the war in Germany.[21]

The issue of a second front in Europe, however, created significant tensions. Stalin's suspicious nature and fears for Soviet security, combined with his ideological preconceptions, disposed him to assume the worst of Western motives and to discount their explanations. His desire to maintain control of his people and to limit contact with the West caused friction when he limited landing rights for Allied bombers or fraternisation by Western servicemen in the northern port of Murmansk where convoys ran intermittently during the war. Yet these frictions were not necessarily signs that Cold War had broken out. Anglo-American frictions were occasionally as abrasive, especially in the Far East.

The key wartime Anglo-American priority was to secure Soviet participation in the Pacific War after German resistance had collapsed. This was finally achieved at the Yalta conference, a factor that is often overlooked by those who criticise Western concessions at that conference.[22] The British and the Americans remained confident that they could deal with Stalin even as they began to suspect that that co-operation might not be as easy as they had hoped. Suspicion remained strong on both sides; no-one assumed that good relations could be achieved easily and, on all sides, there were advisers who pushed their political masters towards greater caution, even confrontation. In 1946 Averell Harriman noted the downgrading of Maisky and Litvinov as a sign of a Soviet move away from co-operation.[23]

During the Second World War the term 'superpower' was coined to describe the three major Allied powers. Among them, the USA was a new, and greater, power than the world had ever seen. With its financial and military might and its technological lead over other countries, it was in a league of its own. On Roosevelt's death in April 1945 Harry S. Truman became president and learned of the Manhattan[24] and Ultra projects, which he had not known about as a senator or vice-president, but which Stalin had long known about. Spies in the atom bomb project and highly placed agents in Washington and London kept Stalin informed. Stalin's suspicions about Allied goodwill had increased as he knew that Roosevelt and Churchill were trying to keep secrets from him. The secrecy and spies indicate the high levels of suspicion within the Grand Alliance throughout the war. At the Potsdam conference Stalin kept remarkably calm when Truman spoke of a new weapon of awesome power that would soon be at his disposal. Whatever his public demeanour, though, Stalin soon had NKVD (the predecessor of the KGB) chief Beria heading up a breakneck programme to develop an atomic bomb. This bore fruit, with significant help from the spies, in 1949.[25]

The literature on the decision to use atomic bombs against Japan in August 1945 is rich in controversy. Some historians have asserted that the last actions of one conflict were the first major shots in another. Some interpretations stress Truman's desire to impress, deter or intimidate Stalin, others discount this motive entirely. Some argue that the rapid advance of the Red Army in Manchuria accentuated the need for a rapid end to the war. In the mid 1990s, as the USA debated how its national museum should commemorate the 50th anniversary of the flight of *Enola Gay* (the plane that dropped the Hiroshima bomb), historians, politicians, journalists, veterans and lobbyists conflated interpretation of the past with contemporary polemics. Cold War themes remained prominent.[26]

In the new, nuclear age all three of the victorious powers also derived lessons from past experience and history that affected their post-war conduct. The phrase 'never again' sums them up. For Roosevelt, Truman and the men who advised them, the memory of the economic chaos they saw as leading inexorably to war and the isolationism in the 1930s was crucial. The perceived mistakes of 1919 (rejection of collective security behind a US lead) and the 1930s (appeasement of dictators, US apathy in the face of aggression) were joined in their minds by the surprise attack on Pearl Harbor in December 1941. Late in the war Congress held hearings on the failure of intelligence before Pearl Harbor. The feeling was that this generation of Americans must never again be caught unawares. For Truman and senior figures such as Dean Acheson or George C. Marshall, relatively junior men like Dean Rusk and John F. Kennedy, and even young refugees such as Madeleine Albright,[27] the 'lessons' of the 1930s seemed clear. Their country must take a leading role in the world. It must do so to build a world of prosperous and stable democracies according to precepts laid out in wartime pronouncements such as the Atlantic Charter. Collective security must be pursued through new bodies such as the UNO, the Bretton Woods financial system, the IMF and the World Bank. Those who denied democracy or refused to be bound by international law and norms must be resisted. These ideas, later summarised as the 'Munich analogy', were common throughout the US and British policy establishments.

These negative 'lessons' were reinforced by the strength of the positive memories of the war years: a united country had performed prodigious feats and had projected its power abroad for good. For the generation that experienced it, this was a 'good' war. Depression gave way to prosperity, lethargy to activism and both the world and the USA were remade. When the Kennedy administration took office, the wife of one senior official commented that this was the moment when the young officers of the Second World War took command. Long after that, the personal and collective memories of the bad peace of 1919–39 and good war of 1941–45, as well as the institutional legacies of that war, continued to influence US conduct.

Ideas of collective security and post-war co-operation informed US and British plans for the post-war world. Economic interdependence, democracy, self-determination and peace were interlocking pieces of a global jigsaw conceived in Wilsonian idealism and matured in the crucible of experience. However, even during the war, this caused problems. Churchill staunchly resisted US pressure on the British Empire, especially Secretary of State Hull's attempts to attach conditions to imperial tariff preferences to US aid. They also had differences over France's status and over the future of conquered French, Dutch and British colonies in Asia.

The post-war world

A number of issues brought these principles and models into sharp conflict with Stalin's vision of a post-war world, especially over those areas, like Poland, where there were competing exiled governments. The London Poles found compromise with Stalin almost impossible. This was complicated by accusations of Soviet responsibility for the massacres of Polish officers during 1940–41, revealed by the mass graves in the Katyn woods. Stalin denounced these claims as black propaganda and blamed the Germans; for nearly 50 years the USSR denied responsibility. Over questions of post-war world order such as the fate of Poland, the Western allies ran into the Soviet policy of 'never again'.

Just as the Western powers warmed to the idea of collective security, Stalin tired of it. He wished to keep the USSR in control of its own destiny, even if this meant forsaking aid. He also anticipated communist revolution in Germany and friendly governments elsewhere in liberated Europe.[28] He also did not expect two elements of US behaviour to change from the pre-war period. He assumed that the capitalist powers would fall out among themselves after the war. Marxist-Leninist ideology, as interpreted by Stalin and his approved thinkers, predicted post-war conflict among capitalists. Marxist historical theory seemed to prove scientifically that this was a recurrent feature of imperialist behaviour and a guide to future conduct. Stalin also assumed that the USA would retreat to political isolationism and would lack the will to involve itself in European security affairs. Both assumptions were proved wrong.

Soviet leaders seem to have cherished a hope of continued co-operation with the Anglo-Americans. They also wished never again to be vulnerable to attack from the western lands of the Russian empire acquired since the time of Peter the Great. Their country's security must not again be endangered as it had been in 1812, 1914, 1919 and 1941. They planned for a westward movement of Soviet borders and for friendly regimes beyond them. The Poles, Czechs, Hungarians, Finns and probably also the Romanians and Bulgarians would have to be prepared to work out compromises that effectively limited their sovereign control over foreign affairs; in return they would be allowed control of their internal affairs. Instructions from Moscow to local communists about internal affairs were ambiguous:

> Do not put the Sovietisation of Czechoslovakia on the imminent agenda. We must not try to guess when the appropriate moment will come . . . As Stalin has rightly said, we must proceed step by step, and before taking any new step we should consolidate positions already conquered.[29]

From an early stage it was clear that the Poles would be harder than the rest to pull or push into line.

The second great stumbling block to post-war inter-allied co-operation was the future of Germany. All parties believed that Germany would rise again within two or three decades – the history of 1919–39 suggested so. The westward movement of Poland (accepted by the Allies) and Russia's seizure of territory around Königsberg (now Kaliningrad) – to be part of the Russian Federation and not of neighbouring Soviet republics – did shrink Germany and removed some of the old Prussian heartlands. Nevertheless, fears about Germany's potential remained. Everyone wanted and needed a peaceful, friendly, democratic, denazified Germany with reduced war-making potential, but history's lessons led to very different ideas about how to achieve this. Even during the war Gromyko worried that the US approach would be markedly different from the Soviet's.[30]

For Stalin, the lead was taken in the reports of his Reparations Commission written by Maisky and Litvinov. They presented schemes calling for huge German payments to compensate for the wartime destruction, factories to be dismantled, experts to be forced to work in Russia and billions to be taken as the spoils of a bitter, brutal war. They wanted Germany to be kept down for decades. Western, especially US, views were radically different. After the flirtation of Treasury Secretary Henry Morgenthau with a scheme to create a series of deindustrialised states, US policy gradually moved to more tolerant attitudes. Germany was to be reduced in industrial capacity only to the point where it could no longer wage aggressive war. Western thinking reflected ideas that the draconian terms of 1919 had fed revanchism and soured Germans to their new democratic institutions. Democratisation was to be pursued by education and persuasion as well as the exclusion of Nazis from German public life.[31]

At the Potsdam conference in July 1945 the US delegation received reports about Russian dismantling that caused Truman and his advisers grave disquiet. One suggested:

> All these removals were in complete violation of all efforts to maintain 'non-war potential' industries in Germany. The effect of the removals will be the complete destruction of employment opportunities in the area. What we saw amounts to organised vandalism directed not alone against Germany, but against the US forces of occupation. Incidentally, under the techniques used, Russia will withdraw two or three times as much from any area as would be withdrawn by the US or UK under similar circumstances. In the area which we captured and turned over to the Russians we made no removals except for a few samples of unique equipment.[32]

New reports reinforced old fears and suspicions about Soviet behaviour, especially when delays about access to the Western zones of Berlin compounded problems. Some historians see the Anglo-American stance as provocative and insufficiently sensitive to Stalin's security needs or the repercussions of the eastern war.[33] Others see the US attitude more favourably and tend to blame either Stalin himself[34] or his East German partners, Soviet troops' behaviour and local Soviet commanders' attitudes for antagonising the West.[35] Opinions vary on how quickly Stalin became reconciled to the idea of a separate East German state. Raack suggests that Stalin changed his mind in favour of dismemberment as early as mid 1945 and that popular front politics were for show only. Loth suggests that it was not until 1952 that Stalin finally gave up the idea of a reunified Germany in which he would retain influence rather than control.

Steininger goes further and argues that only Western intransigence prevented reunification, but his views have been challenged by evidence from Soviet bloc archives.[36]

The historiographical pattern is repeated when historians have looked at other parts of eastern and central Europe, including western Germany and Austria. The rapacity of Soviet economic exploitation was more than matched by the rapine of the Soviet soldiers.[37] The consequences for communist parties became clear as soon as local elections were held and pre-war levels of support for the German and Austrian communist parties were not achieved as they were in Italy, France or in the liberated lands of central Europe. Those who work mainly from US and British archives tend to attribute the decisive role to those whose words they read. Others who work from German, Russian or other sources tend to privilege the players upon whose written records they concentrate. Whatever the interpretation, however, a pattern quickly emerged of worsening relations between the Anglo-Americans and the Soviets. This was as true of reports from alarmed diplomats in countries liberated from German occupation as of soldiers and civilians in the areas which had been part of the Third Reich and which perceived the Soviets as probing for Western weakness at the periphery.[38]

The Potsdam Agreements covered Germany's denazification, democratisation, deindustrialisation and demilitarisation. In each occupation zone it soon became clear that drawing a line about whom to include and exclude from the normal day-to-day life on the basis of past records would prove problematic. All civil servants and administrators had compromised to some extent with the old regime, but their expertise was desperately needed. Viewed through ideological prisms, and sometimes exaggerated by local informants, their recruitment could easily be interpreted as deliberate cultivation. Definitions of democracy and of which parties and individuals should be allowed to participate also saw divergence between Soviet and Anglo-American policies. Politicians such as Adenauer and Schumacher with whom the Western allies sought to collaborate were bitter opponents of the KPD. Stalin's representatives tended to look to returning exiles and former KPD prisoners for advice and to promote them into responsible positions. They, in turn, had little time for the SPD or the new Christian Democrats. Recriminations followed.

These patterns bred a tendency towards dividing Germany. There were those, represented in all the victorious powers, who felt from an early date that it might not be the worst of outcomes, given assumptions of rapid German regeneration and the need to contain a resurgent Germany. No-one set out, however, to create two Germanies. Fear of a new Reich was compounded by assumptions about each occupying power's own wellbeing. The French were in no hurry to see all-German institutions reborn and were reluctant to accept German control of the Saar. They delayed any four-power co-operation during the summer and autumn of 1945. If this tended to promote division of Germany, the French minded less than others.[39] Policies and institutions that tended to promote economic, social and political divergence between the Western and Soviet zones were put into place. The British were primarily concerned about reducing the burden that occupying the industrial areas of northern Germany placed on them. The Americans were probably most inclined, early in the occupation, to seek solutions involving all four powers. The Soviets wished for revenge, reparations and also to gain access to plant and other riches from the Ruhr. This produced a clash with the British over interpreting the Potsdam decisions. The Soviets wanted a higher level of reparations, partly to rebuild their economy, partly to weaken Germany's. The British wanted a lower level to reduce the burden on their resources. By 1946 Bevin and Bidault favoured a divided Germany.[40]

There were also tensions over the occupation regime in Berlin, involving recriminations about partisan activities and complaints about restrictions on free speech from the 'bourgeois' parties. Similar developments in Austria reinforced Western alarmists' fears that Soviet behaviour amounted to wilful violation of promises and agreements made at Yalta and Potsdam and were part of a pattern of Sovietisation and expansion. British perceptions moved 'from ally to enemy' as food supplies from the Soviet zone dried up and Bevin reacted sharply to Soviet efforts to play a role and promote the SED in the British zone.[41]

Problems elsewhere

Truman introduced another potential source of friction when he abruptly terminated lend-lease aid and with his efforts at atomic diplomacy at Potsdam. In both cases Stalin became less inclined to compromise as he perceived these to be US tactics to pressure him for concessions. He reacted in a similar way to the Americans' failure to grant a post-war loan and claims that they had 'lost' the Soviet application.

In late 1945 and early 1946, the geographical focus of US attention widened from Poland and Germany to a broader Eurasian setting. The war reinforced geopolitical theories as a very influential paradigm in Western thinking about international relations. These theories held that control of the 'world island' (the western Eurasian landmass stretching from the Urals to the Atlantic) was vital to dominance in world affairs. Again deriving lessons from their experience with Hitler, Western policy makers began to interpret Soviet behaviour as part of a pattern of expansion towards that end. A reading of communist ideology reinforced this tendency to see the USSR as naturally expansionist and committed to spreading revolution. At the same time, US policy makers were committed to maintaining the USA's dominance in world affairs.

In the winter of 1945–46 matters grew worse, despite efforts to compromise. The Moscow Foreign Ministers conference in December saw some movement towards compromise, especially over Germany, but reparations and differences over the permissible level of German industry continued to cause dissension. Elsewhere, other situations reinforced suspicions and suggested to US leaders that a tough stance worked. Perceptions and misperceptions affected policies with regard to Soviet influence in northern Iran. Truman and others came to believe that a tough stance here, as on Soviet ambitions in the Dardanelles, had forced Stalin to climb down. In reality, Stalin opportunistically tried to expand

Soviet influence and, when he encountered opposition, he quickly abandoned local communists in favour of a deal on oil concessions with Iranian government ministers and the Shah. The deal was never accepted by the Iranian parliament, the Majlis.[42] At the time and afterwards, however, the US belief was that the Munich analogy was correct and that dictators backed down when confronted by resolute opposition.

Something similar occurred during war scares with Yugoslavia (still regarded as a Soviet puppet) over Trieste in the spring of 1945,[43] then Turkey and the Balkans in the spring and summer of 1946. In the latter case, alarmist intelligence was transmitted to Washington and London. A strong Western reaction ensued and Stalin's British spies communicated to Moscow that the West would fight. Stalin backed off. Diplomatic pressure on Turkey for a variety of concessions eased.[44] The 'lesson' of not appeasing dictators was reinforced.

By this time, Churchill had weighed in with his speech at Fulton, Missouri, in which he described an 'iron curtain' across Europe from Stettin to Trieste and called for vigorous Western policies. This was of a piece with George Kennan's February 1946 Long Telegram in which he advocated policies of firm and persistent containment of aggressive Soviet power.

Based at the time in Moscow, Kennan composed his Long Telegram in response to a Treasury request for information about why the USSR would not take up a loan. The brief answer was that Stalin did not wish to have any strings attached. Just as they bargained hard with the British, the Americans would not loan money to the USSR without strings. Kennan took the opportunity to stress again views he had put forward for some time. His telegram followed shortly after Stalin expressed his views in a speech he gave in February 1946. This speech was widely taken in the West as a declaration of inevitable conflict, almost a declaration of war. Yet it seems that Stalin's intention was that both these ideological remarks and other, more temperate, phrases would be heard clearly in the West. The combination of Western preconceptions and Stalin's rhetoric meant that the speech was interpreted as more hostile than it really was. Truman's alarmist advisers seized upon Kennan's telegram: Navy Secretary Forrestal had it copied and circulated to dozens of top policy makers.

Kennan was not alone in seeing in Soviet ideology, rhetoric and action a match that confirmed historical patterns of totalitarian behaviour in foreign affairs.[45] Geopolitical and economic arguments stressed that the USA must remain involved in world affairs and that democracy must be defended against aggression in the enlightened self-interest of the nation. There were dissenters and consensus evolved gradually. Under-Secretary of State Dean Acheson seems to have shifted during the first six months of 1946 to the belief that a more confrontational approach was required, convinced by the Turkish war scare.[46] Clark Clifford, counsel to the president, had long believed that there was a need for a tough policy. He summarised his view in a memorandum to President Truman that was opposed by the former vice-president, Secretary of Commerce Henry Wallace, who held out for more conciliatory policies.[47] Speaking out publicly in September 1946 led to Wallace's resignation from Truman's cabinet.

On the Soviet side there were also competing visions. Zhdanov, Molotov and the harder liners in Europe, such as Walter Ulbricht in Germany, favoured a Soviet presence there, opposed compromise and favoured rapid Sovietisation.[48] Ulbricht inclined towards partition from the time that elections revealed SED weakness at the polls; in his opinion, it would be better to run a quarter country than to be a marginal in the whole country. Those such as Litvinov, Maisky and the economist Evegnii Varga who favoured a less unilateral approach, while still expecting inter-imperialist dissension, were marginalised.[49] Stalin seems to have vacillated and played advisers off against each other. Negotiations still took place. Non-communists participated in Polish, Czech and Hungarian government. Germany's future and the status of Berlin remained uncertain. More and more, the economics and politics of the Soviet zone diverged from those of the others. More and more, there was talk of merging the British, US and, perhaps, the French zones.

During 1946 Soviet relations with its wartime allies grew increasingly fraught. Old suspicions were revitalised in disagreements over the future of Europe. Competition and rivalry bedevilled day-to-day relations in Germany and Austria. Civil war in Greece, diplomatic pressure on Turkey, and efforts to organise governments friendly to the USSR in the Balkans and eastern Europe all contributed to the deterioration of Western impressions of Stalin's ambitions. On the Soviet side, memories of the years before 1941 and conduct in the liberated lands contributed to policies that were not necessarily designed to alienate the West but frequently had the effect of doing so. Those who did not wish to see co-operation continue were gaining the upper hand in most major capitals.[50]

Document case study

The emergence of the Cold War

1.1 Soviet planning for post-war Europe, January 1944

The question of Germany's future is, of course, fundamental to our interests . . . [we propose] occupation of strategic points for not less than ten years . . . Breaking Germany up into a number of more or less independent state formations . . . Military, industrial and ideological [reparations, especially] reparations in labour . . . The USSR's aim must be to create an independent and viable Poland, but we are not interested in creating a Poland too large and too strong. In the past Poland was always Russia's enemy . . . [We must] carefully shape post-war Poland within frontiers as narrow as possible . . . [Czechoslovakia] can be an important transmitter of our influence in Central and South-Eastern Europe . . .

The USSR is interested in seeing to it that the state structure of [occupied] countries shall be based on the principle of broad democracy, in the spirit of the people's front idea. There are grounds for supposing that in such countries as Norway, Denmark, Holland, Belgium, France and Czechoslovakia these principles will be adequately realized without any pressure from without. The situation is different with such countries as Germany, Italy, Japan, Hungary, Romania, Finland, Bulgaria, Poland, Yugoslavia, Greece and Albania. There it may be necessary in order to secure the establishment of democratic regimes, to apply various measures of intervention from outside, by the USSR, the USA and Britain . . .

There are grounds for thinking that, where democratization of the regime in post-war Europe is concerned, it will be possible for the USSR, the USA and Britain to co-operate, though this will not always be easy.

Source: Memorandum from the Maisky Commission to Molotov, January 1944, quoted by A. M. Filitov, 'Problems of Post-war construction in Soviet foreign policy during World War 2' in F. Gori and A. Pons (eds.), *The Soviet Union and Europe in the Cold War, 1943–53*, London, 1996, pp. 8–11

1.2 An alternative Soviet vision, November 1944

[An understanding with Britain] could only be achieved on the basis of an amicable delimitation of security spheres in Europe, according to the principle of relative proximity. The maximum sphere of interest for the USSR can be defined as Finland, Sweden, Poland, Hungary, Czechoslovakia, Romania, the Slav countries of the Balkans and also Turkey. The British sphere can certainly embrace Holland, Belgium, France, Spain, Portugal and Greece . . .

The third, neutral sphere will include Norway, Denmark, Germany, Austria and Italy, wherein both sides will co-operate on the same footing and with regular mutual consultation.

Source: Litvinov Commission report to Molotov, 15 November 1944, quoted by Filitov, pp. 12–13

1.3 US reactions to Soviet behaviour in Germany at the war's end

Payment of reparations should leave sufficient resources to enable the German people to subsist without external assistance . . . If the Control Council fails to agree, each zone commander may still import into his own zone such supplies as his Government considers essential . . .

. . . all these removals were in complete violation of all efforts to maintain 'non-war potential' industries in Germany. The effect of the removals will be the complete destruction of employment opportunities in the [American zone]. What we saw amounts to organized vandalism directed not alone against Germany, but against US forces of occupation.

Source: Working paper of the US delegation at the Potsdam conference and E. W. Pawley to the secretary of state, 27 July 1945, *FRUS*, 1945, vol. II, 'The conference of Berlin', Washington, DC, 1960, pp. 812–89

1.4 Secretary of War Stimson reports on Europe, July 1945

We have immediate interests in a return to stable conditions – the elimination of distress conditions to ease our problems of administration and the speed and success of our redeployment. But our long-range interests are far greater and more significant. One hope for the future is the restoration of stable conditions in Europe, for only thus can concepts of individual liberty, free thought and free speech be nurtured. Under famine, disease and distress conditions . . . the opposite concepts flourish . . . If democratic interests are not given an opportunity to grow in western and middle Europe, there is little possibility they will ever be planted in Russian minds.

I therefore urge . . . that Germany shall be given an opportunity to live and work; that controls be exercised over the German people only in so far as our basic objectives absolutely require . . . The Russian policy on booty in eastern Germany, if it is as I have heard it reported, is rather oriental. It is bound to force us to preserve the economy in western Germany in close co-operation with the British so as to avoid conditions in our areas which, in the last analysis, neither British nor American public opinion would tolerate.

Source: Stimson report to Truman, 22 July 1945, on prospects for European rehabilitation, *FRUS*, 1945, vol. II, 'The conference of Berlin', Washington, DC, 1960, p. 808

1.5 The Novikov telegram, Washington, 27 September 1946

[All underlining replicates that of Foreign Minister Molotov.]

The foreign policy of the United States, which reflects the imperialist tendencies of American monopolistic capital, is characterized in the postwar period by a striving for <u>world supremacy</u> . . .

we have seen a failure of calculations on the part of US circles which assumed that the Soviet Union would be destroyed in the war or would come out of it so weakened that it would be forced to go begging to the United States for economic assistance . . .

At the same time <u>the USSR's international position is currently stronger than it was in the pre-war period</u>. Thanks to the historical victories of Soviet weapons, the Soviet armed forces are located on the territory of Germany and other formerly hostile countries, thus guaranteeing that these countries will not be used again for an attack on the Soviet Union . . .

incidents such as the visit by the American battleship *Missouri* to the Black Sea straits, the visit of the American fleet to Greece . . . have a double meaning. On the one hand, they indicate that the United States has decided to consolidate its position in the Mediterranean basin to support its interests in the countries of the Near East . . . On the other hand, these incidents constitute a political and military demonstration against the USSR . . .

The current relations between England and the United States, despite the temporary attainment of agreements on very important questions, are plagued with <u>great</u> internal <u>contradictions</u> and cannot be lasting.

in accepting the loan, England finds herself in a certain financial dependence on the United States from which it will not be easy to free herself . . .

The <u>objective</u> has been to impose the will of other countries on the Soviet Union . . .

In Germany, the United States is taking measures to strengthen reactionary forces <u>with the purpose of opposing democratic reconstruction</u> . . .

preparation by the United States . . . is being conducted with the prospect of <u>war against the Soviet Union</u>, which in the eyes of the American imperialists is the main obstacle in the path of the United States to world domination. This is indicated by . . . the siting of American strategic bases in regions from which it is possible to launch strikes on Soviet territory . . . and attempts to prepare Germany and Japan to use those countries in a war against the USSR.

Source: Extracts taken from 'Cold War origins', CWIHP; http://cwihp.si.edu/cwihplib.nsf

1.6 Kennan's Long Telegram, February 1946

[W]e have here a political force committed fanatically to the belief that with the US there can be no permanent *modus vivendi*, that it is desirable and necessary that the internal harmony of our society be disrupted, our traditional way of life be destroyed and the international authority of our state be broken, if Soviet power is to be secure . . . It has an elaborate and far-flung apparatus for exertion of its influence in other countries . . . Soviet power, unlike that of Hitlerite Germany, is neither schematic nor adventuristic. It does not work by fixed plans. It does not take unnecessary risks. Impervious to the logic of reason, it is highly sensitive to the logic of force . . . if the adversary has sufficient force and makes clear his readiness to use it, he rarely has to do so . . . World communism is like a malignant parasite which feeds only on diseased tissue . . . Many foreign peoples, in Europe at least, are tired and frightened by experiences of the past, and are less interested in abstract freedom than in security. They are seeking guidance rather than responsibilities. We should be better able than Russians to give them this. And unless we do, Russians certainly will.

Source: Extracts from J. L. Gaddis and T. H. Etzold (eds.), *Containment: documents on American policy and strategy, 1945–1950*, New York, 1978, pp. 61–63

Document case-study questions

1 What conclusions about US policy can be drawn from documents 1.3, 1.4 and 1.6?

2 What does Novikov's view of the British economic relationship to the USA, in document 1.5, reveal about Soviet priorities?

3 Evaluate Kennan's appraisal of Soviet conduct in document 1.6.

4 Compare the extracts from Soviet sources in documents 1.1, 1.2 and 1.5. What do they reveal about changing priorities?

5 In the light of these extracts and your wider knowledge, evaluate the assumptions underlying Soviet and US policies at the end of the Second World War.

Notes and references

1 J. L. Gaddis, *We now know. Rethinking Cold War history*, Oxford, 1997, chs. 1–3. See also H. Adomeit, *Imperial overstretch: Germany in Soviet policy from Stalin to Gorbachev: an analysis based on new archival evidence, memoirs, and interviews*, Baden-Baden, 1998; and G. Lundestad, *The American 'empire'*, Oxford, 1990.

2 See V. Mastny, *The Cold War and Soviet insecurity. The Stalin years*, Oxford, 1996, which builds on his previous work.

3 J. Halsam et al, 'Soviet archives: recent revelations and Cold War historiography', *Diplomatic History*, vol. 21 (1997).

4 C. Kennedy-Pipe, *Stalin's Cold War. Soviet strategies in Europe, 1943 to 1956*, Manchester, 1995.

5 R. Craig Nation, *Black earth, red star. A history of Soviet security policy, 1917–91*, London, 1992, pp. 110–60.

6 M. Leffler, 'The interpretive wars over the Cold War, 1945–60', in G. Martel (ed.), *American foreign relations reconsidered*, London, 1994; and the 1997 *Diplomatic History* symposium.

7 M. Leffler, *A preponderance of power: national security, the Truman administration and the Cold War*, Stanford, 1992; and M. Leffler, 'National security and US foreign policy', and M. McGwire, 'National security and Soviet foreign policy', in M. Leffler and D. S. Painter (eds.), *Origins of the Cold War. An international history*, London, 1994.

8 M. Hogan, *The Marshall Plan. America, Britain, and the reconstruction of western Europe, 1947–1952*, Cambridge, 1987; and his *A cross of iron. Harry S. Truman and the origins of the national security state, 1945–1954*, Cambridge, 1998.

9 T. Smith, *America's mission. The United States and the worldwide struggle for democracy in the twentieth century*, Princeton, 1994.

10 B. Kuniholm, *The origins of the Cold War in the Near East: great power diplomacy in Iran, Turkey, and Greece*, Princeton, 1980; or G. Lundestad, *America, Scandinavia, and the Cold War, 1945–49*, New York, 1980.

11 D. Reynolds, 'The European dimension of the Cold War', J. Kent, 'British policy and the origins of the Cold War', and C. Maier, 'Hegemony and autonomy within the Western alliance', in Leffler and Painter, *Origins of the Cold War*. Z. Karabell, *Architects of intervention. The United States, the third world and the Cold War, 1946–1962*, Baton Rouge, La., 1999, has good chapters on post-war Greece and Italy.

12 D. Welch Larson, *Anatomy of mistrust: US–Soviet relations during the Cold War*, London, 1997.

13 L. C. Gardner, *Safe for democracy. The Anglo-American response to revolution, 1913–1923*, Oxford, 1987; and N. Gordon Levin, jr, *Woodrow Wilson and world politics. America's response to war and revolution*, Oxford, 1968.

14 N. N. Petro and A. Z. Rubinstein, *Russian foreign policy. From empire to nation*, Harlow, 1997, pp. 19–23, 31.

15 Nation, *Black earth*, pp. xii–xiii.

16 Speech to the Seventeenth Congress of the CPSU (Bolshevik), January 1934, quoted in Petro and Rubinstein, *Russian foreign policy*, p. 30.

17 Kennedy-Pipe, *Stalin's Cold War*, p. 27.

18 Gaddis, *We now know*, pp. 23–24.

19 V. O. Pechatnov, 'The big three after World War II', *CWIHP Working Paper*, no. 13 (1995), on which this interpretation is based.

20 Quoted in S. M. Miner, 'His master's voice: Viacheslav Mikhailovich Molotov as Stalin's foreign commissar', in G. A. Craig and F. L. Lowenheim (eds.), *The diplomats, 1939–1979*, Princeton, 1994, p. 82.

21 J. E. Haynes and H. Klehr, *Venona. Decoding Soviet espionage in America*, London, 2000, p. 34 and footnotes 17–19, p. 398.

22 Sir Frank Roberts interview, *Cold War*, programme 1, Turner/ BBC, 1998.

23 Late in the war Averell Harriman, a confidant of Roosevelt's, was the US ambassador to Moscow. Maisky was the Soviet ambassador to London until 1943 and a top foreign policy adviser. From 1943 until 1946 he was Molotov's deputy in the Commissariat of Foreign Affairs.

24 During the Second World War, the USA and Britain collaborated in developing and building an atomic bomb. The US codename was the Manhattan Project.

25 D. Holloway, *Stalin and the bomb: the Soviet Union and atomic energy, 1939–1954*, New Haven, 1994, pp. 116–71; and 'The Soviet Union and the origins of the arms race' in Leffler and Painter, *Origins of the Cold War*. For an insider's account, see P. and A. Sudoplatov, *Special tasks: the memoirs of an unwanted witness – a Soviet spymaster*, tr. J. L. and L. P. Schechter, London, 1994.

26 An early example is G. Alperovitz, *Atomic diplomacy: Hiroshima and Potsdam: the use of the atomic bomb and American confrontation with the Soviet Union*, London, 1966. For summaries of the literature and political controversies, see M. J. Hogan (ed.), *Hiroshima in history and memory*, Cambridge, 1996; and E. T. Linenthal and T. Engelhardt (eds.), *History wars: the Enola Gay and other battles for the American past*, New York, 1996.

27 At her confirmation hearings in 1997 Albright stressed Munich's role in shaping her world view.

28 N. Khrushchev, *Khrushchev remembers. The glasnost tapes*, tr. and ed. J. Schechter, London, 1990, pp. 99–100.

29 Instructions from Georgii Dimitrov to Czechoslovakian communist leaders in December 1944, quoted in E. Aga-Rossi and V. Zaslavsky, 'The Soviet Union and the Italian communist party, 1944–48', in F. Gori and S. Pons (eds.), *The Soviet Union and Europe in the Cold War, 1943–53*, London, 1996, p. 180.

30 Pechatnov, 'The big three', pp. 8–9.

31 Smith, *America's mission*, pp. 27–30, hints that lessons from the reconstruction after the civil war may have suggested a policy that would, in Lincoln's phrase, 'let 'em up easy'.

32 US representative to the Allied commission on reparations to the president, 27 July 1945, *FRUS*, 1945, vol. II, 'The conference of Berlin', Washington, DC, 1960, p. 889.

33 For example, C. Eisenberg, *Drawing the line: the American decision to divide Germany, 1944–1949*, Cambridge, 1996.

34 Mastny, *Soviet insecurity*, pp. 24–25; Kennedy-Pipe, *Stalin's Cold War*, pp. 78–102; and Nation, *Black earth*, pp. 151–68.

35 W. R. Smyser, *From Yalta to Berlin: the Cold War struggle over Germany*, New York, 1999, ch. 2; N. Naimark, 'The Soviets and the Christian Democrats: the challenge of a 'bourgeois' party in eastern Germany, 1945–49', in Gori and Pons, *Soviet Union and Europe*, pp. 37–56.

36 R. C. Raack, 'Stalin plans his postwar Germany', *Journal of Contemporary History*, vol. 28 (1993); W. Loth, *Stalin's unwanted child: the Soviet Union, the German question and the founding of the GDR*, tr. R. Hogg, London, 1998; and his essay in Gori and Pons, *Soviet Union and Europe*, pp. 23–36, place the blame firmly on Soviet inability and SED unwillingness to conduct democratic politics. Compare R. Steininger, *The Stalin note of 1952 and the problem of reunification*, New York, 1990, which uses Western sources and blames Western politicians. See also Adomeit, *Imperial overstretch*, pp. 51–92.

37 G. Bischof, *Austria in the first Cold War, 1945–55: the leverage of the weak*, Cambridge, 1999, pp. 30–41, 75–87; and N. Naimark, *The Russians in Germany. A history of the Soviet zone of occupation, 1945–1949*, London, 1995.

38 On the last point, see Bischof, *Austria in the first Cold War*, pp. 78, 85–86; and the report from General Mark Clark on Austrian affairs, 26 February 1946, *FRUS*, 1946, vol. V, 'The British Commonwealth; western and central Europe', Washington, DC, 1969, pp. 312–15.

39 W. I. Hitchcock, *France restored: Cold War diplomacy and the quest for leadership in Europe, 1944–54*, Chapel Hill, 1998, pp. 44–54.

40 Smyser, *Yalta to Berlin*, p. 30. Ernest Bevin was the British foreign secretary and Georges Bidault his French counterpart.

41 G. Warner, 'From "ally" to enemy: Britain's relations with the Soviet Union, 1941–48,' in Gori and Pons, *Soviet Union and Europe*, esp. p. 302.

42 N. Yegorova, 'The "Iran Crisis" of 1945–1946: a view from the Russian archives', *CWIHP Working Paper*, no. 15 (1996).

43 R. S. DiNardo, 'Reconsidering the Trieste Crisis of 1945', *Diplomatic History*, vol. 21 (1997).

44 E. Mark, 'The war scare of 1946 and its consequences', *Diplomatic History*, vol. 21 (1997).

45 Frank Roberts on the British side offered London a similar analysis, and Ambassador Novikov in Washington sent Moscow reports that were also significant. See K. M. Jensen (ed.), *Origins of the Cold War: the Novikov, Kennan and Roberts 'Long Telegrams' of 1946*, Washington, DC, 1991.

46 R. L. Beisner, 'Dean Acheson joins the Cold warriors', *Diplomatic History*, vol. 20 (1996).

47 See Leffler, *A preponderance of power*, pp. 130–49, for a summary of the debate. The text of the report is in J. L. Gaddis and T. H. Etzold (eds.), *Containment: documents on American policy and strategy, 1945–1950*, New York, 1978, pp. 64–71.

48 At this stage Andrei Zhdanov was Stalin's favourite adviser on ideological matters and remained so until his death in 1949. Ulbricht was the pro-Moscow leader in the SPD/SED, but not yet the dominant force he was to become. Kennedy-Pipe, *Stalin's Cold War*, pp. 93–98, suggests that Zhdanov prevailed over Malenkov's and Beria's isolationism and the assumption that the occupation of Germany would be brief. Roberts, 'Moscow and the Marshall Plan', suggests that Varga's influence waned during 1947.

49 Pechatnov, 'The big three'; G. Roberts, 'Moscow and the Marshall Plan: politics, ideology and the onset of the Cold War, 1947', *Europe-Asia Studies*, vol. 46 (1994); and on Ulbricht, see Smyser, *Yalta to Berlin*, pp. 33–42;

50 As well as Henry Wallace in the USA, British Prime Minister Attlee's hopes for co-operation gave way to Bevin's more confrontational approach. G. Warner, 'Ernest Bevin and British foreign policy, 1945–1951', in Craig and Loewenheim, *The diplomats*; Hitchcock, *France restored*; and G. Dalloz, *Georges Bidault biographie politique*, Paris, 1992, chronicle French assumptions. In Moscow something similar happened with the rise of Molotov and Zhdanov, and the exclusion of Litvinov.

2 The Cold War takes shape, 1947–51

1947 *12 March:* Truman Doctrine speech
April–May: Moscow Foreign Ministers' conference ends in deadlock
June: Marshall Plan speech
July: Paris conferences on the Marshall Plan
September: Cominform founded; Zhdanov makes his 'two camps' speech

1948 *June:* Berlin Blockade and Airlift begin; Yugoslavia expelled from Cominform

1949 *April:* NATO established
May: Berlin Blockade ends; FRG established
29 August: USSR explodes its first atomic bomb
October: DDR and PRC come into existence

1950 *February:* Sino-Soviet treaty of friendship concluded
25 June: Korean War breaks out
October: China enters the Korean War

1951 *Spring:* Korean front stabilises

1952 *March–April:* Stalin's notes on the German question appear

1953 *5 March:* Stalin dies
17 June: Crisis in East Germany ends Beria's scheme for unification
27 July: Korean armistice signed at Panmunjon

The period from early 1947 to 1951 marked the crucial phase in the shaping of the Cold War. By the time aid under the Marshall Plan ended in 1951, the confrontation had frozen into the pattern that dominated world affairs for three decades: a globalised, militarised confrontation in which the two superpowers led alliance systems that threatened nuclear conflagration. In 1947 only one of those two powers had nuclear weapons and there were no institutions connecting other countries to their blocs. Some efforts at compromise over Germany had recently been given up, others were still, at least technically, ongoing. At this stage, confrontation was diplomatic, economic, psychological and political.

In the early months of 1947 Cold War attitudes had not yet frozen into glacial solidity. The fact that Europe was literally freezing in the winter of 1946–47 was, however, of great significance. The economies of the West were descending into disarray. Some Western leaders feared that to Germans the Soviet zone in Germany might seem to be better off than the Western ones: as General Clay put it, there was no choice between being a communist on 1,500 calories a day and a capitalist on 1,000.[1] In September 1946, US Secretary of State Byrnes, trying to bolster German morale, made a speech in Stuttgart that seemed to imply that Germany might be able to redraw its new border with Poland in its favour. Movietone News characterised the speech as 'marking the end of America's appeasement of Russia'. The Russians used the speech (which they and their Polish allies considered 'shocking') to consolidate their hold on Polish opinion, claiming that only they stood between the new Poland and German revanchist aggression.[2] In the January 1947 elections the Polish communists came to power amid Western allegations of fraud and intimidation.

By 1951 the USSR had exploded an atomic bomb and the CCP had formed a government in China which declared that it would 'lean to one side' in the Cold War. There was fighting in Korea that pitted US and allied forces under a UN banner against Chinese (and a few Soviet) troops allied to North Korea. The Berlin Airlift and coup in Czechoslovakia helped to speed the advent of a peacetime US security guarantee to western Europe through NATO. After 1950 all major powers rearmed rapidly, decisions were taken to develop hydrogen bombs and the new structure of the Cold War confrontation solidified. By the time of Stalin's death and Eisenhower's inauguration in early 1953, it was embedded at the very centre of global politics.

The Truman Doctrine and the Marshall Plan

In the winter of 1946–47 the British economy was close to collapse. Finances were overstretched as a result of a combination of global commitments, efforts to build a welfare state at home that would serve as an alternative to US capitalism and Soviet communism, and persistent internal problems that necessitated dollar loans.[3] In early 1947 the decision was taken to cut back aid to Turkey as well as to the Greek government in its struggle against communist insurgency. Britain asked the USA to assume the burden.

This handed Truman a major problem. There was a growing consensus in government that aggressive communism posed a threat to vital US interests, including the security of the Middle East and the eastern Mediterranean.[4] If country after country fell to communism, the USA might eventually stand alone against a hostile world. Yet the new Republican Congress was determined to cut taxes and retained pockets of isolationist or 'Asia-first' sentiment.[5] When Congressional leaders were briefed, the administration argued that failure to defend Greece and Turkey would encourage communist aggression and lead other countries 'to fall like apples in a barrel infected by one rotten one'.[6] They told the administration that if Truman made the same case publicly, Congress would pass an appropriations bill for aid to the two countries. A rallying call, intended to mobilise a public suspected of latent isolationism, resulted. Truman addressed both Houses and the nation on how democracy must be defended wherever it faced aggression. He argued that the investment they had made in freedom in the Second World War must not be lost for want of the funds – and for only a fraction of the cost of the war – now needed to help those fighting totalitarian subversion, oppressive minorities and external threats to their self-determination. The call for a US commitment against tyranny and the juxtaposition of slavery and freedom soon became known as the Truman Doctrine. Not all of the money sought by the administration was approved, but the USA did take up the burden.

Although this ran against Soviet predictions of US post-war behaviour, Stalin did not react openly or finally. The meetings of the foreign ministers' conference in Moscow between April and May 1947, however, convinced Secretary of State Marshall that no progress would be made on Germany or on other issues. He thought Stalin was playing for time in the hope that the situation in western Europe would worsen. Despite pleas from various quarters for more patience, Marshall moved swiftly to adopt George Kennan's vision of building a European bulwark against Soviet expansion. In June he proposed a programme of aid to Europe, emphasising to Congress that 'the situation is critical in the extreme'.[7] Aid would be open to all European countries that chose to participate, but would come with strings attached. The reaction from Britain and France was immediate and positive, while that of the USSR, although not an outright rejection, was guarded.

The USA offered aid with a number of ends in view. As the US economy would benefit, aid was an enlightened form of self-interest. Marshall assumed that the creation of strong economies in a stable Europe would underpin democracy and that Germany could be integrated into this system. This would help to avoid a return to the conditions of the 1930s when the failure of democracy to withstand totalitarian aggression was perceived to have occurred because economic chaos had undermined the will to resist. The USA had not been able to avoid being drawn into the ensuing conflict and thus protect Americans from war. The plan would consolidate European security by promoting prosperity. It also had a clear ideological message, noted by Molotov. Marshall's declaration that 'Our policy is directed not against any country or doctrine but against hunger, poverty, desperation and chaos . . . Governments, political parties or groups which seek to perpetuate human misery in order to profit therefrom politically or otherwise will encounter the opposition of the United States'[8] struck the Soviets as an aggressive speech that sought to bring Germany into the Western fold and bring US economic influence into eastern Europe. However, they did not reject bilateral aid, as long as there were very few strings and Germany was not a beneficiary.

Certain assumptions underlay the ensuing Paris talks of July 1947. Aid was to be centrally planned, not bilaterally negotiated. Not least to satisfy a reluctant Congress, it was to involve opening economies to outside scrutiny and to greater trade with the USA and among European countries. This was assumed to be anathema to Stalin by Assistant Secretary Will L. Clayton and his British and French counterparts when they met in London prior to the Paris conference. By the time Molotov led the Soviet delegation to the first round of talks, he knew, through Stalin's British espionage network, that the intention was to preclude Soviet participation.[9] A struggle ensued over whether the countries of eastern-central Europe would follow Moscow's lead or participate and receive aid. Soviet leaders experienced difficulty in persuading the Poles and Czechs not to partici-pate in the second round of Paris talks. Their interest in participating seemed to provide evidence that the aid posed a threat to the Soviet buffer zone. The Czech leaders were summoned to Moscow and instructed as to what line to adopt, leading Foreign Minister Jan Masaryk to conclude that he had left home the representative of a sovereign state but returned 'as a lackey of the Soviet Union'.[10]

The episode illustrates the 'security dilemma'. The Americans, French and British assumed that they were acting to secure their interests, preserve ideals and institutions which made their societies safer and bolster and extend systems they saw as beneficial. Their efforts to make themselves more secure were perceived in Moscow as threatening. Misperceptions of the other side's efforts to defend its interests were a feature of Cold War reasoning, but they were never more important than at this moment. Stalin's advisers assumed that Marshall was deliberately putting together an anti-Soviet bloc and both sides underestimated the other's genuine apprehensions.

Soviet responses

In September 1947 Andrei Zhdanov described to the newly established Cominform how Europe was now irrevocably split into two camps. He said that the Americans were building up Europe as a base from which to attack the USSR and they must respond accordingly; concessions were futile, unilateral action was the best tactic. By early 1948 this resulted in the vestiges of pluralism being purged from the eastern European regimes and in new strategies of resistance by communist parties in western Europe.

Communist responses to the events of the summer of 1947 show a clear break from the previous pattern in national and international affairs. Along with the exclusion of communists from government in Italy and France in May, they mark the true onset of Cold War. Where communists were already in power, they instituted purges. Where they dominated coalitions, there first occurred a series of moves to consolidate communist control, then came purges.[11] From September 1947 the Cominform exercised vigilant supervision of European communist movements. In Germany there was a distinct toughening in Russian and SED dealings with both the bourgeois parties and the Western powers.[12] The toppling of the democratic government in Prague in February 1948 followed rigged elections in Hungary in August 1947 and the ejection of non-communists from the government of Poland after January 1947.[13] Events in Czechoslovakia, in turn, were crucial in persuading a hesitant US Congress to vote the appropriations for Marshall aid.

Purges of those who deviated from the Cominform line began, ironically, with Yugoslavia's Tito, previously a loyal Stalinist. Yugoslavia's lack of consultation with Moscow over Albania and internal Yugoslavian politics produced a split in which the Soviet embassy backed its men in the Politburo. Tito ousted them. By March 1948 the split was open and bitter ideological polemics followed. In June Yugoslavia was expelled from Cominform. For about two years there seemed a real possibility of military action. Stalin also moved to purge real, imagined and potential Titoists from other parties. Future communist leaders such as Gomulka of Poland and Husak of Czechoslovakia were arrested. Among the victims of the show trials and purges were top communists, starting in October 1948 with Lazlo Rajk in Hungary and culminating with the trial of Rudolf Slansky in Czechoslovakia in 1952.[14] In the latter, the trial transcript 'reads as if it had been translated from Russian word by word. In identifying the defendants by their last names first, as well as by nationality, it followed Soviet rather than Czechoslovak practice'.[15]

Such efforts at consolidation and retrenchment were viewed in the West as evidence of Moscow's plans for Soviet expansion. On both sides, fear dominated thinking. In the absence of hard evidence, Westerners drew on historical parallels to divine Moscow's intentions. In the absence of effective means to analyse intelligence,[16] Stalin fell prey to his insecurities and mistrust.

The Berlin Blockade and NATO

Events in Germany now took centre stage. Four-power co-operation had never worked as intended. In Berlin there had been persistent problems over Western access, local politics, judicial affairs, trade union activities and policing.[17] On both sides the fear that a revived Germany, allied to a superpower, would pose an overwhelming threat contributed greatly to each occupying power accepting division instead of risking reunification. Stalin, for example, wanted a united Germany only if Soviet influence, reparations and a sure role for the SED were guaranteed.[18] In 1947 the merger of the British and US zones and the rebirth of democratic institutions in this Bizone worried the Soviets profoundly, especially as their spies relayed evidence of secret discussions in London about the German economy.[19] Efforts to incorporate the French zone strengthened fears that the Western powers wished to divide Germany in two and harness the industrial might of the Ruhr against the USSR.

By 1947 many in London and some in Washington feared Soviet power more than they did German. In the Western zones Marshall aid was part of a rebuilding process that took on many aspects of state creation, and rebuilding the German economy took on the added quality of bolstering democracy. The crunch came over currency reforms. Western efforts to bring these in and to extend the new currency to western Berlin were the trigger that caused Stalin to cut off most access to that city in June 1948.

Stalin's main aims seem to have been to avert the incorporation of western Germany into the Western alliance and to retain some access and influence there, especially in the Ruhr. By cutting road and rail access to Berlin he may have hoped to carve out a position of strength from which he could negotiate on larger questions and to sow doubts in the minds of west Germans about the West's will and ability to aid them. As with many of his Cold War gambits, this backfired and helped bring about the very things he sought to avert. Truman did not back down. He took up the British idea of an airlift. By May 1949 over 275,000 flights had carried 2.3 million tons of supplies into the city and hundreds of thousands of tons of Berlin products out. Truman rejected General

Lucius Clay's advice to force a convoy down the *Autobahn* to Berlin as he had no wish to risk war. For the same reason the Soviets controlled their harassment of the airlift planes very carefully. By the time Stalin backed down in May 1949, the airlift of supplies had kept the city viable and west German opinion had consolidated against him. The crisis helped create the political conditions in which a West German state was founded in May 1949.

The mood of crisis and confrontation forms a key part of the explanation for the acceptance by the US people and Congress of a peacetime security guarantee to western Europe. The creation of NATO in April 1949 marked a watershed in British and US diplomacy. In Lord Ismay's[20] phrase, the alliance was formed to 'keep the Russians out, the Germans down and the Yanks in'. For both powers such a commitment in peacetime marked a departure from traditions of isolation. Bevin, Monnet, Bidault, Spaak and the other west European leaders co-operated to create a new institution for US influence and assistance in which the double containment of Germany and the USSR was a key consideration, as was the desire to build on the achievements of the war and cement the USA into the European security architecture. With the US guarantee, doubts about the wisdom of rapid progress towards a German state, and even its rearmament, were eased. Alongside NATO came other structures that drew on the experience of the Marshall Plan and, with US encouragement, the process of the integration of Europe began.[21]

To win domestic support for the new departures of 1947 to 1949, the Truman administration's rhetoric referred to a clear and present danger to US national security. In Acheson's phrase the message had to be 'clearer than truth'. An alarm bell was sounded to rally support for controversial new measures that would cost taxpayers significant sums, make commitments to foreigners that might cost US lives and would help build up economic competitors so that they would be better able to withstand the USSR. In the name of containment sceptical Congressmen were persuaded to offer dollar aid to Europe's social democracies and welfare states. New national security bureaucracies – an integrated Defense Department in the Pentagon, the CIA, the National Security Council – were created in 1947.[22]

The cost of the rhetoric was exaggerated alarm over the Soviet threat that spilled into domestic politics. Truman 'red-baited' Henry Wallace to win liberal support in 1948.[23] Internal security programmes and vetting of government employees heightened concerns about communist subversion, as did politicians from both parties who prominently agitated the issue. We now know that Venona project decrypts led the FBI and British security services to greater knowledge of Soviet penetration.[24] Even though most Soviet agents had ceased activity, knowledge of previous espionage fuelled fears that subversion was a real threat. Leaks of sanitised material helped keep the issue alive.[25]

Rising tensions

Following events in 1947 and 1948, international tensions rose. The CIA intervened in the Italian elections and French trade union affairs to counter

The Soviet intelligence message that, when decrypted as part of the Venona project, gave away British spy Donald McLean (no-one else in the British embassy had a pregnant wife in New York in July 1944).

communist influence. The USA also backed the anti-communists in the Greek Civil War's closing stages.[26] Covert operations were mounted in Albania (betrayed by Kim Philby), the Baltic states, Poland and the Ukraine, where anti-communist resistance persisted into the early 1950s. This must have fuelled Stalin's fears that enemies within were linked to those without. The testimony of a US defector and former OSS agent, Noel Field, may have helped seal the fate of the victims of the purge in Czechoslovakia and elsewhere. His links to Rajk and Slansky were brought to the local authorities' notice by a Polish security official who was a CIA agent and was later to defect.[27] Although actual US agents were never traced, the Americans did obtain transcripts of Czechoslovakian Politburo meetings and suspicion of the presence of US agents was a key part of the purges.[28]

On the one side, the NATO alliance was facilitated by fears about Berlin and the changes in government in what were now called the 'satellite states'. On the other, the communists' hold on power was dramatically consolidated. The split in Germany appeared to be more and more permanent with the creation of two states in May and October 1949 and the DDR's recognition the following year of its eastern frontier with Poland, which was not matched by Bonn.[29]

Other events heightened fears on both sides that the confrontation was going badly and that the other might be planning to unleash a third world war. The successful Soviet atom bomb test at the end of August 1949, three or four years earlier than the CIA had estimated, had a profound effect. That it happened so quickly was due to espionage, a fact that soon became public. Thanks to Venona (though publicly other sources were cited), Klaus Fuchs in Britain, David Greenglass and Julius and Ethel Rosenberg were convicted of atomic espionage. Other key spies, notably Theodore Hall, were not prosecuted for fear that the Venona decrypts would be revealed or that the case would not stand up in court.[30] In January 1950 Alger Hiss, also named in the decrypts, and who had been with Roosevelt at Yalta, was found guilty of perjury arising from testimony connected to allegations of his spying. The proclamation of the People's Republic of China on 1 October 1949 deepened US gloom. Despite the State Department's publication of a mass of evidence showing what efforts had been made, the allegation was made that the administration, because it was soft on communism or worse, had 'lost' China.

On the Soviet side there was a mixture of insecurity and optimism. Stalin was insecure because of Tito and extended the search for Titoists and imperialist agents into the satellite states and throughout the USSR. The Berlin Blockade had been a failure. West Germany seemed poised to enter the Western alliance and there were already Western voices arguing for its rearmament. The creation of a loyal DDR under Walter Ulbricht was scant consolation. Nevertheless, the explosion of the bomb helped to diminish fears of war and, although Stalin feared that Mao Zedong would prove another false friend, he found more hopeful signs in Asia and so the focus of his attention shifted. Closer co-operation with the PRC followed. Leaders there were told that they should take the lead in promoting communism in Asia.

Global confrontation

The new China's main priority was military action against nationalist remnants in Hainan, Tibet, Laos and Burma as well as Taiwan. This led to the Cold War becoming a global confrontation. The war in Indochina, a colonial struggle in which the USA was critical of France's rule and the USSR ignored Ho Chi Minh's insurgency, was transformed into a Cold War battleground. First China (18 January 1950) and then the USSR (30 January) recognised the Vietminh Democratic Republic of Vietnam. The first commitment of dollars by the USA to the other side came in February 1950 from funds appropriated for fighting communism in the vicinity of China. Then Truman recognised Bao Dai's French-backed government.[31] French leaders loudly proclaimed that they were fighting communism. They also stressed the global nature of the Cold War, telling the Americans how their efforts in the Far East were weakening them in Europe and led them to fear German rearmament. Secretary Acheson saw Ho as a hardened communist and sought to bolster French resolve in Europe through US aid to the anti-communist cause in Asia.

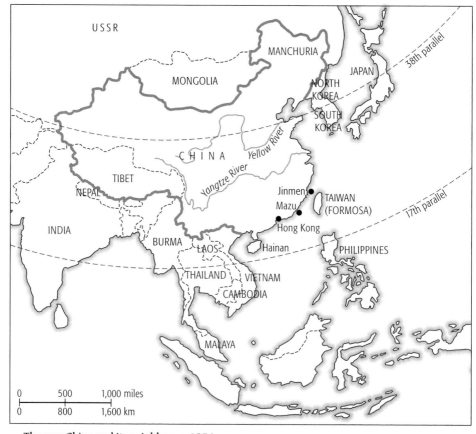

The new China and its neighbours, 1954.

The USA also mounted a fundamental review of its security needs in Asia as well as of its national security strategy. The ensuing documents formed the basis of an important shift in the US strategy of containment and changed the Cold War.[32] Influence over policy shifted with the replacement of Kennan by Paul Nitze as head of the State Department's policy planning staff. Henceforth there would be more emphasis on the military aspects of containment: Nitze was the main author of NSC 68, which was the chief result of the national security strategic reappraisal of the winter of 1950, approved by Truman in April. Nitze was largely responsible for the change in emphasis from psychology, economics, politics and careful selection of interests to a globalised, militarised system of alliances and arms races that the new statement of policy foreshadowed. Envisaged as a bureaucratic and political tool 'to bludgeon the mass mind of "top government"', the document became a blueprint for US rearmament and alliances.[33]

The Korean War

The new US strategy had a significant influence on its response to the outbreak of the Korean War in June 1950. The origins of that war lie within the rivalries of Korean nationalist leaders in the north and south, Kim Il Sung and Syngman Rhee. As long as the two superpowers maintained a military presence in Korea their 'clients' were restrained by the patrons' fears of the escalation of hostilities. The withdrawal of US troops and the scaling down of the Soviet presence in 1948–49, therefore, had a destabilising effect. In their drive for reunification, local forces became more aggressive. When the communists triumphed in China, Kim Il Sung, a veteran of the Soviet Army and Comintern, became more impatient in pressing for support for his schemes to unite Korea. Stalin repeatedly put him off and continued to do so into early 1950.[34] In February he wrote to his ambassador in Pyongyang:

> I understand the dissatisfaction of Comrade Kim Il Sung, but he must understand that such a large matter in regard to South Korea such as he wants to undertake needs large preparation. The matter must be organised so that there would not be too great a risk . . .

> I have a request for Comrade Kim Il Sung. The Soviet Union is experiencing a great insufficiency in lead. We would like to receive from Korea a yearly minimum of 25,000 tons of lead. Korea would render us a great assistance if it could yearly send to the Soviet Union the indicated amount of lead.[35]

Stalin still held back his client and held out for a high price if the USSR was to help. By the end of March, things had changed.

There are a number of possible explanations for Stalin's change of mind. He seems to have become somewhat more confident in the wake of the successful A-bomb test. The success of the Chinese Revolution was also important, especially the conclusion of the February 1950 Sino-Soviet treaty of friendship. This created a safe rear base area in China from which North Korea could be supported at less risk to the USSR. It also made Stalin fear encirclement and

Mao Zedong (second from the left) and other communist leaders visited Moscow to celebrate Stalin's seventieth birthday in December 1950. In February 1950 China and the USSR had concluded a treaty of friendship.

Japan rather less.[36] Further, if the USA had not fought to keep Jiang Jieshi[37] in power, why should it do so for Syngman Rhee? A speech to the Washington Press Club by Secretary of State Acheson may have given the impression that the USA had defined its vital interests in Asia as excluding the mainland. It stated a commitment to defend Japan and the Philippines and sought to warn off potential aggressors. Acheson later claimed that his stress on the offshore security perimeter was intended to demonstrate what the USA had already done 'to defend vital interests in the Pacific, not to speculate on what it might do in the event of various exigencies in Asia'. His speech was followed by a vote in Congress to cut aid to South Korea (although it was restored in a bill giving aid to Taiwan). Acheson later reflected that these steps and long-term Congressional pressure for troop cuts in Korea may have made more impression on Stalin than statements of resolve.[38] Pyongyang, Beijing and Moscow did see the USA's commitment to South Korea as being weak. China also began to expedite the return to Korea of two divisions of ethnic Korean soldiers from the PLA in readiness for action.[39]

Negotiations between Kim Il Sung, Stalin and Mao went on into the spring, with Stalin being careful not to put himself in a position that risked US–Soviet war. He manoeuvred Mao into backing North Korea's plans for a war of reunification, which meant that he neatly avoided having to become involved in China's planned invasion of Taiwan in 1950 which had to be shelved. The clinching circumstance was Kim's confident promise of a rapid victory. As averse to risk as ever, Stalin was assured that uprisings in the south, combined with the superiority of the Soviet-equipped and -trained North Korean army, would lead to victory in days. Under these conditions, Stalin allowed Soviet officers to play an important advisory role in the planning and execution of the 25 June attack. Stalin was so confident of success, and of the weakness of the US reaction, that he did not order the return of his delegation to the UNO which the USSR was boycotting in protest at the UNO's refusal to seat communist China.[40] It came as a huge shock when the USA rapidly mobilised a wide coalition to condemn North Korean aggression and pass resolutions mandating UN action to support South Korea.

This decisive reaction was the result of the strategic reappraisal that had taken place as well as domestic and international circumstances. NSC 68 reflected new views on the world situation, especially the need to avert the loss of any further territory and resources. Its alarmist mood and apocalyptic vision of the Soviet threat combined with McCarthy's assault on the administration's record and Truman's reading of history to make the choice of whether to intervene no choice at all. Truman's and Acheson's memoirs testify to the way in which there seemed to be no alternative to US support for South Korea against aggression that seemed reminiscent of the 1930s and early 1940s. Truman recalled:

> In my generation, this was not the first time that the strong had attacked the weak. I recalled some earlier instances: Manchuria, Ethiopia, Austria. I remembered how each time the democracies failed to act, it had encouraged the aggressors to keep going ahead. Communism was acting in Korea just as Hitler, Mussolini, and the Japanese had acted . . . If this were allowed to go unchallenged it would mean a third World War, just as similar incidents had brought on a Second World War.[41]

Ernest May has traced the broad influence of the 'lessons' of the past on early Cold War US policy: it was not only Kennan who drew on past behaviour and historical patterns to predict Soviet behaviour and suggest how to respond.[42] Like the Americans, the British identified appeasement of totalitarian regimes as a key mistake of the 1930s. As a result, they and other allies rapidly followed the US lead into Korea and a multinational force under the command of General Douglas MacArthur helped stabilise a defensive perimeter around the port of Pusan in south-eastern Korea. A desperate defence succeeded in August and early September. Then in an operation involving amphibious landings at Inchon, Chinese warnings of which were ignored by Kim, MacArthur struck northwards.

There followed a turning point in the Korean War, indeed in the whole Cold War. The rout of the North Koreans meant that Truman was faced with the issue of where to stop. Domestic political considerations (with off-year elections coming up in November, it was important for Truman to demonstrate his anti-communist credentials and succeed in rolling back a communist-controlled area) and the confidence of his field commander mingled with his anti-communism and the pressure from Rhee, who wished to reunify Korea under his leadership. On the other hand, the British and other coalition partners were wary of risking

Chinese intervention. Beijing's diplomatic warnings that a push north would provoke just that were discounted and UN forces raced northwards at the end of September. Kim, steered in that direction by Stalin, requested direct Chinese aid. There followed two weeks of complex negotiations and internal Chinese politicking. Fearing encirclement and imperialist influence on his borders, Mao was inclined to give full backing, but other leaders were more cautious. Intervention would divert Chinese resources from reconstruction after the civil war and mean that attempts to invade Taiwan would have to be postponed. The key issue for the Chinese became the extent of Soviet support, especially given the vulnerability of Chinese forces to US air power. China hesitated to commit troops without Soviet air support and equipment.

Stalin was reluctant to undertake a step carrying the risk of direct Soviet–US confrontation and escalation. By 11 October a compromise, which minimised the risks for Stalin, was reached. Soviet-manned planes with Korean markings would operate behind friendly lines. There was a desire on all sides to avoid actions that carried a significant risk of escalation towards a third world war. When UN pilots' reports and radio traffic revealed the Soviet presence, Western leaders chose not to make a big issue of it. The Chinese committed troops as 'volunteers' rather than as an official PLA contingent.[43]

The war now entered a new phase. After initially underestimating their opponents, a prolonged and costly retreat taught the Americans respect for the PLA. Truman made comments at a press conference that seemed to threaten nuclear escalation, thus risking the rupture of his alliance. Prime Minister Clement Attlee hastened to Washington on behalf of the allies and neutrals to seek and receive reassurance. In late December 1950 and January 1951 the Chinese reached the 38th parallel (see map on p. 42). Then Mao, like Truman, decided to try to clear the peninsula of his enemies. Encouraged by Kim and not restrained by Stalin, he ordered his forces to press forwards. As communications lines grew longer they became more vulnerable to allied air power. After a failed Chinese offensive in April and limited counter-offensive by the UNO, the front stabilised in the general area of the 38th parallel.

MacArthur's replacement by General Ridgway (for insubordination) was part of a shift from a war of movement to a war of position that lasted for another two years. The armistice negotiations lasted from June 1951 until July 1953 because of the intransigence of all sides. On the issues of where exactly the line of demarcation should be and whether Americans and Chinese would negotiate directly with each other, there was reasonably rapid progress. The issue of prisoner repatriation delayed matters. Most allies supported Truman's insistence that no prisoners should be repatriated against their wishes. His opponents were equally determined that all prisoners should be repatriated.[44] Willingness to compromise varied inversely to battlefield fortunes and at all times at least one major player resisted settlement.

Initially neither side was enthusiastic for compromise. By the middle of 1952 the Chinese and Americans had accepted that the costly war might be better settled. Stalin remained obdurate. For him, the war diverted and tied down US resources, it created strains in the Western alliance (as over the 1951 UN resolution condemning Chinese aggression)[45] and there was the hope that war-weariness could lead to difficulties for his main adversaries. The war yielded valuable intelligence and, above all, proved Chinese loyalty to him and deepened Sino-US estrangement.

In October 1952 Stalin made his position clear to Zhou Enlai:

Stalin answer [sic] that we want the return of all POWs. This also concurs with the Chinese position . . .

Stalin says that [a proposal to deal through India] can be acceptable, but we must keep in mind that the Americans will not want to deliver all POWs, that they will keep some captives, with the intention to recruit them . . .

Stalin emphasises that UN is an American organisation and we should destroy it, while keeping up the appearance that we are not against the UN . . .[46]

Stalin drove hard bargains. He insisted on explicit Chinese agreement that war supplies would be paid for in full. This rankled with the Chinese, whose human and material sacrifices had been great. The war had also brought the US fleet into the Taiwan Straits and caused repeated postponements of their invasion plans, thus preventing reunification with Taiwan.

The logjam on prisoner repatriation was broken after Stalin died in March 1953. His successors moved quickly to improve relations with the West. This included progress towards an armistice for which President Eisenhower claimed credit in his memoirs, suggesting that his tough stance and nuclear diplomacy had forced compromise on his foes. New research suggests otherwise.[47] Economic, domestic and alliance considerations were more important to Stalin's successors than they had been to Stalin. Final delays were caused by South Korean efforts to prevent an armistice, but these were overcome and it was signed at Panmunjon on 27 July 1953.

The Cold War had changed. Fighting on the Pacific Rim was accompanied by US security commitments to Japan, Australia and New Zealand. The USSR backed China and it, in turn, supported the Vietminh and the North Koreans. US and British troops were committed to western Europe with no set time limit on their stay. The arms race took new turns with both sides moving to the development of thermonuclear weapons and accelerating work on ballistic missiles. Spending on conventional weapons rose in all the major Cold War countries.[48] NATO and the Cominform were organised. The CMEA (or Comecon) was formed to tie the economies of the satellites more closely to that of the USSR. Germany was divided into two ideologically antagonistic states. Although Stalin continued to hope that he might detach West Germany from the West and prevent its rearmament and/or integration into NATO, he was unable to do so. McCarthy's and his collaborators' campaigns in the USA, China's 'Hate America' campaign and Stalin's purges all, in their own ways, intensified the Cold War and encouraged the rooting out of subversion and the encouragement of conformity. Loyalty, whether to 'One nation under God', the system or the new China was the order of the day. The Cold War had taken shape.

International and domestic politics in the early Cold War

2.1 Secretary of State Marshall announces his plan, June 1947

It has become obvious during recent months that this visible destruction was probably less serious than the dislocation of the entire fabric of European economy . . . Aside from the demoralising effect on the world at large and the possibilities of disturbances arising as a result of the desperation of the people concerned, the consequences to the economy of the United States should be apparent to all. It is logical that the United States should do whatever it is able to do to assist in the return of normal economic health in the world, without which there can be no political stability and no assured peace. Our policy is not directed against any country or doctrine but against hunger, poverty, desperation and chaos. Its purpose should be the revival of a working economy in the world so as to permit the emergence of political and social conditions in which free institutions can exist . . . Any government which maneuvers to block the recovery of other countries cannot expect help from us. Furthermore, governments, political parties, or other groups which seek to perpetuate human misery in order to profit therefrom politically or otherwise will encounter the opposition of the United States.

Source: *FRUS*, 1947, vol. III, 'The British Commonwealth; Europe', Washington, DC, 1972, pp. 237–39.

2.2 Zhdanov's speech at the founding of the Cominform, September 1947

A new alignment of political forces has arisen. The more the war recedes into the past, the more distinct become two major trends in post-war international policy, corresponding to the division of the political forces operating on the international arena into two major camps[:] the imperialist and anti-democratic camp, on the one hand, and the anti-imperialist and democratic camp on the other . . . The vague and deliberately guarded formulations of the Marshall Plan amount in essence to a scheme to create blocs of states bound by obligations to the United States, and to grant American credits to European countries as a recompense for their renunciation of economic, and then of political, independence. Moreover, the cornerstone of the Marshall Plan is the restoration of the industrial areas of Western Germany controlled by American monopolies.

There has devolved upon the Communists the special historical task of leading the resistance to the American plan for the enthrallment of Europe, and of boldly denouncing all coadjutors of American imperialism in their own countries . . .

Source: M. Hunt (ed.), *Crises in U.S. foreign policy: an international history reader*, New Haven, 1996, pp. 159–61.

2.3 China declares its Cold War alignment, July 1949

New China will follow the following principles: (a) we will persist in fighting against the imperialist countries so that the complete independence of the Chinese nation will be realised; (b) we will stand on the side of the Soviet Union and other new democratic countries in international affairs, against the danger of new wars and for the maintenance of world peace and democracy; (c) we will try to take advantage of the contradictions existing between capitalist countries; and (d) we will pursue commercial and trade relations, under equal and mutually beneficial conditions, with foreign countries, especially with the Soviet Union and the new democratic countries . . . Some non-communist figures in China criticise us for our policy of leaning to the side of the Soviet Union. Comrade Mao Zedong has responded to them, emphasising that it is our established policy to lean to the side of the Soviet Union . . . In this regard it is very important for the Soviet Communist Party to give us suggestions and assistance. We are urgently in need of help in that regard.

Source: Liu Shaoqi, memorandum to Stalin, 4 July 1949, in Shuguang Zhang and Jian Chen (eds.), *Chinese communist foreign policy and the Cold War in Asia. New documentary evidence, 1944–1950*, Chicago, 1996

2.4 The top-secret US National Security Council report, NSC 68, on national security objectives and programmes, April 1950

During the span of one generation, the international distribution of power has been fundamentally altered. For several centuries it had proved impossible for any one nation to gain such a preponderant strength that a coalition of other nations could not in time face it with greater strength . . . Two complex sets of factors have now basically altered this historical distribution of power. First the defeat of Germany and Japan and the decline of the British and French Empires have interacted with the development of the United States and the Soviet Union in such a way that power has increasingly gravitated to these centers. Second the Soviet Union, unlike previous aspirants to hegemony, is animated by a new fanatic faith, antithetical to our own, and seeks to impose absolute authority over the rest of the world. Conflict has, therefore, become endemic and is waged, on the part of the Soviet Union, by violent or non-violent methods in accordance with the dictates of expediency. With the development of increasingly terrifying weapons of mass destruction, every individual faces the ever-present possibility of annihilation . . . Any substantial further extension of the area under the domination of the Kremlin would raise the possibility that no coalition adequate to confront the Kremlin with greater strength could be assembled . . .

There is a basic conflict between the idea of freedom under a government of laws, and the idea of slavery under the grim oligarchy of the Kremlin . . .

In the absence of affirmative decision on our part, the rest of the free world is almost certain to become demoralised. Our friends will become more than a liability to us, they can eventually become a positive increment to Soviet power.

Source: As quoted in J. L. Gaddis and T. H. Etzold (eds.), *Containment: documents on American policy and strategy, 1945–1950*, New York, 1978, pp. 385–404

2.5 A Czech exile, formerly with access to the archives of the Central Committee, explains the connections of domestic and foreign policy

The Slansky Trial['s] . . . form and exterior facade had certainly been conditioned by local needs and interests, but its genesis had been very much subordinated to the grand designs of the Kremlin's foreign policy. These were the determining motives, surely, especially when one recalls Moscow's attachment to articulating its bloc around the principle of an absolute dependence and unconditional obedience of all the satellite countries. At the start of the cold war, when Yugoslavia appeared to be the generator of centrifugal tendencies, the first great trials were intended to serve as an example to all those who might have been tempted to rethink their links to Moscow, or to place national interests ahead of those of the USSR . . . At a moment when the Soviet Union hastened its preparations for a global conflagration which it considered inevitable in the short term, the Prague trial was meant to demonstrate in the first instance that the imperialists, through their local agents, were engaged in preparations in all sectors of society to make the country tip into the opposite camp. In order to consolidate Soviet hegemony, it was thus imperative to separate from command posts all those with notorious links to the West, including those who, until then, had given every appearance of being loyal servants.

For in effect this second generation of trials signalled a general relieving of cadres to replace the apparently docile with the much more docile again, often those under obligations to Moscow for various reasons . . .

Source: K. Kaplan, *Procès politiques à Prague*, Paris, 1980, p. 51 (author's translation)

2.6 Why China decided to enter the Korean War, October 1950

We have decided to send a portion of our troops, under the name of Volunteers, to Korea . . . If Korea were completely occupied by the Americans and the Korean revolutionary forces were substantially destroyed the American invaders would be more rampant, and such a situation would be unfavourable to the whole East . . . Meanwhile our troops will be awaiting the arrival of Soviet weapons and becoming equipped with those weapons. Only then will our troops launch a counteroffensive . . . The enemy will control the air while our air force, which has just started its training, will not be able to enter the war with some 300 planes until February 1951.

Source: Telegram, Mao Zedong to Stalin, 2 October 1950, in Zhang and Chen (eds.), *Chinese communist foreign policy*, pp. 162–63

Document case-study questions

1 How far does the evidence in these extracts support the view that Cold War policy makers perceived their actions as defensive?

2 What do documents 2.1 and 2.4 tell us about changes in US attitudes to security between 1947 and 1950?

3 What do documents 2.2, 2.3, 2.5 and 2.6 reveal about Soviet relations with the countries in their emerging bloc?

4 What is the significance of the following phrases: 'new democratic countries' (2.3); 'centrifugal tendencies' (2.5); 'volunteers' (2.6)?

5 Compare the relationships between foreign and domestic considerations as revealed in these extracts.

Notes and references

1 M. Trachtenberg, *A constructed peace. The making of a European settlement, 1945–1963*, Princeton, 1999, p. 52. Major General Lucius Clay was the commander of the US occupation forces.

2 Byrnes speech, Movietone coverage and General Jaruzelski interview, *Cold War*, programme 1, Turner/BBC, 1998. For Soviet reactions, see C. Kennedy-Pipe, *Stalin's Cold War. Soviet strategies in Europe, 1943 to 1956*, Manchester, 1995, p. 101.

3 G. Warner, 'Ernest Bevin and British foreign policy, 1945–51', in G. A. Craig and F. L. Loewenheim (eds.), *The diplomats, 1939–1979*, Princeton, 1994, pp. 103–34. See also S. Greenwood, *Britain and the Cold War, 1945–91*, London, 2000, chs. 1 and 2; and P. Weiler, 'British Labour and the Cold War: the foreign policy of the Labour governments, 1945–1951', *Journal of British Studies*, vol. 26 (1987), pp. 54–82.

4 See B. Kuniholm, *The origins of the Cold War in the Near East: great power diplomacy in Iran, Turkey, and Greece*, Princeton, 1980.

5 Supporters of 'Asia-first' sentiment, like Senator Taft, were sceptical of aid to social democracies in Europe and of support for NATO. Many of them were later at the heart of the China lobby.

6 Dean Acheson, *Present at the creation. My years in the State Department*, London, 1969, p. 219.

7 Congressional testimony, *Cold War*, programme 2, Turner/BBC, 1998.

8 The quotation appears in S. Parrish and M. M. Narinsky, 'New evidence on the Soviet rejection of the Marshall Plan: two reports', *CWIHP Working Paper*, no. 9 (1994). On p. 14 Parrish indicates Molotov's underlinings on the copy of the speech sent to him from Washington.

9 Parrish and Narinsky, 'New evidence', pp. 45–46.

10 The analysis here follows that of Parrish and Narinsky, 'New evidence', p. 51. See also K. Kratky, 'Czechoslovakia, the Soviet Union and the Marshall Plan', in O. A. Westad et al (eds.), *The Soviet Union and eastern Europe, 1945–89*, New York, 1994, pp. 9–25.

11 See K. Kaplan, *Dans les archives du Comité Central, 30 ans de secrets du bloc Sovietique*, Paris, 1978, pp. 132–79.

12 W. Loth, *Stalin's unwanted child: the Soviet Union, the German question and the founding of the GDR*, tr. R. Hogg, London, 1998, pp. 72 ff.; N. Naimark, 'The Soviets and the Christian Democrats', in F. Gori and S. Pons (eds.), *The Soviet Union and Europe in the Cold War, 1943–53*, London, 1996, pp. 46–49.

13 Kennedy-Pipe, *Stalin's Cold War*, pp. 120–24; and V. Mastny, *The Cold War and Soviet insecurity. The Stalin years*, Oxford, 1996, pp. 63–79.

14 C. Andrew and O. Gordievsky, *KGB. The inside story of its foreign operations from Lenin to Gorbachev*, London, 1990, pp. 292–96, 343–46, give a good account of the process by which governments were undermined and of the active role played by the Soviets in the process.

15 Mastny, *Soviet insecurity*, p. 154. K. Kaplan, *Procès politiques à Prague*, Paris, 1980, p. 48, testifies to Moscow's close supervision of the trials.

16 There was no proper analytical division in the Soviet intelligence community until the mid 1980s. Politically correct analyses confirmed the Moscow line. See C. Andrew and O. Gordievsky, *Instructions from the centre*, London, 1993.

17 A. Tusa and J. Tusa, *The Berlin Airlift*, London, 1988, pp. 67–94. Trachtenberg, *Constructed peace*, chs. 2 and 3. C. Eisenberg, *Drawing the line: the American decision to divide Germany, 1944–1949*, Cambridge, 1996, is thorough, but its title reflects its emphasis on the USA. See also N. Naimark, 'The Soviets and the Christian Democrats: the challenge of a "bourgeois party" in eastern Germany, 1945–49'; and V. Narinskii, 'The Soviet Union and the Berlin Crisis, 1948–49', in Gori and Pons, *Soviet Union and Europe*.

18 W. R. Smyser, *From Yalta to Berlin: the Cold War struggle over Germany*, New York, 1999, p. 68.

19 Interviews with former Soviet military administration personnel, *Cold War*, programme 3, Turner/BBC, 1998.

20 Lord Ismay was a senior British policy maker, Second World War general, minister under Churchill from 1951 and secretary-general of NATO from 1952.

21 G. Lundestad, *'Empire' by integration: the United States and European integration, 1945–1997*, Oxford, 1998, pp. 28–46.

22 M. J. Hogan, *A cross of iron. Harry S. Truman and the origins of the national security state, 1945–1954*, Cambridge, 1998, esp. pp. 23–68; and M. Leffler, *A preponderance of power: national security, the Truman administration and the Cold War*, Stanford, 1992, esp. pp. 141–81.

23 Truman's campaign depicted Wallace's Progressives as unduly pro-Soviet and communist influenced, prefiguring what the Republicans did to Truman during the McCarthy years.

24 Venona was the ultimate codename of a long-term project working on Soviet material, during and just after the Second World War. The first decrypted messages were produced by military intelligence, and subsequently the FBI, during 1946. By 1948 there was a significant amount of material on atom spies and other Soviet activities. The project ran until the late 1970s, but most significant material was decrypted by the mid 1950s. The bulk of Soviet activity was curtailed after the defections of a cypher clerk at their Ottowa embassy in 1946 and Helen Bentley's testimony to the FBI the previous year. Some spies (Philby, Burgess and Maclean in Britain and a number of those in the USA) remained active for longer. By the early 1950s the success of Soviet spying in the USA was much reduced.

25 The Venona decrypts incriminated Maclean, Klaus Fuchs and Alger Hiss (as a recruiter as well as a spy) and contained nearly 350 codenames, about half of which were identified. In the USA the disbanding of OSS, changes in top government personnel and security vetting procedures meant that the CIA and Department of Defense were not penetrated. The NSA was, and Stalin knew of Venona from an early date. See C. M. Andrew, *For the president's eyes only*, London, 1995, pp. 180–81. Decrypts cast suspicion on senior figures in the Roosevelt Treasury (Harry D. White) and State departments (Larry Duggan) as well as on Roosevelt's entourage. These had been Soviet sources of information and were suspected by the FBI of being agents. In Duggan's case the suspicions may have helped drive him to suicide; in White's case the debate still rages over whether there was any actual wrongdoing in his wartime contacts, with the president's knowledge, with what was then an Allied power.

26 S. Lucas, *Freedom's war: the American crusade against the Soviet Union*, New York, 1999, pp. 43–46. Z. Karabell, *Architects of intervention. The United States, the third world and the Cold War, 1946–1962*, Baton Rouge, La., 1999, pp. 17–36.

27 Field spied for the USSR from the 1930s through to the Second World War. When he began to fear that he would have to testify in the Hiss case he fled to eastern Europe just as Stalin's purges there were beginning. He was arrested and accused of being the link between the targets of the purges and the USA. Rehabilitated after Stalin's death, he lived in Hungary until his death in 1970. Mastny tells us that comments made by him connected the Stalin–Tito split to Laszlo Rajk, the former interior minister of Hungary, who was the most

senior Hungarian victim of the purges. Slansky was general-secretary of the Czech Communist Party under Gottwald. The agent Josef Swiatlo worked for the Polish Security Police and it was he who drew the attention of the authorities to Field's connections.

28 Mastny, *Soviet insecurity*, pp. 70–71, 131; and R. Garthoff, *Assessing the adversary: estimates by the Eisenhower administration of Soviet intentions and capabilities*, Washington, DC, 1991, p. 52 note 125.

29 In 1945 Poland's borders were moved west by Stalin (much of what is now western Poland had been Germany). Poles worried about German ambitions to reclaim that land and, given memories of the interwar years, these were not necessarily unreasonable. At Moscow's behest, East Germany offered recognition of the border (except for some disputed islands). FRG politics meant that until Brandt's *Ostpolitik* there was no matching guarantee from the West of Poland's new frontiers. This meant that the two German states each claimed to be the basis for a whole Germany – but they did not even have the same definition of German frontiers.

30 C. Andrew and V. Mitrokhin, *The Mitrokhin archive. The KGB in Europe and the West*, London, 1999, pp. 169–75; D. Holloway, *Stalin and the bomb: the Soviet Union and atomic energy, 1939–1954*, New Haven, 1994; and J. L. Gaddis, *We now know. Rethinking Cold War history*, Oxford, 1997, pp. 92–99.

31 R. McMahon, 'Harry S. Truman and the roots of U.S. involvement in Indochina, 1945–1953', in D. Anderson (ed.), *Shadow on the White House: presidents and the Vietnam War, 1945–1975*, Lawrence, 1993, pp. 28–29.

32 J. L. Gaddis, *Strategies of containment: a critical appraisal of American national security policy*, Oxford, 1982, ch. 4.

33 Acheson, *Present at the creation*, p. 374. More generally, see Leffler, *A preponderance of power*, pp. 355–56; and Hogan, *Cross of iron*, ch. 7.

34 V. Zubok and C. Pleshakov, *Inside the Kremlin's Cold War. From Stalin to Khrushchev*, Cambridge, Mass., 1996, pp. 54–62; K. Weathersby, 'Soviet aims in Korea and the origins of the Korean War, 1945–1950: new evidence from Russian archives', *CWIHP Working Paper*, no. 8 (1998); and S. N. Goncharov, J. W. Lewis and Xue Litai, *Uncertain partners: Stalin, Mao, and the Korean War*, Stanford, 1993, ch. 5.

35 Ciphered telegram from Stalin to Ambassador Shtykov in Pyongyang, 30 January 1950, translated and reproduced in *CWIHP Bulletin*, no. 5 (1995).

36 Goncharov et al, *Uncertain partners*, p. 121.

37 Born in 1887, Jiang Jieshi was an early member of the Guomindang (Nationalist) Party. He trained in Moscow and returned to take charge of the military academy set up, with Russian help, to train officers for the Guomindang army. When he seized control in 1925, he began the March to the North campaign in 1926 to re-establish central control over all China. By 1927, after discussions with foreign businesses, he turned on his communist allies and a civil war between nationalists and communists began and continued, on and off, until 1949, when the communists finally won. Jiang then fled to Taiwan (Formosa) where he set up an anti-communist government, with US backing, that claimed to be the legitimate Chinese state.

38 Acheson, *Present at the creation*, pp. 356–58.

39 Goncharov et al, *Uncertain partners*, pp. 140–54.

40 For some time in the 1960s and 1970s US historians used the USSR's absence to argue that Stalin could not have known of the invasion plans, or he would have had Gromyko at the UNO ready to veto a mandate to the forces fighting against North Korea. New evidence suggests just the opposite – Stalin believed he would win easily, so felt no need to reverse the boycott that had been started in protest at the UNO's refusal to seat communist China.

41 H. S. Truman, *Years of trial and hope, 1946–1953*, New York, 1956, p. 351; Acheson, *Present at the creation*, pp. 402–08.

42 E. May, *'Lessons' of the past: the use and abuse of history*, London, 1979, chs. 2–3.

43 W. Stueck, *The Korean War: an international history*, Princeton, 1995, pp. 44–50; Weathersby, 'Soviet aims', pp. 26–31; and her essay 'Stalin, Mao, and the end of the Korean War', in O. E. Westad (ed.), *Brothers in arms: the rise and fall of the Sino-Soviet Alliance, 1945–1963*, Stanford, 1998.

44 The Chinese and North Korean prisoners of war included significant numbers who, if offered the chance, would have preferred to stay in South Korea rather than go back. The USA and Rhee wanted all prisoners to be given that chance. China and Democratic People's Republic of Korea argued that they must be repatriated. Even when some vetting was provisionally agreed, the composition of the international panel to oversee matters was a cause of great wrangling. In the end, not all prisoners were repatriated, partly because Rhee opened the gates of some camps in the last weeks of the war in an effort to prevent armistice.

45 Britain, India and various western European powers believed that the UN resolution was too partisan and unhelpful to secure any negotiated settlement. They recognised the PRC and wanted to deal with it. Britain and Portugal had the added incentives for a careful approach that derived from their colonial possessions in southern China.

46 Record of a conversation between Stalin and Zhou Enlai, 19 September 1952, in Westad, *Brothers in arms*, pp. 330–34.

47 R. Dingman, 'Atomic diplomacy during the Korean War', *International Security*, vol. 13 (1988–89), pp. 50–91; R. Foot, 'Nuclear coercion and the ending of the Korean conflict', *International Security*, vol. 13 (1988–89), pp. 92–112. Zubok and Pleshakov, *Kremlin's Cold War*, p. 155, suggest that his successors may have been somewhat influenced by the threat of escalation.

48 Hogan, *Cross of iron*, ch. 8; Leffler, *A preponderance of power*, pp. 411–17; Greenwood, *Britain and the Cold War*, pp. 97–101; and T. W. Wolfe, *Soviet power and Europe, 1945–1970*, Baltimore, 1970, ch. 3.

3 Brinkmanship, 1951–63

1951 *Spring:* Korean front stabilises

1952 *March–April:* Stalin's notes on German question

1953 *5 March:* Stalin dies
17 June: Crisis in East Germany ends Beria's scheme for unification
27 July: Korean armistice

1954 *June–July:* Geneva conference on south-east Asia
September: First Taiwan Straits Crisis

1955 West Germany enters NATO; Warsaw Pact and Austrian State Treaty concluded

1956 *February:* Twentieth CPSU Congress; Khrushchev makes his 'secret' speech
June: Riots in Poznan, Poland
October–November: Crisis in Poland; Hungary invaded by USSR; Suez Crisis

1958 *September:* Second Taiwan Straits Crisis

1959 NLF takes up armed struggle in South Vietnam
September: Camp David Summit
November: Khrushchev delivers his ultimatum on Berlin

1961 *August:* Berlin Wall built

1962 *October:* Cuban Missile Crisis and Sino-Indian War

1963 *March:* Sino-Soviet split comes out into the open

1964 *August:* Tonkin Gulf Resolution

During the last two years of Truman's presidency and Stalin's life, the Cold War was near to its coldest. Many people felt that a third world war was inevitable.[1] The ensuing years were punctuated by crises, notably over Berlin, Poland, Hungary, the Middle East, Taiwan and Cuba. Their ferocity triggered pressure for détente as world leaders recoiled from the horror that war between the superpowers would bring. They also felt pressure from world public opinion and from their allies to prevent war and resume diplomatic exchanges. (The Chinese were less inclined to compromise.) The story of the 1950s and early 1960s is one of competitive co-existence, or limited conflict, rather than limitless escalation into disaster.

Change and continuity

By 1951 the main features of the Cold War were in place. These included a globalised, militarised, ideological confrontation between alliance systems, the arms race, limited wars, covert conflict, proxy warfare and vigorous propaganda campaigns. After 1951 both sides developed thermonuclear weapons and raced to develop intercontinental delivery systems, learning to fear their vulnerability to the other's retaliatory power. Fear of superpower war, deterrence and efforts to avoid escalation featured prominently in both Moscow's and Washington's priorities. The willingness of the Chinese and US leaders to go 'to the nuclear brink' in crises over the islands of the Taiwan Straits in 1954–55 and 1958–59 re-emphasised the danger. It also highlighted how confrontation had now spread to the developing world.

The major powers, acutely aware of the costs and dangers of the Cold War, sought to manage their antagonism. The period from the early 1950s to the onset of détente in the aftermath of the Berlin Wall and Cuban Missile crises, therefore, presents contradictory aspects. An early example is the fighting in Korea that dragged on into the summer of 1953 while negotiations foundered. Summit diplomacy resumed with the Geneva summits of 1954 and 1955, but achieved little. Although there were crises that threatened nuclear war, the nuclear powers were cautious not to escalate them beyond the brink. Efforts began to limit nuclear testing even as bigger bombs and missiles were developed.

Underlying assumptions about the other side were not suddenly or profoundly transformed. Arms budgets remained large, even if both superpowers tried to trim them in the mid to late 1950s. By the 1960s their growth resumed and nuclear arsenals continued to expand. Security policies and alliance priorities showed more continuity than change. Confrontation remained the order of the day. The superpowers concluded cultural exchanges and other agreements, but deep rivalry and antagonism between the two social systems remained the dominant theme.

The crises that marked Khrushchev's rise to power reflected confrontation but their very nature also stimulated efforts to promote 'peaceful co-existence' between the two superpowers and their blocs. Signs of détente appeared, especially in bilateral superpower relations and European affairs, as the risks of escalation constrained the superpowers. Both tacitly accepted limitations to their ambitions; an example is when the US National Security Council reviewed the satellite states of eastern Europe in July 1956 and concluded that US interest in their liberation was not worth the risk of global war. Khrushchev took a similar view in justifying Soviet reluctance to follow China to the nuclear brink in September 1958 or in telling Anatoly Dobrynin that he would not actually risk war, but would only bluff to gain concessions. War was inadmissible.[2]

The tendency of the superpowers to veer between détente and confrontation owed something to the personalities of their leaders. Some historians have made much of Secretary of State John Foster Dulles' unbending Presbyterian morality.[3] Even if recent work has shown that the secretary of state's views were more complex, Christian values (communism was frequently described as godless) influenced US policy makers. Khrushchev is often described as impulsive, even rash, in a way that Stalin or Brezhnev would never have been. Even filtered through bureaucracies, their policies often reflected Khrushchev's opportunism and Dulles' strongly held Christian beliefs.

Stalin's last years

Confrontation was predominant in the last two years of Stalin's life. Negotiations over Korea stalled, plans for possible invasion of Yugoslavia by his forces were laid, purges and trials racked the USSR and eastern Europe. Both sides were rapidly rearming and both feared that the other might unleash war. After his defeat in the Berlin Airlift, Stalin accepted the division of Germany and Ulbricht obtained his long-held wish for a separate state. The outbreak of the Korean War stimulated Western fears of Soviet aggression in Europe and led directly to the decision to rearm West Germany.[4] In his German notes of March 1952, Stalin responded by suggesting a neutral, disarmed and reunified Germany. Historians remain divided over whether they represented a genuine attempt to resolve the German question. The initial Western reaction was that the notes were a mere propaganda ploy. Historians followed this line for some years, viewing the notes as a bid to influence West German public opinion against Adenauer's policy of embedding his country in the Western alliance. In the 1970s and 1980s some historians, influenced by contemporary developments in West German politics, found evidence in newly opened Western archives that suggested Stalin may have been sincere in seeking reunification and neutralisation. More recent revelations from Soviet, DDR and other Eastern bloc sources have moved the balance of probability back towards the view that the West was right to treat the overture as insincere; the essential condition seems to have been that the West would have had to accept Stalin's terms on communist influence and future security arrangements.[5] One scholar has concluded that Stalin's insistence on an SED veto over any scheme suggests that he 'neither expected nor hoped for a positive western response to result'.[6] As Adomeit has stressed, Stalin sought to use the issue of unification as a lever while holding out for some of his stated aims as a prize.[7] Stalin was rebuffed by the West's insistence on certain conditions concerning Germany's future freedom to choose diplomatic alignments and the guarantee of democratic elections. Much to the relief of the SED leadership in the East and Moscow hardliners, Stalin's suggestion was dropped amid diplomatic exchanges that sought to shift the blame for the failure of reunification onto the other side.

A chance for peace?

Stalin died less than two months after the inauguration of Dwight David Eisenhower as president of the USA. The superpowers' new leaders moved quickly to make conciliatory gestures. Economic considerations played a role in this shift. Eisenhower, with strong Treasury support, repeatedly warned that economic strength at home was the basis of US hopes. A garrison state that devoted too much to military expenditure would endanger these hopes. Eisenhower's 'New Look' policy was based on limiting spending and relying on nuclear weapons as the most cost-effective way of deterring Soviet aggression. Khrushchev also tried to reduce the USSR's military budget.[8] The new Soviet leaders' rapid move to end the fighting in Korea immediately after Stalin's death was based, in part, on concerns about the strains the continued fighting might place on their economy.

This new turn was about more than economic concerns. Costs in Korea had gone beyond dollars and roubles. The new men wished to manage affairs differently from their predecessors and those who had long been statesmen joined in the pressure for talks. Prime Minister Churchill wanted to reduce the prospects of nuclear war and for Britain to play a leading role in world affairs, as during the war. Between the moves to end the Korean War (discussed in the previous chapter) in the spring of 1953 and the Twentieth Congress of the CPSU in early 1956, a number of developments testified to a new mood in the continuing Cold War rivalry.

Responding to hints of a new tone from the post-Stalin leaders, Eisenhower made conciliatory overtures such as the 'Chance for Peace' speech of April 1953 and the 'Open Skies' proposal of 1955. These initiatives were constructed in ways that made rejection likely and when that happened the Americans gained propaganda advantage. However, the fact of the proposals being made at all was itself significant. Behind Dulles' stern facade was a willingness to compromise. Movement towards agreements in certain areas started with the Korean armistice and the Austrian State Treaty, the Geneva conferences of 1954 and 1955, the USSR withdrawing from Finnish bases occupied since 1940 and the US and Chinese ambassadors in Warsaw meeting to discuss the release of US prisoners of war from Korea.

The Austrian State Treaty of 1955 was the most significant of these developments. Negotiations had stalled for years. With Austria divided into occupation zones like Germany, the Soviets had sought economic benefits from their occupation and the Western powers had moved to aid their zones during the crisis times of 1947. Austrian leaders in the Western zones, like Julius Raab, played up fears that their country could go the way of Czechoslovakia in order to sustain high levels of Western support. Moves for a treaty foundered repeatedly. By 1952 Western priorities were dominated by their global strategy and some US leaders had come to view Austria as 'Europe's Korea'. Moves were made to step up the secret rearming of the government in the Western zone, begun in 1948. The shift from posturing to serious negotiations showed both the importance of Kremlin politics (Khrushchev's dominance over Molotov by 1954) and the leverage of local leaders (Raab's acceptance of neutrality for domestic reasons). The Soviets saw neutrality as better than partition, in line with Khrushchev's acceptance of Finnish and Yugoslavian neutrality. It also allowed them to signal their intention to negotiate seriously on other matters. The USA accepted Raab's preferences and a diminution of their direct influence in Austria. Under the treaty all troops were withdrawn from Austria in return for its neutrality.[9]

Discussions began that led to increased cultural and economic contacts between the superpowers. Fear of war, domestic pressures and a desire to court international opinion were key considerations in leading the superpowers to resume summit diplomacy. Eisenhower and Dulles were not always keen. The

Europeans were more influential in Geneva than the Americans. Dulles refused to sign the accords on Indochina and little progress was made on Taiwan but, compared to the Truman–Stalin years, the very fact that talks took place was of the utmost significance.

This was due to the fears of what the new weapons might do if they were ever used. Ordinary citizens and policy makers alike shared a dread of nuclear war. US efforts at civil defence planning were hampered by the alarm provoked by exercises and shelter building, and tests of new weapons had a profound impact on senior Soviet figures.[10] The spectre of conflict haunted the world. Given the risks, both sides sought to pursue their geostrategic rivalry by any means short of war. Intelligence communities waged covert conflict. Subversion and counter-subversion were preoccupations on all sides. U-2 spy-planes roamed the skies over the communist bloc, above the range of Soviet missiles and planes, from 1955 until 1960. The Berlin tunnel, copied from one dug in Vienna, was used to tap Soviet communications until it was revealed by the British spy George Blake. His career and those of Georges Paques, Oleg Penkovsky and Greville Wynne demonstrate the extent of espionage activity.[11] Commander Crabbe, a Royal Navy diver, disappeared and died near Soviet ships in Portsmouth harbour during Khrushchev's visit to Britain.

The propaganda competition continued unabated. The KGB and CIA spread disinformation through the world's media, creating and perpetuating myths about each other.[12] Stalin combined repression and retrenchment inside the Soviet bloc with a vigorous peace campaign that reflected the Soviets' genuine fear of war and an attempt to stir up Western public opinion against their governments' rearmament and alliance building. The Soviet intelligence community helped to promote demonstrations of anti-war sentiment alongside government-sponsored meetings and other events behind the Iron Curtain. For both sides, radio broadcasts carried propaganda far and wide. Western efforts to reach into the Soviet bloc involved balloon releases to carry propaganda into communist central Europe.[13] Efforts continued to solidify support for the superpowers within their own blocs. Soviet domination of eastern Europe was upheld through force. The CIA intervened widely in European trade union affairs and the politics of the non-communist left to bolster native anti-communism. Journals such as *Encounter*, political parties, intellectuals and workers' movements were all targeted by the CIA in the competition for friends.[14]

The covert Cold War extended into the non-European world. In Iran in 1952–53 Britain and the USA plotted to overthrow Prime Minister Mossadeq when they suspected that he posed a threat of neutralism, expropriation of property and possible friendliness to the USSR. Encouraged by local elites, covert action saw the return to power of the Shah and less anti-Western forces.[15] Ideological anti-communism dominated US assumptions regarding Iran; a similar pattern emerged with regard to the Arbenz government in Guatemala. Here again, local groups manipulated the USA, but ideological blinkers predisposed the Eisenhower administration to perceive a communist threat far greater than it really was. US officials came to prefer dictatorship to left-leaning democracy and misperceived the threat from Arbenz.[16] The limited communist influence in a reformist government was exaggerated within and without Guatemala by a major US disinformation campaign, opposition was fomented, arms were planted and 'discovered' and economic sanctions were imposed. Under pressure the Guatemalan government turned to the Soviet bloc for weapons to keep the army supplied and loyal. Despite resistance to US claims at the OAS and UNO, Arbenz's government collapsed. The destabilisation became a model for subsequent adventures, as covert means were employed with varying degrees of success against governments deemed pro-communist or anti-American, notably in Cuba.[17]

Crisis in the Taiwan Straits

Two crises particularly highlighted the risk of war in the mid 1950s. One was over the Taiwan Straits. Although Eisenhower and Dulles declaimed about 'rolling back' communism during the 1952 election campaign, their behaviour in office was more circumspect. Some of the best experts on China were hounded from the State Department in the McCarthy years, and for years policy towards that country was dominated by political exigencies, including a wish to avert more witch-hunts. The 'China lobby' was vocal in its support of Jiang Jieshi and in its condemnation of the PRC. When the USA opened negotiations with Jiang in 1954 and concluded the SEATO Pact, Mao retaliated by invading one island and shelling others.[18]

Domestic priorities – reconstruction, reunification and consolidation of his power – affected Mao's foreign policy. His ideological commitment to peasant revolution, combined with his fear of encirclement by the imperialist camp, led him to give significant support to Ho Chi Minh in neighbouring Vietnam.[19] By playing up international crises and external threats, he also created greater loyalty at home. For the USSR, China was a different type of ally from those it had in eastern Europe where, Beria quipped, the DDR only existed because of the presence of Soviet tanks. The Chinese Revolution was home grown and its leaders were strong nationalists, sensitive to anything that smacked of European condescension. After the Korean War the Sino-Soviet alliance entered its golden age. Co-operation was close and Soviet aid was plentiful. Advisers and ideas poured into China and there were few points of friction.

Khrushchev backed the Chinese strongly in the 1954 Taiwan Straits Crisis. All sides, however, were careful to guard against escalation.[20] The world was taken towards the brink over Jinmen, Mazu and other offshore islands, but not beyond it. The crisis was managed and Chinese shelling of nationalist outposts was first reduced and later stopped. Eisenhower disappointed the China lobby and Jiang by failing to live up to campaign rhetoric of unleashing the nationalists to topple Mao. Mao had asserted China's status, taken some small islands and backed down once clear, if limited, US commitment to the fight was demonstrated. He was also keen to avoid criticism at the forthcoming Bandung meeting of non-aligned nations.[21]

Germany in crisis

The other acute crisis followed the failure of Stalin's German notes in 1952. Ulbricht pressed for rapid and extensive Sovietisation of East Germany to help resolve its economic crisis. As such a step would tend to perpetuate the division of the country and push West Germany closer to NATO, Moscow approached it with some reluctance. After March 1953 Molotov, Khrushchev (for his own political reasons) and those concerned with party-to-party relationships followed the trend of Stalin's last year and allowed Ulbricht his preference, but would not subsidise the DDR's ailing economy. The Soviet leadership agreed, however, that the rapid Sovietisation that had been taking place must be slowed down and Ulbricht was obliged to change policies in early June.

Beria and Malenkov (who downplayed party contacts) may have been 'ready to sell the Socialist GDR for détente with the West',[22] which could have resulted in a renewed bid by the Soviets to agree with the West on a neutralised, demilitarised, reunited Germany with free elections and an end to the SED's power. This never happened because rioting and protests against Sovietisation in East Berlin and other East German cities in June 1953 necessitated the use of Soviet forces to restore order and tarnished the entire scheme.[23]

Soon afterwards Beria fell and Soviet policy turned decisively to backing the DDR. The West had used radio in the US sector to disseminate news of the troubles and were accused by the communists of fomenting them. In Germany and at home there were recriminations about how little, beyond food aid, the West had actually done in the face of overwhelming Soviet power.[24]

After the June 1953 crisis the situation remained tense. Berlin's borders were open, through which considerable numbers of East Germans came and went, many without returning. The East Germans were never quite free of the fear that changing Soviet priorities might bring about their abandonment. They were preoccupied with the issues of the recognition of their state, its economic problems and their desire to push ahead with its Sovietisation. Their first priority was to follow Moscow's lead loyally. They were happy with Khrushchev as he had criticised his defeated rivals' proposals to abandon the DDR. For him, however, the East Germans became a millstone, as their weak state was intimately tied to his prestige.

In the Western alliance the issue was how to rearm the FRG. The preferred scheme was the European Defence Community, but this ran into trouble in France. The French consistently linked this issue to their quest for aid in their war in Indochina. They solicited US aid, and concessions over NATO and the EDC, with suggestions that their National Assembly might not otherwise support US wishes in Europe. The communist left and Gaullist right played on historical fears of German power and nationalist fears of US influence to oppose German rearmament as envisaged under the EDC Treaty. In 1954 France's failure to ratify the EDC Treaty and the subsequent British-brokered terms for West German entry into NATO demonstrated the depth of feeling and difficult alliance politics involved in the issue. The tensions were present throughout the Eisenhower and Kennedy administrations and grew worse when the idea of German access to nuclear weapons arose.[25]

Adenauer and Ulbricht had strong personalities that affected their states' relations with the superpowers. Once a commitment was made, the weak acquired leverage that made it difficult for the patron to abandon the client. Adenauer played this game in attempts to keep the British and Americans committed to policies of which he approved. He thought Macmillan and Eden too prone to compromise and warned them that he did not trust his own people and, therefore, was worried about the preparedness of the Anglo-Americans to contemplate reunification with no pre-arranged limits on German freedom to make alliances:

> Dr Adenauer wished us to know that he would deprecate reaching this position. The bald reason was that Dr Adenauer had no confidence in the German people. He was terrified that when he disappeared from the scene a future German

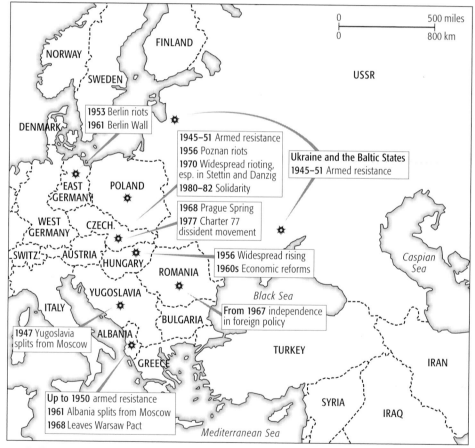

Challenges to the pro-Soviet regimes in eastern and central Europe demonstrated the continuity of resistance to its policies.

government might do a deal with Russia at the German expense. Consequently he felt that the integration of Western Germany with the West was more important than the unification of Germany. He . . . hoped that we would do all in our power to sustain him in this task.

The minute of this conversation was so sensitive that it was held back from full availability in the Foreign Office from early 1956 to 1961.[26]

Poland and Hungary, 1956

Soviet allies were able to put pressure on Khrushchev through party connections as well as through state contacts. The creation of the Warsaw Pact in 1955 introduced another channel through which influence could flow. This was a two-way process and the Soviet side wielded great influence in the affairs of its partners. The agreement to form the Warsaw Treaty Organisation was signed the day before the Austrian State Treaty in May 1955 and as West Germany entered NATO. The Soviets needed the new treaty to legitimate the presence of their troops in Hungary and Romania once occupation duties ended. At this point, alliance matters intersected with Soviet domestic politics to dramatic effect. Khrushchev's thawing of relations with Yugoslavia went along with his dramatic moves in early 1956 to distance himself from aspects of Stalin's policies. The 'secret' speech to the Twentieth Congress of the CPSU in February not only broached liberalisation at home, it promised change in the satellites. Like Beria in 1953, however, Khrushchev found that opening the door to reform could quickly degenerate into challenges to Soviet domination.[27]

The twin crises in Poland and Hungary were a product of these policies, nationalism in the satellites and international tensions. The new Soviet leadership was committed to a foreign policy of co-existence with the West, stability in the satellites, repairing the breach with Yugoslavia and expanding Soviet influence outside Europe. They did not contemplate any serious change to the eastern European status quo, though concern for stability sometimes led them to allow limited reforms. The countries of eastern Europe were allowed to find their own ways to socialism on two conditions: they were not to leave the bloc nor were they to undermine the system of Soviet rule.

Strikes and riots in Poznan, Poland, in June 1956 led to the promotion – at Moscow's behest – of once purged reformers in Hungary, such as Imre Nagy, to prevent the Polish unrest from spreading. At the same time, clear signals were sent that a breach in the bloc's front line would not be tolerated.[28] Ulbricht and other bloc leaders adopted a hard line towards the reformists, seeing change as a threat to their rule at home.[29]

Many Hungarians wished to go further than their neighbours would tolerate: they were encouraged to unrealistic hopes of freedom by US propaganda, wondering how far they could exploit the circumstances of de-Stalinisation and hopeful that they might follow a Yugoslavian or even an Austrian model. In negotiations with high-ranking Soviet delegations Nagy tried to balance popular nationalist and democratic aspirations with the reality of Soviet power; on

24 October he called for Soviet intervention to help him head off revolution. At this point, the Polish crisis ended in a compromise that saw nationalist communist leaders promoted against Moscow's wishes in return for pledges on the leading role of the party and loyalty to the bloc.

Nagy then reversed his position on intervention in the hope of a similar compromise. As they had done in Yugoslavia in 1948, Soviet representatives made common cause with local Moscow loyalists. Ambassador Andropov's reports reflected the alarm of the Stalinists and exaggerated fears of Hungarian defection, which provoked Soviet intervention. That, in turn, drove desperate reformists in Hungary to try to abandon the bloc. The Soviets appeared to be withdrawing, but Moscow would not actually tolerate a threat to bloc solidarity. Soviet forces moved in on 4 November and the revolution was crushed.

Western reaction was much less than the Hungarians had hoped. After the Polish strikes and their violent suppression, Dulles had stated on US television that the use of force to help the cause of freedom was not an option for his government as it carried too great a risk of global war.[30] Britain and France were distracted by their own problems with Egypt.[31] Eisenhower and Dulles used Suez as a convenient shield to deflect domestic criticism of their inaction. A State Department paper dated 16 October 1956 stressed: 'It should be a matter of the highest priority to prevent the outbreak of a war, either general in character, or a serious local action which might develop into large-scale conflict.' Pressed by a former close adviser to do more to help Hungary beyond the 'pitifully small things' that had so far been tried, Eisenhower replied: 'I assure you that the measures taken there by the Soviets are just as distressing to me as they are to you. But to annihilate Hungary, should it happen to become the scene of a bitter conflict, is in no way to help her.'[32]

The aftermath of the Hungarian invasion

In effect the USA had accepted a Soviet sphere of influence in eastern Europe. Dulles reflected in the aftermath of this crisis that 'a showdown with Russia would not have more than one chance in three of working, and two chances out of three of making global war inevitable'.[33] Western reactions amounted to rhetorical condemnation, propaganda (now more carefully vetted to ensure that false hopes were not raised) and declarations at the UNO and elsewhere that portrayed the USSR as an imperialist power. The last step was important in that Khrushchev had striven to display his anti-imperialist credentials at the end of the Suez Crisis. Although Hungary remained on the UNO's agenda until 1962, the dominance of the USSR in its bloc had been established. The 'Polish road' won limited leeway and in the 1960s and 1970s Kadar's Hungary experimented in economic policy, but the fundamental lesson was that the Soviet political system and the alliance must be respected at all times.

As Eisenhower began his second term in January 1957 it seemed as though the Cold War had returned to bitter, inflexible confrontation. This was not quite the case. In July 1956 NSC 5608 considered propaganda, covert operations, aid to

Two pages from a top-secret briefing book of the late 1950s illustrate the view of the Joint Chiefs of Staff of the Cold War confrontation.

exile groups, diplomatic and economic pressure and anything that looked as if it might encourage evolutionary change (such as greater contact through travel and exchanges) to foment nationalism, even communist nationalism, as acceptable alternatives to war.[34] After the Polish upheavals were resolved without Soviet intervention, the USA offered a relatively generous economic aid package to Poland, designed to encourage the Gomulka government down a national road. The policy, later known as differentiation, continued to the end of the Cold War.

At the same time, the efforts of Poland's foreign minister Adam Rapacki to carve out an independent Polish policy and create a nuclear-free zone in eastern and central Europe grew out of a mix of national aspirations, Soviet dominance of the bloc, Western alliance politics and fears of nuclear war.[35] These efforts owed much to both historical fears of Germany and concerns about NATO's deployment of tactical nuclear weapons. The problem for the superpowers was to manage the responses of their allies to such suggestions.[36] In both NATO and the Warsaw Pact the notion of double containment lived on. Rapacki was happy to see the continued division of Germany: there was an abiding Soviet and Polish fear of revanchism underlying their German policies that lasted until the 1980s. Western responses to Rapacki did create tensions in the alliance: at that time and during discussions of multilateral European nuclear forces controlled by NATO, the British, French and Americans sought ways of keeping Germany tied to NATO while denying Adenauer's bid for nuclear weapons.

Western rejection of the Rapacki plan came at a time of heightened fears in the USA about Soviet strength. There were scares in the mid 1950s about an alleged bomber gap. The Soviet launch of Sputnik in 1957, before the USA had a satellite in orbit, caused something close to panic. The Gaither Committee brought together government, academic and business experts who recommended emergency action to bridge the science gap.[37] For the rest of Eisenhower's presidency, Democrats and elements in the armed forces made much of US vulnerability. Due to U-2 and other intelligence, Eisenhower knew that the gaps were non-existent. In the face of highly questionable airforce intelligence estimates that exaggerated Soviet capability (for reasons of Pentagon bureaucratic politics) that were used by his critics, he did not make the information public: he was concealing the U-2 flights and feared that too much publicity about the USA's advantage might encourage Congress to cut spending too far. John F. Kennedy campaigned in 1960 against the administration's supposed weakness in the face of Khrushchev's boasts about his arsenal. Within weeks of taking office, however, the Kennedy administration acknowledged the reality of a major US lead in missiles and other delivery systems.

China and the superpowers

In the aftermath of the Suez Crisis, the Middle East remained an area of tension. The Lebanese Christian leader Camille Chamoun was instrumental in drawing the USA into Lebanon in July 1958. In an attempt to prolong his own premiership, he manipulated a domestic crisis. Then, by stressing Nasser's threat, he made an international crisis out of a domestic one and brought the Eisenhower Doctrine into play. The Eisenhower Doctrine committed the USA to intervention in the Middle East whenever a friendly government asked the USA to help it resist 'power-hungry communists', whose motives were likened by Dulles to those of

Hitler in the 1930s.[38] US intervention may have helped maintain an uneasy status quo in that region, but it had important ramifications on the Pacific Rim.

By the mid 1950s there were growing problems in the Sino-Soviet alliance. Soviet advisers had caused some resentment in China when their nationalist susceptibilities were ruffled by perceived arrogance. Soviet insistence on payment for material supplied during the Korean War did not help matters. The key to the growing friction was ideology. De-Stalinisation and attacks on the cult of the personality went down badly in Beijing, as did Soviet critiques of the Great Leap Forward, Mao's radical economic policy (which had had disastrous consequences). Although China initially welcomed the intervention in Hungary, there was a measure of ambivalence about such forceful Soviet leadership. Personal relations between the leaders were poor and Mao resented criticism of Molotov and the 'anti-party group' for views that resembled his own.

Sino-Soviet relations were thus changing by the time Mao initiated the second Taiwan Straits Crisis in 1958, in part to punish the USA for intervening in Lebanon. He may also have hoped to prevent further moves towards peaceful co-existence between the two superpowers. Given that he wanted to make China once more into a major power recognised as an equal by enemies and allies, he resented Khrushchev's lack of consultation and his détente policies. Mao's ideological aversion to settling with the USA meant that the so-called spirit of Camp David held little attraction.[39] To him the intervention in Lebanon suggested that imperialist ambitions were unchanged by détente with the USSR. Shelling Jinmen and Mazu demonstrated that he was cowed neither by nuclear bombs nor by Soviet–US détente. In addition, a new crisis and pressure on Taiwan secured support for a nationalist external policy in the chaos that followed innovations in economic and social policy, and served to silence domestic criticism. Mao failed to anticipate Khrushchev's reaction: he was horrified by Mao's willingness to call Dulles' nuclear bluff and threaten (Soviet) retaliation and quickly distanced himself from China in September 1958. Dulles vowed that there would be 'no appeasement'[40] and, by the time Mao climbed down, the superpowers' allies had increased tension locally in an attempt to derail US–Soviet détente. Neither Mao nor Jiang Jieshi wished to see the sort of 'two Chinas' compromise that the superpowers might have accepted and they were successful in preventing any such outcome.[41]

In the aftermath of the crises Mao's suspicions of foreign domination turned to the Soviets. He avoided Soviet efforts to involve the Chinese in co-operative ventures in submarine deployments, radar and signal facilities and other naval matters that he feared might give the USSR too much influence. In 1959, after more tensions and a disastrous meeting which strengthened Soviet fears about Mao's reliability on nuclear matters, the USSR recalled its advisers and abruptly terminated nuclear co-operation.

In the spring of 1960 the Soviets and Chinese criticised each other at a gathering of communist leaders in Bucharest. Ideological rivalry soon extended to the developing world, where both sides began to compete for friends and influence. Each criticised the other's revisionism, deviations or adventurism.

By 1963 Sino-Soviet tensions were at breaking point and the polemics open. In May 1963 the British prime minister's private secretary noted that a Soviet diplomat:

> . . . several times expressed worry about China . . . Russia and Britain both wished for peace in Laos but . . . they could not put much pressure on the Chinese to fall into line. He also seemed worried about the Chinese position in relation to a possible [nuclear] non-dissemination agreement.[42]

State as well as ideological interests were involved. In supporting progress towards a nuclear test ban and, especially, non-proliferation treaties, the nuclear powers acted together against China and, to some extent, France. The Johnson administration even considered the prospect of joint Soviet–US action against Chinese nuclear facilities.[43]

Vietnam and Indochina

Another problem for China was the renewal of warfare in Vietnam. Ngo Dinh Diem, a northern Catholic exile whose nationalist credentials were sufficient to make the French prefer Bao Dai, rose to power south of the 17th parallel after the USA refused to sign the Geneva Accords in 1954. There British, Soviets and Chinese had pressured North Vietnam into accepting temporary partition at the 17th parallel. After the fall of their stronghold at Dien Bien Phu, the French too accepted partition. Reunification elections were planned for 1956.[44] Diem shouldered aside Bao Dai and the USA backed his efforts to create an independent South Vietnam. When Diem's regime proved to be both corrupt and inefficient, they were then faced with a dilemma: their prestige and resources were committed and threatening to give up on Diem might weaken the steadfastness of other allies who might interpret the situation as the USA failing to honour its commitments. Like Khrushchev with Ulbricht, US credibility was staked on Diem's survival.

US aid bolstered South Vietnam and the consolidation of communist power in the North precluded any action until 1959. Soviet and Chinese policies also backed peaceful reunification. That year those resisting Diem formed the National Liberation Front and decided upon armed struggle to hasten reunification. The authorities in the North went along with this in the face of Soviet and Chinese reluctance.[45] Diem's regime fared badly against the Chinese-backed insurgency. US aid increased in 1960 and again under Kennedy. He inherited a situation where there were over 1,000 military advisers aiding Diem as well as a significant CIA presence in Saigon. By the time of Kennedy's assassination in November 1963 the advisers numbered over 16,000. Arguments have raged ever since over whether Kennedy might have pulled out after a successful re-election campaign in 1964. He had accepted a neutral Laos in accords brokered with Khrushchev in 1962 and some former advisers claimed that a similar solution would have been found in Vietnam.[46]

Diem consistently manipulated local US representatives to ensure a continued flow of aid with a minimum of strings. Although Eisenhower had promised aid only to a viable southern state, he had also formulated the domino theory to demonstrate the importance of poor and faraway places like Indochina: if one fell, a whole row would follow. The Americans had committed themselves to keeping friendly regimes in place. In so doing they created a Vietnamese state that became progressively more dependent on US aid to build itself into a nation. The need to assist grew in proportion to Vietnamese weakness. This was starkly illustrated by the deposition of Diem in November 1963: coup-plotting generals acted only when they felt they had the backing of the US ambassador. Lyndon Johnson inherited a difficult situation, made worse by his domestic political concern with not seeming weak.

The USSR barely concerned itself with Vietnam until the massive US escalation of 1965. Before then Stalin had left the region to Mao, and Khrushchev had been satisfied with a compromise in 1954. The Soviets advised against the resumption of fighting in 1959 and approved the neutralisation of Laos in 1962. As US prestige became involved, Soviet interests were dictated by a reflex to oppose anything their main adversary did. Moscow also felt obliged to react to Chinese support for Hanoi once tensions spilled into rivalry for leadership within the communist bloc.

Neutrals and new nations

Elsewhere in the developing world the decade between the Geneva conference and the Tonkin Gulf Resolution of August 1964 (see p. 95) saw an intensification of Cold War rivalry. Both superpowers worried about their allies' loyalty and both strove for ways to deal with neutralist states such as Egypt and India. The superpowers relied on the support of new nations emerging from European colonial rule for UN votes, resources, strategic locations and propaganda value. Winning friends was seen as important in bolstering the morale of other allies. It fostered a reassuring sense that history was vindicating one's ideology or a romantic attachment to regimes that seemed to mirror one's own. To the ageing Soviet leadership the young revolutionaries in Cuba seemed to bring back memories of their youth.[47] Nationalist and other politicians, eager to secure 'rent' for their nation, also stimulated the process as they sought alliances outside their countries.[48] The superpowers were motivated partly by their respective anti-colonial traditions, partly by a desire to pre-empt each other. They were also spurred on by fear of Chinese communism's appeal to new nations.

The Soviets were quick to make propaganda points of US race politics.[49] A British diplomat saw Southern resistance to civil rights as 'a present for communist propaganda in Asia and Africa'. It was especially embarrassing when ambassadors from newly independent African states were denied basic highway services on grounds of their colour. Secretary of State Dean Rusk, a Southern liberal, spoke out in 1963: 'This issue deeply affects the conduct of our foreign relations . . . Our voice is muted, our friends are embarrassed, and our enemies are gleeful, because we have not really put our hands fully and effectively to this problem . . . '.[50]

These matters were considered important because US leaders viewed neutralism with suspicion and wished to cultivate friendships around the world. Eisenhower and Dulles cut back on Truman's assistance to the anti-Moscow communists in Yugoslavia and they allowed their Cold War priorities to influence their judgements about Nasser's militant pan-Arabism and nationalism. His regime was viewed as more of a Soviet proxy than was really the case and they came, as they had in the Lebanese Crisis or that over Jordan in 1958, to view Egyptian influence as synonymous with Soviet influence.

Rhetorically at least, the Kennedy administration dealt with these matters better than its predecessors had but, as Rabe and others have demonstrated, the reality was that no-one handled neutralism well.[51] Forced to choose, Kennedy backed Portugal, a NATO ally, over its African critics. Although he tried to build aid policies that would allow co-operation with the likes of Nkrumah's Ghana or through the efforts of the Peace Corps, the reality was that rhetoric was rarely matched by actions. This was demonstrated by the Alliance for Progress in Latin America. Intended to place the USA on the progressive side of that region's politics and head off the appeal of Castro, the Alliance's policies channelled funds to regimes that rarely used them to assist popular reforms. Johnson reverted to the assumption that it was preferable to back local anti-communist elites rather than risk upheaval through reform.

Khrushchev's January 1961 declaration of Soviet support for wars of national liberation demonstrates the complex interactions of the superpowers in developing-world affairs. It was aimed more to fend off Chinese criticism than to threaten the USA's allies, but it was perceived in Washington as a challenge. This rediscovery of Lenin's enthusiasm for aid to peasant revolutionaries affected Kennedy's perceptions of developments in Cuba, the Congo and Indochina. It also became the basis for costly interventions around the world as the USSR fell prey to the leverage of weak allies.

Berlin again

At the time, however, another weak ally closer to home dominated Soviet foreign policy. West Germany entered NATO in 1955 and it seemed only a matter of time before its rearmament produced a strong military, perhaps armed with nuclear weapons. This prospect alarmed Soviet and DDR leaders and they took steps to prevent it. Diplomatic pressure and propaganda strove to divide the Americans, West Germans and other Europeans.

This situation arose as Khrushchev sought to consolidate his power. His strategies for maximising his influence in Soviet decision-making processes led him to undertake ever-riskier initiatives in foreign affairs. His economic priorities entailed cuts in the armed forces and greater reliance on nuclear weapons. Although de-Stalinisation implied a measure of co-existence, his domestic opponents sought a return to harder Cold War policies alongside their commitment to a more hardline domestic ideology. Party leaders such as Molotov or Mikhail Suslov were critical of Khrushchev's foreign and domestic policies and tended to fall out with reformers. Those involved in the armed forces, heavy industry and the party bureaucracy were more inclined to be critical; those responsible for light industry, the foreign affairs bureaucracy and policy experts less so. According to Richter, as Khrushchev's reforms ran into trouble, he strove to legitimise his leadership with foreign policy successes.[52] Berlin became vital to the prospects of reform at home.

In late 1958, feeling confident after the successful testing of a hydrogen bomb and the launch of ICBMs (inter-continental ballistic missiles), keen to impress the Chinese with his resolution and to focus minds at home on his strengths, Khrushchev initiated a new crisis. Closely supervised East German moves to put pressure on West Berlin were followed by Soviet demands for a four-power peace treaty. Khrushchev's ultimatum gave the West six months before he would hand over control of the borders and access corridors of West Berlin to the DDR and conclude a separate treaty with that state.[53] Richter interprets the ultimatum as an effort to force negotiations that might split the West while offering hope of fending off West Germany's rearmament and bids for nuclear weapons as well as bolstering the struggling East German regime. The gambit was also intended to force respect for Soviet power and prove that Khrushchev's policies were not weakening the USSR as domestic critics had alleged, thus boosting his prestige.[54]

A Western outpost in the heart of the bloc might sometimes have been an annoyance, but it also gave Khrushchev a pressure point whenever he wished to create a crisis. He viewed Berlin as a lever with which he could win larger concessions over West German (especially nuclear) rearmament, European frontiers and statehood for the DDR. Ulbricht and his government saw West Berlin as a prize and sought to exclude the West, stop the exodus to West Germany and control a city on their soil. Their weak economy gave them leverage over Khrushchev, who had prestige invested in their success. The USA and West Germany were constantly concerned that the British and French were too much inclined to compromise in the face of Soviet bluster. In 1959 Adenauer became extremely agitated at Macmillan's eagerness for summit talks with Khrushchev to resolve the crisis before the ultimatum expired. Adenauer emphasised that dividing the allies was a standard Soviet ploy and that the British were playing into Soviet hands in their willingness to compromise. Eisenhower shared this concern and resisted British efforts to push for early talks in 1959.[55]

Given Ulbricht's ability to manipulate Khrushchev and given Khrushchev's fears that he could 'lose' the DDR to an aggressive, rearmed West, the Soviet position was essentially defensive. In the light of internal power struggles, the need to watch for Chinese challenges and his tendency to retreat to assumptions dating back to before 1941, the collapsing East German economy combined with Western intransigence to put Khrushchev in a difficult position. Khrushchev wanted to demonstrate that his nuclear arsenal (or rather his rhetoric about having a big nuclear arsenal) could and did pay diplomatic dividends, yet he also needed to resist Ulbricht's pressure for an immediate and hardline solution as that would have called his bluff (that he might resort to a nuclear exchange if no solution satisfactory to him was reached). Khrushchev veered from using diplomacy to threatening force, but his attempts to achieve a resolution came to nothing.

The DDR leaders' problems were economic and social as well as ideological. By 1960 the country was losing thousands of mainly young and often professional citizens to the West each month, as it had in 1952–53. After the failure of the Paris summit in April, Khrushchev put off his ally with pledges that he would deal with the new US administration the following year. Both Ulbricht and the Chinese were critical of this stance. The East Germans appealed for massive Soviet aid while also courting the Chinese and staging provocations around Berlin. The Soviet emphasis on Berlin gave Khrushchev a chance to demonstrate a toughness that reassured critics of his reforms at home. He also seems to have hoped that he might be able to pull off a diplomatic coup at a summit meeting that would allow him to portray himself as a tough Cold warrior and demonstrate the merits of co-existence to domestic and Chinese critics. His moderation exasperated Ulbricht, who craved a solution to his domestic problems and reportedly commented that 'we cannot compete with capitalism with open borders'.[56]

At Vienna in June 1961 Kennedy proved just as obdurate as Eisenhower and some of the most chilling moments of the summit concerned Germany. The prospect of 'a cold winter' of confrontation, perhaps even war, loomed.[57] Neither Eisenhower (whom Bundy quotes as saying: 'I don't know how you could free anything with nuclear weapons') nor Kennedy were prepared to wage nuclear war for the city, even though they did wish to be seen to resist Khrushchev's nuclear diplomacy. British views were somewhat similar, despite US and German fears of their willingness to appease.[58] Before summer was over, however, a dramatic new development occurred which stabilised the Berlin Crisis. Ulbricht made statements that hastened the exodus of East Germans to over 20,000 a month, probably to provoke a crisis. Pressed by the East German leadership, Khrushchev accepted drastic measures, but insisted that Ulbricht go 'not one millimetre' beyond them.[59] The Warsaw Pact leadership met between 3 and 5 August to fix dates for sealing off the borders. The decision was eased (deliberately or otherwise) by the Kennedy administration's rhetoric, which suggested strong US commitment to West Berlin but restraint on the issue of its borders. Kennedy's view was that the wall was 'not a very nice solution but . . . a hell of a lot better than a war'.[60]

When the barriers went up on 13 August the West's less than vigorous response disappointed many West Germans. Rhetorical denunciation and prominent displays of armed resolve by US tanks in Berlin were the extent of it. The Soviet response was designed to show that they, not Ulbricht, were really in charge. Throughout the crisis Khrushchev was careful not to risk war, even as the tanks faced each other. Berlin's status seemed unresolved. For both sides, consideration of how to deal with the city remained a high priority.[61] The outcome did not fulfil anyone's maximum ambitions. Massive Soviet aid and the end of mass emigration eased the DDR's economic problems, but Khrushchev continued to defer any discussion of a separate peace treaty. The West's firm reaction, combined with continued gestures and statements from the USA about Germany, was enough to deter Khrushchev. Both the Chinese and Ulbricht were disappointed by Khrushchev's compromise solution for preserving East Germany while not provoking the West.[62] Ulbricht had been able to influence Khrushchev's options, and the wall restrained him as much as it did anyone.

The atmosphere remained tense throughout 1962. Berlin played a major part in both Western and communist actions during the Cuban Missile Crisis. The Kennedy administration was deeply concerned about allied, specifically German, reactions lest the USA be seen as more willing to fight for Cuba than it had been for West Berlin. The situation only shifted after the Cuban Missile Crisis had demonstrated Kennedy's resolve. His tough stance then saw Soviet ambitions in Germany scaled down and Kennedy grow in confidence. He reversed his German policy in 1963 and abandoned ideas of any compromise in his stirring oratory during his visit to Berlin in June. The outcome of the crisis was that Khrushchev made very limited gains, if any. Ulbricht stabilised his regime but saw West Germany and West Berlin embedded more firmly in the Western alliance.[63] In future, all parties would have to seek new ways to manage intra-German relations.

Co-existence

The summits of the years 1959–61 offer a flavour of the ambivalent nature of the Cold War at that time. Efforts to negotiate on nuclear testing, Berlin, Indochina and other matters did not succeed in significantly reducing tension, still less in ending confrontation. Certain episodes sum up the mood of competitive co-operation: as Khrushchev travelled by train across the USA he asked for, and was given, a map. This outraged the Soviets as it showed military facilities and was assumed to be a CIA provocation. The Americans finally overcame the suspicions of their guests and persuaded them that this was standard in US atlases. The US exhibition in Moscow in 1959 was testimony to improved relations and resulted from the conclusion of the Cultural Agreement in 1958. Loved by Muscovites, the exhibition manifested the tensions that underlay improved relations. The Soviet authorities prevented the Americans from installing up-to-date restrooms, distributing free cosmetics or toy cars and from playing jazz. They objected to tacit encouragement of book pilfering, especially of Bibles. When Vice-President Nixon attended, Khrushchev met him and they engaged in sparring about the merits of their social systems.[64]

Eisenhower's meeting with Khrushchev in Paris in May 1960 was intended to deal with the Berlin Crisis among other issues. Both leaders wished to meet so that they could defend themselves against domestic criticism that their foreign policies were ineffective. They were also responding to Western public opinion that sought reassurance in manifestations of co-existence. The summit was brought to an abrupt halt when the shooting down of a US U-2 deep over the USSR became public and Eisenhower refused to apologise. The underlying mutual mistrust was too great to overcome and the wish not to back down in such a public stand-off was too strong. By then the Soviet leader knew that the meeting would yield no Western concessions, but he paid a domestic price for the dénouement. Khrushchev came to believe that this was the moment when everything started to go wrong. The shooting down of the US plane was publicised by his domestic critics and the failed summit weakened him at home.

In the early 1960s US schoolchildren were drilled on what to do in the event of a nuclear attack. The arms race, the launching of satellites, the spy-planes, the bigger and bigger kilotonnages of the bombs tested were the backdrop to efforts to manage the Cold War and to build better relations. The tensions reached a peak in the twin crises over Berlin and Cuba in 1961–62. The apparent imminence of nuclear war increased the urgency of finding ways to co-exist peacefully, causing the Cold War to change again.

Responses to crisis

3.1 US evaluation of eastern Europe, July 1956

The elimination of Soviet domination of the satellites is . . . in the fundamental interest of the United States . . .

One alternative is to take direct action for the liberation of the satellite peoples from the USSR by military force, either through direct military intervention or through armed support of revolutionary movements. Such use of military force would in all probability start a global war. This alternative is not in accordance with current US policy and must therefore be rejected . . .

In its efforts to encourage anti-Soviet elements in the satellites and keep up their hopes, the United States should not encourage premature action on their part which will bring upon them reprisals involving further terror and suppression . . .

Source: Annex to NSC 5608, 6 July 1956, record no. 79194, Soviet Flashpoints Collection, National Security Archive, Washington, DC, pp. 14–15, paras 31 and 35

3.2 Account of a meeting at the CPSU Central Committee, 24 October 1956, on the situation in Poland and Hungary

Comrade Khrushchev . . . The Soviet comrades are very worried because the [Polish] comrades who were removed from the Politburo were known to the Soviet party as old, trustworthy revolutionaries who were faithful to the cause of socialism. Among them is also Comrade [Defence Minister] Rokossovskii, who is of Polish origin but never gave up his Soviet citizenship . . .

Gomulka several times emphasized that they would not permit their independence to be taken away and would not allow anyone to interfere in Poland's internal affairs . . . [Gomulka] further emphasized that the presence of Soviet troops on Polish territory was necessary because of the existence of NATO and the presence of American troops in

West Germany . . . It was the view of Comrade Khrushchev that this speech by Comrade Gomulka gives hope that Poland has now adopted a course that will eliminate the unpleasant state of affairs.

. . . Comrade Zhukov informed [Khrushchev] that Gero had asked the military attaché at the Soviet embassy in Budapest to dispatch Soviet troops to suppress a demonstration that was reaching an ever greater and unprecedented scale . . .

Shortly thereafter, a call came through from the Soviet embassy in Budapest saying that the situation is extremely dangerous and that the intervention of Soviet troops is necessary . . . The situation developed in such a way that Comrade Zhukov was given orders to occupy Budapest with Soviet military units . . .

Comrade Ulbricht emphasized . . . the situation had arisen because we did not act in time to expose all the incorrect opinions that had emerged in Poland and Hungary.

Source: *CWIHP Bulletin*, no. 5 (1995), tr. M. Kramer, pp. 50–57

3.3 Records of meetings of CPSU and CCP delegations, Moscow, July 1963

Deng Xiaoping: [A] whole series of disagreements of a fundamental character which exist today in the international Communist movement started at the Twentieth Congress of the CPSU . . . From April to July of 1958 the CPSU put to China the issue of the creation of a long wave radar station and a joint fleet, trying thereby to bring China under its military control . . . Following that you started both in statements and in actions to carry out anti-Chinese activities in an intensified manner . . . In June 1959 you unilaterally annulled the agreement on rendering help to China in developing a nuclear industry and in producing atom bombs . . . On August 25, 1962, the Soviet government informed China that it was ready to conclude an agreement with the USA on the proliferation of nuclear weapons. In our view, you were pursuing an unseemly goal in coming to such an agreement, namely: to bind China by the hands and feet through an agreement with the USA . . . Your position on the issues of the Indian–Chinese border conflict received praise from the United States.

Source: O. A. Westad (ed.), *Brothers in arms: the rise and fall of the Sino-Soviet alliance, 1945–1963*, Stanford, 1998, pp. 376 ff

3.4 Foreign Secretary Lord Home sends the British ambassador in Washington, Ormsby Gore, his reflections on the Berlin Crisis, February 1962

[Concessions would produce difficulties with Germany and France and run counter to Anglo-American desires not to abandon Western positions,] unless we are absolutely convinced that such concessions are necessary to avoid the danger of war or that they will buy for us a new situation which is both tolerable and stable . . . The Russians are fully conscious of American superiority in the nuclear field. The fact that they have postponed their deadline and are now careful to name no deadline at all, undoubtedly reflects this, and I think we are right to assume that they will think very hard before risking a showdown over Berlin. On the other hand, as we well know, Khrushchev is deeply committed to achieve a peace treaty. There is also the fact that the Russians must be ~~deeply~~ [sic] concerned about the growing economic and military power of the Federal Republic on the one hand and the continued instability and ill-success of the East German regime on the other . . . They feel an urgent need to obtain recognition and international standing for the regime and a more general acceptance of the 'finality' of the division of Germany and of the frontiers of all Germany . . . We do not ourselves want to see Germany reunited, though we will never deny the right of self-determination . . . It suits us best that [East Germany] should remain as it is, a very bad advertisement for Communism and a burden to the USSR . . . These are . . . not the sort of [ideas] we could discuss with the Germans at the present time . . .

Source: Home replying to Ormsby Gore's letter, 5 February 1962, FO371/163567, Public Record Office (hereafter PRO), London

Document case-study questions

1 Explain the significance of the phrases 'satellite peoples' (3.1) and 'incorrect opinions' (3.2).

2 Compare the Soviet attitude to the Polish and Hungarian crises in extract 3.2 with the Chinese criticism of their attitude in extract 3.3. What conclusions can we draw about the motives of the Chinese?

3 What do extracts 3.1 and 3.4 reveal about attitudes towards the prospect of war?

4 Evaluate the evidence of extracts 3.3 and 3.4 regarding changes in the Cold War between 1951 and 1963.

5 Using the documents and your wider knowledge, assess the importance of alliance politics in the crises of the period between 1951 and 1963.

Notes and references

1 K. Kaplan, *Procès politiques à Prague*, Paris, 1980, pp. 51–52, for an account of Eastern bloc assumptions at the time of the Slansky trial in Czechoslovakia.

2 Annex to NSC 5608, 6 July 1956, record no. 79194, Soviet Flashpoints Collection, National Security Archive, Washington, DC, pp. 14–15, paras 31 and 35, explicitly rejects war. The same document appears in *FRUS*, 1955–1957, vol. XXV, 'Eastern Europe', Washington, DC, 1996, pp. 198–209, but was not completely declassified and the sections on military and covert action are missing. O. A. Westad, 'The Sino-Soviet alliance and the United States', in O. A. Westad (ed.), *Brothers in arms: the rise and fall of the Sino-Soviet alliance, 1945–1963*, Stanford, 1998, pp. 175–77, also p. 22 of his Introduction; C. Pleshakov, 'Nikita Khrushchev and Sino-Soviet relations', in the same volume, pp. 236–37. In A. Dobrynin, *In confidence. Moscow's ambassador to America's six Cold War presidents*, New York, 1995, p. 53, Dobrynin recounts that before going to take up his post for the first time, Khrushchev told him, '"Don't ask for trouble." He plainly told me that I should always bear in mind that war with the United States was inadmissible; this was above all.'

3 T. Hoopes, *The devil and John Foster Dulles*, Boston, 1973. Compare R. H. Immerman, *John Foster Dulles. Piety, pragmatism and power in U.S. foreign policy*, Wilmington, Del., 1999. On Dean Rusk's similar views, see T. W. Zeiler, *Dean Rusk: defending the American mission abroad*, Wilmington, Del., 2000.

4 W. R. Smyser, *From Yalta to Berlin: the Cold War struggle over Germany*, New York, 1999, p. 107.

5 R. Van Dijk, 'The 1952 Stalin note debate: myth or missed opportunity for German unification?', *CWIHP Working Paper*, no. 14 (1996), summarises the debate; also J. Richter, 'Re-examining Soviet policy towards Germany in 1953', *Europe–Asia Studies*, vol. 45 (1993), p. 675.

6 G. Wettig, 'The Soviet Union and Germany in the late Stalin period, 1950–53', in F. Gori and S. Pons (eds.), *The Soviet Union and Europe in the Cold War, 1943–53*, London, 1996, p. 365. He also characterises Stalin as 'terrified' of Western rearmament and of a Western attack.

7 H. Adomeit, *Imperial overstretch: Germany in Soviet policy from Stalin to Gorbachev: an analysis based on new archival evidence, memoirs, and interviews*, Baden-Baden, 1998, pp. 80–92.

8 R. R. Bowie and R. H. Immerman, *Waging peace. How Eisenhower shaped an enduring Cold War strategy*, Oxford, 1998, esp. p. 75; M. Evangelista, '"Why keep such an army?": Khrushchev's troop reductions', *CWIHP Working Paper*, no. 19 (1997).

9 G. Bischof, *Austria in the first Cold War, 1945–55: the leverage of the weak*, Cambridge, 1999, pp. 104–56.

10 J. L. Gaddis, *We now know. Rethinking Cold War history*, Oxford, 1997, pp. 223–30.

11 C. Andrew and O. Gordievsky, *KGB. The inside story of its foreign operations from Lenin to Gorbachev*, London, 1990, pp. 358–73, 419–20; T. Wolton, *Le KGB en France*, Paris, 1986, pp. 202–05, 279–87; and D. E. Murphy, G. Bailey and S. A. Kondrashev, *Battleground Berlin. CIA vs KGB in the Cold War*, London, 1997.

12 C. Andrew and V. Mitrokhin, *The Mitrokhin archive. The KGB in Europe and the West*, London, 1999, esp. chs. 14, 27, describes 'active measures' by the KGB from the 1940s to the 1980s. See also Wolton, *KGB en France*, pp. 301–400. N. Cullather, *Secret history. The CIA's classified account of its operations in Guatemala, 1952–1954*, Stanford, 1999, describes CIA disinformation operations in Guatemala.

13 W. L. Hixson, *Parting the curtain. Propaganda, culture, and the Cold War, 1945–1961*, London, 1998, recounts US propaganda efforts.

14 S. Lucas, *Freedom's war: the American crusade against the Soviet Union*, New York, 1999, pp. 46, 110–21.

15 Z. Karabell, *Architects of intervention. The United States, the third world and the Cold War, 1946–1962*, Baton Rouge, La., 1999, pp. 50–135, on Iran and Guatemala.

16 Cullather, *Secret history*, pp. 60–63.

17 S. Rabe, 'Dulles, Latin America and Cold War anticommunism', in R. H. Immerman (ed.), *John Foster Dulles and the diplomacy of the Cold War*, Princeton, 1990; and Rabe, *The most dangerous area in the world*, Chapel Hill, 1999. On Kennedy, see Karabell, *Architects of intervention*, pp. 173–77, 204–08; R. M. Bissell and J. E. Lewis, *Reflections of a Cold warrior: from Yalta to the Bay of Pigs*, New Haven, 1996, pp. 140–204; and Cullather, *Secret history*, pp. 109–12 and afterword.

18 Qiang Zhai, *The dragon, the lion and the eagle: Chinese–British–American relations, 1949–1958*, London, 1994, p. 159.

19 Qiang Zhai, *China and the Vietnam wars, 1950–1975*, Chapel Hill, 2000, pp. 20–26.

20 Westad, 'The Sino-Soviet alliance', p. 173; N. B. Tucker, 'John Foster Dulles and Taiwan', in Immerman (ed.), *Dulles and the diplomacy*, pp. 235–62; and V. Zubok and C. Pleshakov, *Inside the Kremlin's Cold War. From Stalin to Khrushchev*, Cambridge, Mass., 1996, pp. 210–16. Shu Guang Zhang, *Deterrence and strategic culture: Chinese–American confrontations, 1949–1958*, London, 1992, pp. 189–224.

21 Qiang Zhai, *The dragon, the lion*, pp. 165–74.

22 Zubok and Pleshakov, *Kremlin's Cold War*, p.160–61.

23 Smyser, *Yalta to Berlin*, pp. 119–26; Adomeit, *Imperial overstretch*, pp. 92–100; and J. Richter,

'Reexamining Soviet policy towards Germany during the Beria interregnum', *CWIHP Working Paper*, no. 3 (1992).

24 V. Ingimundarson, 'The 1953 East German uprising', *Diplomatic History*, vol. 20 (1996); C. F. Ostermann, 'The United States, the East German uprising of 1953, and the limits of rollback', *CWIHP Working Paper*, no. 11 (1994); Murphy et al, *Battleground Berlin*, pp. 163–82.

25 Smyser, *Yalta to Berlin*, pp. 140–43; W. L. Hitchcock, *France restored: Cold War diplomacy and the quest for leadership in Europe, 1944–1954*, Chapel Hill, 1998, chs. 5 and 6; M. Trachtenberg, *A constructed peace. The making of a European settlement, 1945–1963*, Princeton, 1999, ch. 4.

26 Memo by Sir Ivone Kirkpatrick, permanent under secretary, 16 December 1955, FO371/118254, top secret, PRO, London.

27 Gaddis, *We now know*, pp. 208–10.

28 This section is based on C. Bekes, 'The 1956 Hungarian Revolution and world politics', *CWIHP Working Paper*, no. 16 (1996).

29 V. Zubok, 'Khrushchev and the Berlin Crisis (1958–1962)', *CWIHP Working Paper*, no. 6 (1993), p. 6, stresses protests in the DDR.

30 Dulles on 'Face the Nation', *Cold War*, programme 7, Turner/BBC, 1998.

31 Britain and France's long-standing animosity to Nasser of Egypt was exacerbated by his nationalisation of the Suez Canal. In October 1956, together with Israel, they intervened militarily against Egypt, believing that the USA would support them. After they invaded the canal area, they found that Dulles and Eisenhower would not back them. Late in the crisis Khrushchev announced that he might contemplate drastic action if the invasion were not called off. The British were forced to climb down. Many in the developing world believed that Khrushchev's announcement was the key moment but, in fact, the change of policy resulted from US economic diplomacy, and the Soviet ultimatum came after the British had made their key decision.

32 L. W. Fuller, 'Concepts and principles of a long-term foreign policy', record no. 66024; and exchange of letters between C. D. Jackson and DDE, 19 November 1956, box no. 3, record nos. 64716 and 64717, Soviet Flashpoints Collection, National Security Archive, Washington, DC.

33 Quoted in J. L. Gaddis, 'The unexpected John Foster Dulles', in Immerman (ed.), *Dulles and the diplomacy*, p. 57. See also R. Garthoff, *Assessing the adversary: estimates by the Eisenhower administration of Soviet intentions and capabilities*, Washington, DC, 1991, pp. 16–17.

34 Annex to NSC 5608, 6 July 1956, record no. 79194, Soviet Flashpoints Collection, National Security Archive, Washington, DC.

35 Rapacki put forward denuclearisation proposals in a speech to the UNO in October 1957. They would have had an impact on both Polish–German relations and German–NATO relations.

36 P. Wanzcyk, 'Adam Rapacki and the search for European security', in G. A. Craig and F. L. Loewenheim (eds.), *The diplomats, 1939–1979*, Princeton, 1994, pp. 289–317.

37 D. L. Snead, *The Gaither committee, Eisenhower and the Cold War*, Columbus, Ohio, 1999.

38 S. Ambrose, *Eisenhower the president, 1952–1969*, London, 1984, pp. 381–83, 463–66, 469–75; and Immerman, *John Foster Dulles. Piety, pragmatism and power*, pp. 161–66.

39 R. Foot, *The practice of power. U.S. Relations with China since 1949*, Oxford, 1997, pp. 124–30, 150–1; G. Chang, *Friends and enemies. The United States, China, and the Soviet Union, 1948–1972*, Stanford, 1990, pp. 183–94; Westad, *Brothers in arms*, pp. 149–52, 175–77, 236–37.

40 Immerman, *John Foster Dulles. Piety, pragmatism and power*, p. 184.

41 Tucker, 'John Foster Dulles and Taiwan', pp. 254–59.

42 Memo by P. de Zulueta, 3 May 1963, PREM 11/4495, PRO, London.

43 Chang, *Friends and enemies*, p. 250.

44 J. Cable, *The Geneva conference of 1954 on Indochina*, London, 2000; Qiang Zhai, *China and the Vietnam wars*, ch. 2.

45 I. Gaiduk, *The Soviet Union and the Vietnam War*, Chicago, 1996, pp. 5–6; Qiang Zhai, *China and the Vietnam wars*, pp. 81–86.

46 See M. R. Beschloss, *Kennedy and Khrushchev: the crisis years, 1960–1963*, New York, 1991, pp. 395–98, on Laos. R. D. Schulzinger, *A time for war: the United States and Vietnam, 1941–1975*, Oxford, 1997, ch. 5. R. S. McNamara with B. VanDeMark, *In retrospect. The tragedy and lessons of Vietnam*, New York, vintage edn, 1995, p. 96, concludes that Kennedy would have pulled out of Vietnam.

47 Zubok and Pleshakov, *Kremlin's Cold War*, pp. 206–07. Mikoyan quoted in A. Fursenko and T. Naftali, *'One hell of a gamble': the secret history of the Cuban Missile Crisis*, London, 1997, pp. 38–39.

48 A. Shlaim and Y. Sayigh (eds.), *The Cold War and the Middle East*, Oxford, 1997. 'Rent' is money coming to local government either as outright aid or, for example, from rent for training areas, bases or other facilities.

49 See C. Fraser, 'Crossing the color line in Little Rock: the Eisenhower administration and the dilemma of race for U.S. foreign policy', *Diplomatic History*, vol. 24 (2000).

50 M. Sewell, 'British responses to Martin Luther King, jr. and the civil rights movement', in B. E. Ward and A. J. Badger, *The making of Martin Luther King, jr.*, London, 1996, p. 197; 'Mr Dean Rusk denounces colour discrimination', in *Times* (London), 29 May 1963.

51 Rabe, *The most dangerous area*; 'Dulles, Latin America and Cold War anticommunism'; and Karabell, *Architects of intervention*, pp. 206–25.

52 G. Arbatov, *The system: an insider's life in Soviet politics*, New York, 1992, pp. 69–79; J. Richter, *Khrushchev's double bind. International pressures and domestic coalition politics*, London, 1994, pp. 37–50, 64–68, 126–28, 135–39.

53 This draws on H. Harrison, 'Ulbricht and the "concrete rose": new archival evidence on the dynamics of Soviet-East German relations and the Berlin crisis, 1958–1961', CWIHP Working Paper, no. 5 (1993); and Zubok, 'Khrushchev and the Berlin Crisis (1958–1962)'. There was no peace treaty ending the Second World War until 1990 as the victor powers could never conclude a satisfactory one. Khrushchev was threatening to conclude a separate Soviet peace treaty with East Germany.

54 Richter, *Khrushchev's double bind*, pp. 97–103.

55 Correspondence over the Geneva talks, FO371/159671; and memo of a special secret talk between Sir H. Caccia and Eisenhower, 16 June 1959, PREM11/2685, PRO, London.

56 Richter, *Khrushchev's double bind*, p. 116, and *passim* on this issue. Smyser, *Yalta to Berlin*, chs. 8–10; and Zubok and Pleshakov, *Kremlin's Cold War*, pp. 190–201, 248–58.

57 The phrase was Kennedy's. See Beschloss, *Crisis years*, p. 224.

58 M. Bundy, *Danger and survival: choices about the bomb in the first fifty years*, New York, 1988, pp. 359–82, 373; S. Greenwood, *Britain and the Cold War, 1945–1991*, London, 2000, p. 152.

59 Harrison, 'Ulbricht and the "concrete rose"'; p. 48.

60 Quoted in Smyser, *Yalta to Berlin*, p. 161.

61 See the persistent German concerns about Anglo-American tendencies to compromise too much in dealings with the Russians and their view that to talk at all was too much of a concession, February 1962, FO371/163567, PRO, London.

62 Harrison, 'Ulbricht and the "concrete rose"'; p. 56.

63 Smyser, *Yalta to Berlin*, pp. 199–201.

64 Hixson, *Parting the curtain*, ch. 7, esp. p. 190.

4 The Cuban Missile Crisis, hinge of the Cold War, 1962

1959   Cuban Revolution led by Fidel Castro

1960   US–Cuban relations deteriorate

1961   *April:* Bay of Pigs invasion by US-backed Cuban rebels fails

1961–62   US covert action against Castro; Operation Mongoose; USSR backing for the Cuban Revolution

1962   *May:* Khrushchev decides to send nuclear weapons to Cuba

August: US intelligence detect activity but not strategic weapons

September: SAM sites discovered; Kennedy warns against offensive weapons

14 October: Missile sites first discovered by U-2 spy-planes

16 October: ExComm meets for the first time

22 October: Kennedy announces the quarantine (or blockade) of Cuba

24–25 October: Soviet ships turned around

27 October: Key day of the crisis; essentials of compromise agreed

29 October: Khrushchev publicly backs down

November: Soviets withdraw; Castro refuses to allow inspection by the UNO

The crisis over the Soviet deployment of intermediate and medium range nuclear missiles in Cuba was one of the most dangerous moments of the Cold War and a turning point in its history. It is one of the most intensely studied and documented Cold War crises. It also demonstrates – again – the key themes of this study. The historical perspectives of all participants affected their decisions and their perceptions of others. The options open to both superpowers were limited by such considerations as well as by the reactions of allies, their Cuban connections and domestic political processes. Local and international priorities influenced policy decisions, and the superpowers retreated from the brink of nuclear war.

The crisis is known as the 'Cuban Missile Crisis' in the West, the 'Caribbean Crisis' in the USSR and the 'October Crisis' in Cuba. To Americans the focus of the crisis was always on the events of October 1962, to the Soviets its main focus was geographic, while to Cubans it was part of a longer crisis in which the fate of the revolution hung in the balance. It was a key moment when the Cold War changed from being a confrontation focused on the perimeters of the USSR and China to a global one.

Genesis

The crisis had its origins in a number of developments of the 1950s, not least among them new technologies. Thermonuclear weapons lent a new dimension to fears of war. The development of missile technology and the USA's deployment of missiles in Turkey, Britain and Italy significantly increased Soviet insecurity in the years 1959–60. The U-2 spy-planes revealed to US leaders the extent of their lead over the USSR in both missiles and warheads. The U-2 also revealed the missiles in Cuba before they became operational or were acknowledged by either Khrushchev or Castro, a discovery that had a vital impact on the course of events.

The events of the recent past also contributed to the crisis. The success of the revolutionary movement in Cuba and the deterioration of Cuban–US relations in 1959–1960 were crucial.[1] The interaction of domestic and foreign politics was also important: first Fidel Castro's January 1959 revolution ousted the US-backed Batista then turned towards Marxism and a pro-Soviet alignment. This resulted partly from Castro's convictions and partly from US sanctions and pressure.[2] Partisan pressure, business pressure, diplomats' anti-communist or pro-Batista views and Eisenhower's reluctance to compromise with left-leaning nationalists combined to drive Cuban policy away from conciliation during 1960. This situation culminated in the CIA operation to land anti-Castro Cubans on the island as the start of a counter-revolution. Kennedy inherited this plan and changed but dared not stop it, having made much of Cuba in his campaign. The US-backed invasion in April 1961 went disastrously wrong.[3]

As illustrated by their relationship with Cuba, US leaders were sensitive to ideological interests in what they casually termed their 'own hemisphere'.[4] Fear of communism combined with concerns for US economic interests and with older ideas about hemispheric security associated with the Monroe Doctrine. Historic animosity between some Cuban nationalists and the USA was renewed as Cuba sought to regulate, nationalise or limit US interests and power there. Fidel and his communist brother Raul, Che Guevara and other Cuban revolutionary leaders also sought Soviet backing as relations with the Eisenhower administration deteriorated. This increased US fears that Cuba might become a part of the Soviet bloc. Like many Soviet leaders of his generation, Khrushchev enthused over a revolution that recalled his own youthful activities and that had brought communism (Castro declared himself Marxist-Leninist in late 1960) to a country without the aid of the Red Army. By 1960 the USSR was supplying weapons and advice to Cuba and Eisenhower had established a CIA project to undermine or overthrow the revolution there. The scheme to back an invasion of Cuba by anti-Castro rebels came to disastrous fruition in the Bay of Pigs in 1961. After this, the Kennedy administration maintained pressure on Castro through Operation Mongoose. Attorney General Robert Kennedy was intimately involved in this operation, which planned the possible overthrow of Castro as well as sabotage and propaganda against the Cuban regime.

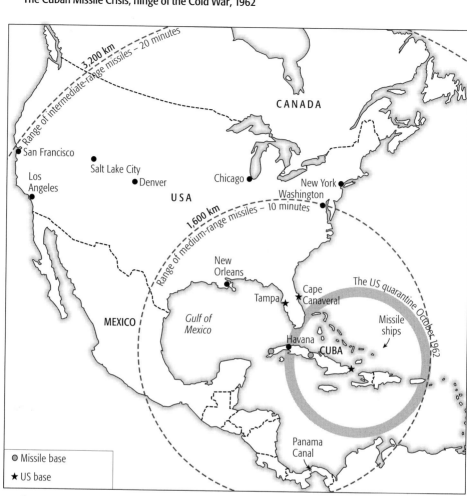

The range of Soviet missiles in Cuba, 1962.

Outside the Caribbean, the ongoing deadlock over Berlin and the poor relations between the leaders highlighted the continuing Soviet–US tension. Khrushchev seems to have been concerned about how vulnerable his country was to a possible US attack. His intelligence services reported the rumours of a surprise nuclear first strike being planned for 1961. The Americans seemed to ignore his protests at their deployments in Turkey and Italy. He faced Chinese competition for support from countries in the developing world. US actions and what were perceived as hints of parallels between Cuba in 1961–62 and Hungary in 1956 alarmed the Soviet leader. In addition, he faced criticism at home for making cuts in the armed forces, for economic failures and for some of his reforms. He believed that a foreign policy coup would improve matters for him.

In February 1961 the USA publicly acknowledged that any missile gap that existed was in its favour, exposing Khrushchev's bluffing. At Vienna Khrushchev was impressed with Kennedy's resolve over Berlin. Khrushchev was alarmed at the new administration's aggressive stance towards Cuba and more generally, and thought that Cuba presented him with a way to meet a number of problems at once. While staying by the Black Sea in Bulgaria and at his *dacha* in Pitsunda in the Crimea in May 1961 and pondering Castro's request for substantial conventional military aid, he hit upon the idea of deploying strategic weapons.[5] This would trump any Chinese criticism of Soviet attitudes to revolutions in the developing world.[6] It would bring home to the USA what it meant to face missiles within a few hundred miles of their territory and alter the global 'correlation of forces' in his favour, perhaps giving him the chance to force the Americans out of Berlin. It would offer a new challenge and extra spending to his military and give him a significant coup in the international arena. Castro's reluctance to accept this idea was overcome by appealing to the solidarity and interests of the communist movement. Khrushchev took the key decision towards the end of May after feasibility studies by the armed forces. In June the deployment, known as Operation Anadyr, began. Forces massed on the inner German border by the late autumn seem to have been intended to reinforce the dual threat.[7]

Evolution

Khrushchev gambled that the deployment would remain secret until the missiles were operational. He was, perhaps, intending to announce a *fait accompli* on a visit to Cuba or in a speech at the United Nations General Assembly after the US off-year elections in November.[8] The Cuban leadership argued persistently for open deployment that could be portrayed as no different in diplomatic or strategic terms from the US missiles in Turkey. Whether the result of habits of secrecy or simply a miscalculation, the covert deployment exacerbated Kennedy's anger when the missiles were discovered. Certainly Khrushchev badly underestimated the capabilities of US imagery intelligence (IMINT) to detect the missiles.

In the summer of 1962 US intelligence noted the arrival of Soviet 'technicians' in Cuba, the huge sea-lift and the build-up of large amounts of equipment. Indeed, with Il-28 planes and SAM-2 anti-aircraft systems being recognised from their packaging crates, the crisis gave birth to the new science of 'cratology' in US intelligence circles. Rumours among Cuban exiles, debriefing of refugees at Opa Loca in Florida, German intelligence on the Soviet sea-lift and surveillance in the Atlantic as well as reports of the scale of the build-up all contributed to heightened tension during August. The Kennedy administration, under pressure from critics such as Senator Keating (Republican, New York), stepped up surveillance. The results suggested that reports of missiles were probably about SAM-2 and SAM-3 air defence weapons. Kennedy issued a statement on 4 September in which he said that there must be no deployment of offensive weapons or Soviet combat troops in Cuba. Ambassador Dobrynin gave him the reassurances he sought on 18 September. In his memoirs, Dobrynin recounts that he was kept unaware of the existence of Anadyr and that the Soviet definition of defensive weapons 'for the defence of Cuba' was understood very differently in

83

IR - 1

PROB NUCLEAR WARHEAD STORAGE SITE

LAUNCH SITE 1

SECURITY FENCE U C

VEHICLE REVETMENTS

STRUCTURE BEING EARTH-MOUNDED 114 X 60

CONTROL BUNKER

BATCH PLANT

CONTROL BUNKER

LAUNCH PADS

PRE-FAB CONSTRUCTION MATERIALS

A U-2 photograph of a ballistic missile launch pad in Cuba, October 1962.

Washington as 'weapons for defense that could only be used in Cuba or its territorial waters'.[9]

Senator Keating continued to claim that he had evidence of nuclear missiles in Cuba. Kennedy rested on the assurances he had received and the findings of his intelligence community. The main sceptic within his administration was CIA director John McCone, who ordered a renewed over-flight effort to check on the island. Exactly why remains unclear, but there is a hint in Soviet sources that a leak from German intelligence led them to believe that US intelligence had evidence of strategic missiles by mid September.[10] After delays caused by bad weather and political concerns, photographs from a U-2 flight on 14 October revealed unmistakable evidence of the construction of ballistic missile launch facilities in western Cuba. The IMINT interpreters were so sure of their judgement largely because of the information passed by an Anglo-American agent, KGB Colonel Oleg Penkovsky, which included manuals and plans for such sites. Soviet confidence in secrecy had been misplaced. The initiative had now passed to the USA.

Crisis

On 16 October the president convened his Executive Committee (ExComm) of the NSC. This body has passed into history as the archetype of successful bureaucratic-political management of a crisis. In reality, the president took major decisions himself together with a much smaller group of advisers, including his brother Robert, Secretary of State Dean Rusk, Secretary of Defense Robert McNamara and National Security Adviser McGeorge Bundy.[11] Using back-channel (unofficial) diplomacy and UN representative Adlai Stevenson as conduits to the Soviet leadership, Kennedy resolved certain key issues outside ExComm and then brought his decisions to that body. Its role was, therefore, as much to create an intra-administration consensus as to formulate policy. It was also useful to the president in that it allowed him to hear all sides of arguments and commit participants to the outcomes. It gave him a forum in which he could overcome the objections of his senior military advisers when they wanted a more aggressive policy.

The transcripts of ExComm have now been published. They reveal that the US leaders focused their discussions on the international and alliance politics of the crisis from the start. There was a widespread assumption that the Soviet action was a ploy to gain advantage in Berlin – perhaps Khrushchev wished to trade Cuban missiles for the Western presence in that city. Throughout the debates, ExComm members were keenly aware of the need to formulate a response that would not split the NATO alliance. They were desperate not to appear to 'sell out' Europe or to seem as if they would risk nuclear war (which would devastate Europe) for Cuba when no such risk had been run over the Berlin Crisis. In addition, toughness in one area increased the chances of US wishes being heeded in the other. This concern extended to the USA making an effort to mollify Turkish (and broader European) sentiments about the implicit trade of the Jupiter missiles in Turkey as part of the resolution of the crisis.

ExComm transcripts reveal a concern that Khrushchev and Castro should not be allowed to bully the USA into concessions. This reaction was linked to the credibility of the USA in world affairs. At the height of the crisis, Chief of the General Staff Maxwell Taylor stated:

> I think we'd all be unanimous in saying that really our strength in Berlin, our strength anyplace in the world, is the credibility of our response under certain conditions. And if we don't respond here in Cuba, [the Chiefs] think the credibility is sacrificed.[12]

Such considerations were a refraction of an older set of apparent lessons from history and experience that influenced participants. Although rarely explicitly mentioned, the analogy of appeasement and Munich informed ExComm debates about dealing with dictatorships. Another analogy that did become spoken concerned Pearl Harbor. Stevenson, George Ball, Robert Kennedy and others used this analogy as they argued against a surprise attack on the missile sites. It was not the only argument that led to this view prevailing, but it was significant in overcoming the advocates of such an attack.

The role of domestic politics in the administration's deliberations was less obvious. Numerous participants have aired their views on the subject. Off-year elections were close and Keating and others had made Kennedy's Cuba policy an issue. While such considerations cannot have been absent from the minds of the president and his advisers, they never predominated in the discussions. Indeed they were rarely explicitly mentioned.

As the crisis developed Kennedy came to see the advantages of a blockade over an air strike. At the start of the ExComm meetings, a majority had been in favour of an invasion or aerial attack that would 'take out' the offending weapons and might have the collateral benefit of bringing down Castro. Both within and away from ExComm, Kennedy came to prefer a more measured approach, which had the advantage of buying time during which secret diplomacy might result in a settlement short of war. He and his closest advisers came to favour a blockade of the island. Preparations for possible air strikes and invasion continued, as did debates in ExComm. Although Kennedy allowed these to range widely, he went on national television to announce the blockade on 22 October.

Resolution

The days from Kennedy's broadcast until Khrushchev's message of 29 October were among the tensest of the Cold War. Khrushchev's message was broadcast via Radio Moscow to avoid delays in communication and announced that the USSR would pull out the missiles and supporting troops from Cuba. Leading participants on both sides have testified to the imminent danger of nuclear war. In Moscow and Washington high officials slept in their offices and worried about whether they would see their families again. Around the world people anxiously watched television and listened to the radio for news of the crisis.

As the first indications of a Soviet climbdown began to emerge Dean Rusk, referring to a childhood game, commented that the adversaries had stared each other eyeball to eyeball and the other guy had just blinked. The tactic of initiating a naval blockade had worked. Kennedy's broadcast had prompted a period of great tension in the Kremlin. Khrushchev took the final decisions, as he had taken the first ones, alone. At the time and subsequently he was reproached by the Cubans for insufficient consultation with them. When Anastas Mikoyan[13] went to Cuba in November to pacify the Cuban leaders he found them angry, bitter and disappointed.

On 24 October Khrushchev ordered his ships in the Atlantic that were carrying sensitive cargoes to stop or turn around. Construction of the sites in Cuba was, however, speeded up. We now know that there were sufficient missiles and warheads already in Cuba for a number of sites to become operational by late October or early November. It took four more days for the *dénouement* to be completed. At the time there were hints of possible deals, but it took years for the full nature of the compromises (and the failed compromises) to emerge. Khrushchev picked up on hints dropped by the US administration through back-channel diplomacy and more regular channels. He also noted commentary from eminent journalists that suggested concluding a deal over the Jupiter missiles. This contributed to a hardening of the Soviet stance as the crisis peaked, between the two messages that Khrushchev sent. The first, his own personal work, was more conciliatory and less conditional than the second, which bore signs of committee drafting and foreign ministry thinking. After some hesitation, ExComm decided that a way forward could be found in ignoring the second message and responding to the first in what became known as the 'Trollope ploy' (after the marital tactics of the novelist's heroines).

Essentially Khrushchev acknowledged that he had miscalculated the reaction of the USA. No estimates had been prepared for him about what their reaction might be if the deployment was discovered – he had never asked for such a briefing. Always fearful of war, he seems to have been swayed by reports from across the Atlantic of preparations for war. A message from Castro about the shooting down of a U-2 was overinterpreted as eagerness for nuclear confrontation. Intelligence reports of troop concentrations in the south-eastern USA were augmented around 22 and 23 October by erroneous reports of Washington press gossip in late-night bars. From these the KGB reported that an invasion of Cuba would come within days. This seemed to be confirmed by reports emanating from Cuban sources at the same time. The Soviet leader had already manifested his caution about the possibility of nuclear escalation in the summer when he changed orders to prevent his man on the spot, General Pliyev, from controlling the battlefield nuclear weapons that, unknown to the Americans until 1990, had been deployed. Khrushchev was determined to keep any decision about escalation to himself, as was Kennedy. As the crisis neared its conclusion he took further steps to tighten his control over nuclear forces and reduce the chances of their use.[14] The shooting down of the U-2 spy-plane on 27 October came against orders. At first it was assumed to be a Cuban action, though it later transpired that a Soviet battery had been responsible. Along with other tokens of US resolve and such incidents as the mistaken entry into Soviet airspace of a US U-2 based in Alaska, it helped Khrushchev decide that his Caribbean gamble was not worth the risk of all-out war.

Khrushchev's motives were complex. Although Kennedy had made him back down, he had dealt with Khrushchev as an equal and had recognised Soviet security interests as legitimate, which was very important to successive Soviet leaders. The balance between this consideration and calculations of Soviet inferiority in the nuclear correlation of forces is impossible to calculate on the evidence available. Khrushchev's messages to Kennedy are suffused with wording that reveal how this perennial anxiety had once more played a part in the Soviet approach to a major issue. There is an emphasis on how the two must act together as equals. In post-crisis justifications he dwelt on the growth in power of the USSR against the odds, drew parallels between Cuba after 1959 and his country after 1917 and stressed how the crisis demonstrated Soviet strengths.[15] The USA had been made aware of what it was like to live so close to enemy missiles and agreed to withdraw some of the NATO missiles closest to the USSR. Khrushchev also testified to how the historically conditioned Soviet fear of war had resurfaced in response to Castro's preparedness to risk war rather than back down. Khrushchev's very personal message to Kennedy at the height of the crisis fused two key Soviet lessons of history:

I have taken part in two wars, and I know that war only ends when it has rolled through cities and villages sowing death and destruction everywhere . . . Why have we undertaken to render . . . aid to Cuba? . . . At one time our people accomplished its own revolution . . . We were the target of attack by many countries. The United States took part in that affair . . . [16]

Castro recalls that memories of June 1941 were prominent in his correspondence with Khrushchev at the height of the crisis.[17] In justifying the climbdown, Mikoyan stressed that it was better to safeguard proletarian internationalism and the Cuban revolution through the deal than to risk nuclear war.[18] In the end, neither leader agreed with his more hawkish advisers that the risks of war were worth the strategic or diplomatic benefits of a refusal to compromise.

The Soviet withdrawal was not as unconditional as was widely assumed at the time. Kennedy pledged secretly to withdraw the Jupiter missiles from Turkey. Evidence has emerged that he was prepared to make a public deal of that nature if that was what it would have taken to bring the crisis to a successful conclusion without war. In addition, he let it be understood by the Kremlin that he would not sanction a future invasion of Cuba. This last pledge did not, however, come into effect. It was linked to UN inspections of the missile sites. Castro absolutely refused such access, deeming it a violation of Cuban sovereignty. As the post-crisis haggling went on, the non-invasion pledge fell victim to the triangular wrangling over inspection and Cuban intransigence.

Conclusions

The significance of the crisis lies in the fact that the world has never been closer to a nuclear exchange. It was also a hinge, or turning point, in the history of the Cold War. Among the experiences that shaped policy makers' approaches to any issue in the post-1962 period was a memory of the way in which crisis management was now crucial to the very survival of life on earth. As Defense Secretary McNamara later put it, the very idea of crisis management was shown to be a dangerous misperception. Crises, by their nature, are unmanageable. Within months the hot line had been created to facilitate communication between the White House and the Kremlin. Kennedy and Khrushchev moved in 1963 to complete and secure ratification of the partial test ban treaty that had been the subject of years of complex negotiations. That the ban was limited to atmospheric testing demonstrated how powerful lobbies in both camps were still wary of any deal. Further, the arms race of the 1960s and beyond was partially fuelled by a Soviet perception that without strategic parity they would remain at a disadvantage in any crisis, as they had been in 1962. The outcome of the crisis cemented the position of Cuba and West Berlin as outposts of their respective blocs and changed both sides' negotiating styles. As Smyser writes: 'The total victory that Kennedy could thus claim in Cuba had a dramatic effect in Berlin. Khrushchev's and Ulbricht's threats had lost credibility, and West Berlin no longer needed to fear neutralisation.'[19]

In appraising the crisis the importance of the personalities of the two leaders is clear. Kennedy's aggressiveness stimulated Cuban insecurity and helped to push Castro to seek closer ties to the USSR in order to preserve his revolution. The mercurial Khrushchev was prepared to go along with this and stepped up aid before the May 1962 decision. His main tactical mistake was to keep the deployments secret. This exacerbated Kennedy's sense of betrayal and suspicion in October. He had asked direct questions of Dobrynin, he had publicly demanded that no offensive weapons be deployed and he had been lied to. Gromyko maintained the pretence when he met Kennedy on 18 October and declared that assistance was given 'solely for the purpose of contributing to the defense capabilities of Cuba'.[20] Perhaps, had the warnings been clearer sooner, the deployment would not have been undertaken. As over Korea, the subtleties of the warnings were missed by the Kremlin. This reflected the absence of analysis of possible US reactions and the keenness of the KGB and CPSU to help their Cuban comrades. It was also a product of the concern of US leaders to address various audiences at once. Kennedy had to issue warnings that would not further inflame the volatile Cuban issue either way in election year. He had to make sure that he did not seem to his European allies to be prepared to risk more for Cuba than he had when the Berlin Wall had gone up.

The crisis bred new perspectives in both superpower capitals and helped contribute to the rise of détente. Although it changed the Cold War confrontation, it did not end it. The crisis also demonstrates the ways in which the two intelligence communities played roles of great significance that were not fully understood publicly for years. None of the three intelligence communities involved emerged from the crisis with a record of unblemished success. The USA, for example, underestimated the size of the Soviet presence by half and did not identify any tactical nuclear weapons.[21]

The crisis once again demonstrated the way in which the superpowers remained the dominant actors in world politics – both were prepared to override the interests and wishes of an ally in the interests of peace. At the same time, it was also obvious that the input of local clients, alliance, and domestic, political concerns played a key role in the genesis of the crisis, even if their importance in its acute phase seems to have been rather less. In the global confrontation that the Cold War had become the crisis stands out as a moment when rivalry in the developing world threatened war more imminently than any event in Europe had in the previous 15 years.

The Cuban Missile Crisis

4.1 Khrushchev's decision, May 1962

An attack on Cuba is being prepared . . . The correlation of forces is unfavourable to us and the only way to save Cuba is to put missiles there . . . [Kennedy] would not set off a thermonuclear war if there were our warheads there, just as they put their warheads in Turkey . . . The missiles have one purpose – to scare them, to restrain them . . . To give them back some of their own medicine . . . Tell Fidel there is no other way out.

Source: Speech at Khrushchev's dacha 27 May 1962, quoted in A. Fursenko and T. Naftali, *'One hell of a gamble': the secret history of the Cuban Missile Crisis*, London, 1997, p. 182

4.2 CIA appraisal of the Soviet action, October 1962

A major Soviet objective in their military buildup in Cuba is to demonstrate that the world balance of forces has shifted so far in their favour that the US can no longer prevent the advance of Soviet offensive power even into its own hemisphere . . . It is possible that the USSR is installing these missiles primarily in order to use them in bargaining for US concessions elsewhere. We think this unlikely, however . . . If the US accepts the strategic missile buildup, the Soviets would continue the buildup of strategic weapons . . . They would probably expect their missile forces in Cuba to make some contribution to their total strategic capability . . . US acceptance of the strategic missile buildup would provide strong encouragement to Communists, pro-Communists, and the more anti-American sectors of public opinion in Latin America and elsewhere . . . There would be a loss of confidence in US power and determination and a serious decline of US influence generally.

Source: Special National Intelligence Estimate (SNIE), 19 October 1962, *FRUS*, 1961–63, vol. IX, 'Cuba', Washington, DC, 1996, p. 123

4.3 ExComm transcript of Friday, 19 October 1962

Chief of the General Staff Taylor: From the outset . . . We were united on the military requirement. We could not accept Cuba as a missile base; that we should either eliminate or neutralize the missiles there and prevent others coming in . . .

President Kennedy: If we attack Cuban missiles, or Cuba, in any way, it gives them a clear line to go ahead and take Berlin, as they were able to do in Hungary under the Anglo war in Egypt . . . We would be regarded as the trigger happy Americans who lost Berlin. We would have no support among our allies. We would affect West Germans' attitudes towards us . . . If we go in and take them out . . . We increase the chance greatly . . . [of] their just going in and taking Berlin by force. Which leaves me only one alternative, which is to fire nuclear weapons – which is a hell of an alternative – and begin a nuclear exchange.

Source: E. May and P. Zelikow (eds.), *The Kennedy tapes: inside the White House during the Cuban Missile Crisis*, Cambridge, Mass., 1997, pp. 174–76

4.4 Khrushchev's letter to Kennedy, 26 October 1962

I propose: we will declare that our ships bound for Cuba are not carrying any armaments. You will declare that the United States will not invade Cuba with its troops and will not support any other forces which might intend to invade Cuba. Then the necessity for the presence of our military specialists in Cuba will be obviated . . . You and I should not now pull on the ends of the rope in which you have tied the knot of war . . . thereby dooming the world to the catastrophe of thermonuclear war.

Source: Document 44 in L. Chang and P. Kornbluh (eds.), *The Cuban Missile Crisis, 1962, a National Security Archive documents reader*, New York, 1992, p. 188

4.5 Fidel Castro recounts a conversation with Khrushchev in 1963

[He read a message from Kennedy]: He said 'we have fulfilled our commitments and we have withdrawn, or we are withdrawing, or we're going to withdraw the missiles from Turkey and Italy.' . . . When I heard that, I imagine that Nikita realized that that was the last sentence I wanted to hear. He knew how I thought and how we were totally against being used as a bargaining chip. That ran counter to the theory that the missiles had been sent to defend Cuba. You do not defend Cuba by withdrawing missiles from Turkey . . . Defending Cuba would have been accomplished by insisting that the United States withdraw from its base at Guantanamo, stop the pirate attacks, and end the blockade [of Cuba]. But withdrawing missiles from Turkey completely contradicted the theory that the main objective of the deployment had been defending Cuba.

Source: Comments by Castro at the Havana conference on the crisis, 1992, in J. G. Blight, B. J. Allyn and D. A. Welch (eds.), *Cuba on the brink: Castro, the Missile Crisis and the Soviet collapse*, New York, 1993, pp. 224–25

Document case-study questions

1 What light do the documents shed on the motives of the Soviet leader in deploying missiles?

2 Compare the US appraisals of the motives behind and consequences of the Soviet build-up in documents 4.2 and 4.3.

3 What light do the documents shed on the relationship between the superpowers and their Cold War allies?

4 Evaluate the usefulness as a source of document 4.5 for the historian.

5 Using the documents and your wider knowledge, assess the forces shaping US reactions to the deployment of missiles in Cuba.

Notes and references

1 T. G. Paterson, *Contesting Castro: the United States and the triumph of the Cuban Revolution*, Oxford, 1994.

2 Paterson, *Contesting Castro*, pp. 254–63.

3 A. Fursenko and T. Naftali, 'One hell of a gamble': the secret history of the Cuban Missile Crisis, London, 1997, ch. 5. P. Kornbluh (ed.), Bay of Pigs declassified, New York, 1998, reproduces a contemporary CIA report on the invasion. R. M. Bissell and J. E. Lewis, Reflections of a Cold warrior: from Yalta to the Bay of Pigs, New Haven, 1996, ch. 7, is by a key insider.

4 The phrase occurs in the Special National Intelligence Estimate (SNIE), 19 October 1962, FRUS, 1961–63, vol. XI, 'Cuban Missile Crisis and aftermath', Washington, DC, 1996, p. 123. Paterson, Contesting Castro, p. 250, suggests there was a 'distorting, hegemonic presumption of "backyardism"' which trapped American policy.

5 F. Burlatsky, Khrushchev and the first Russian spring, tr. D. Skillen, London, 1991, pp. 171–75. Khrushchev's presence across the Black Sea from the Jupiter missiles stationed in Turkey may have set him to thinking of giving the USA a taste of its own medicine.

6 Lenin had initially considered wars of national liberation as central to the global revolutionary struggle. He moved away from this idea, and Stalin further still, hence the latter's lukewarm support for Mao until very late in the Chinese Civil War. In the late 1950s, within communist circles, the Chinese grew critical of Soviet ideology. Part of their critique was that too little support was given to developing world movements of national liberation. The Cubans had hinted in a number of ways that they might consider building ties with China if they did not receive help from the USSR.

7 W. R. Smyser, From Yalta to Berlin: the Cold War struggle over Germany, New York, 1999, p. 186.

8 Off-year elections take place in a year when there is no presidential election. The House and a third of the Senate as well as many local offices were up for re-election in November 1962.

9 A. Dobrynin, In confidence. Moscow's ambassador to America's six Cold War presidents, New York, 1995, pp. 71–72.

10 The hint is in V. Zubok, 'Mikoyan's talks with Castro', CWIHP Bulletin, no. 5 (1995), p. 91.

11 M. Bundy, Danger and survival: choices about the bomb in the first fifty years, New York, 1988, pp. 432–36.

12 E. May and P. Zelikow (eds.), The Kennedy tapes: inside the White House during the Cuban Missile Crisis, Cambridge, Mass., 1997, p. 177.

13 Anastas Mikoyan was a top Kremlin figure and Politburo member who was close to Khrushchev.

14 A. I. Gribkov and W. Y. Smith, Operation Anadyr: US and Soviet generals recount the Cuban Missile Crisis, Chicago, 1994, pp. 43–51, 62–68.

15 Khrushchev to Castro, 31 January 1963 (document 82), in L. Chang and P. Kornbluh (eds.), The Cuban Missile Crisis, 1962: a National Security Archive documents reader, New York, 1992, pp. 319–29.

16 Khrushchev to Kennedy, 26 October 1962 (document 44), in Chang and Kornbluh, Cuban Missile Crisis, pp. 185–87.

17 Comment by Castro in J. G. Blight, B. J. Allyn and D. A. Welch (eds.), Cuba on the brink: Castro, the Missile Crisis and the Soviet collapse, New York, 1993, p. 111.

18 See Zubok, 'Mikoyan's talks'; V. Zubok and C. Pleshakov, Inside the Kremlin's Cold War. From Stalin to Khrushchev, Cambridge, Mass., 1996, p. 268.

19 G. Ball, The past has another pattern. Memoirs, London, 1982, p. 309; Smyser, Yalta to Berlin, p. 190.

20 Memorandum of conversation, 18 October 1962, FRUS, 1961–63, vol. XI, 'Cuban Missile Crisis and aftermath', p. 112.

21 See the recent discussion of this theme in J. Blight and D. Welch (eds.), Intelligence and the Cuban Missile Crisis, London, 1998. It is also one of a number of themes covered in the Roundtable review, 'FRUS on the Cuban Missile Crisis', Diplomatic History, vol. 24 (2000).

5 Détente, 1963-75

1961 *August:* Berlin Wall built

1962 *October:* Cuban Missile Crisis and Sino-Indian War

1963 *March:* Sino-Soviet split comes out into the open
August: Partial Test Ban Treaty signed

1965 *February:* Major US escalation in Vietnam War; France withdraws from NATO military structure

1968 *January:* Tet Offensive
July: Nuclear Non-proliferation Treaty
August: Czechoslovakia invaded

1970 *August:* German–Soviet Friendship Treaty signed
December: Rioting in Poland

1971 *July:* Kissinger visits Beijing
October: Kissinger visits Beijing for the second time

1972 *February:* Nixon visits China
May: Nixon visits Moscow; SALT I and ABM Treaty signed

1973 *January:* Paris Peace Accords on Vietnam
June: Second Nixon–Brezhnev summit

1974 *June–July:* Third Nixon–Brezhnev summit; Portuguese Revolution

1975 *April:* Vietnam War ends; reunification under Hanoi's rule
August: Helsinki Conference on Security and Co-operation in Europe produces Helsinki Final Act (Accords)

In the aftermath of the October 1962 crisis the nature of the Cold War changed profoundly. In Europe and in bilateral superpower relations, there was a trend towards greater understanding, confidence-building, contact and even co-operation. This co-existed with a continuing arms race, the threat of mutually assured destruction, economic and diplomatic rivalry. As one participant put it, 'Détente . . . is compelled by the nuclear stalemate.' It was also profoundly affected by the advent of satellite imagery intelligence that rendered both superpowers and the rest of the world 'transparent' and facilitated the verification of agreements.[1] Outside Europe, Cold War crises coincided with local conflicts. When factions in local disputes sought arms or other backing from the superpowers and their blocs, they transformed themselves into Cold warriors by proxy and their local struggles into Cold War battlegrounds.

Towards détente

The global trend from the 1960s to the early 1970s was towards détente. This culminated in Nixon's overtures to Beijing and Moscow, strategic arms limitation treaties, trade links, numerous accords and the Helsinki summit of 1975. Nixon, Brandt, Brezhnev and Heath's Cold War was markedly different from that of Eisenhower, Adenauer, Khrushchev and Macmillan. The Chinese leadership changed less but, as the Cultural Revolution waned, Mao turned back to pragmatic advisers such as Deng Xiaoping and Zhou Enlai and pro-Soviet advisers such as Liu Shiaoqui and Lin Biao disappeared.

After the October 1962 crisis, the two superpowers moved to create a safer international environment. A hot line was inaugurated between Moscow and Washington to help prevent crises escalating out of control. A number of negotiations, including long-standing efforts to limit testing of nuclear weapons, moved rapidly towards progress. In the 1950s better knowledge of the dangers of fallout had produced intermittent discussions. From November 1958 a pause in testing was observed by the USSR, Britain and the USA, but first Khrushchev (in August 1961) and then Kennedy resumed testing. This was largely due to domestic pressures, concerns not to fall behind the other side in the arms race and to demonstrate resolve.

In 1963, especially after Kennedy's conciliatory speech at American University in June, progress was made towards limiting testing. It proved impossible to agree inspection arrangements for a comprehensive test ban, but a limited ban on atmospheric testing was concluded. The superpowers also initiated progress on non-proliferation of nuclear weapons. This was partly aimed at France and China, which were both causing their allies growing concern. It also headed off the prospects of an independent German nuclear force. Neither France nor China signed up to the test ban treaty and both conducted H-bomb tests within a few years. West Germany did, however, become part of the non-proliferation regime.

Under Johnson, progress was also made towards talks on arms limitations and an Anti-Ballistic Missile (ABM) treaty, though little real headway was made until Nixon's administration was in power. There were also increases in economic contacts between the two superpowers. Johnson was proud that more agreements were concluded between November 1963 and 1968 than had been reached between 1933 and 1963.[2] In 1963, after bad harvests, Khrushchev sought to purchase US grain, something that became a regular feature of Soviet–US relations.

Transparency, mutually assured destruction [MAD] and strategic parity between the superpowers were three key preconditions for détente. The Soviet leadership tried to make concrete the benefits of parity and so demonstrate the superpowers' equal status. Like their US counterparts, they knew that there were domestic economic benefits to be had from reduced spending on armaments as well as the reduced possibility of global conflagration. Khrushchev had fallen out with Mao, retreated from his Berlin ultimatum and backed down over Cuba because of his abhorrence of nuclear war.

On both sides, a perception grew of the need to build greater confidence, improve crisis-time communications, manage problems safely and limit armaments. However, as long as the struggle for supremacy in the Kremlin was unresolved, it remained unlikely that dramatic changes would take place. Advocates of détente included Kosygin who wanted to divert resources for domestic economic reform. It also had powerful opponents such as Shelest and Suslov (from an ideological perspective), Podgorny (from the perspective of the Soviets) and military men such as Grechko, who did his best to derail the turn towards détente. Once Brezhnev committed himself to détente, while making allowances for the military–industrial complex, progress was made.[3]

The Vietnam War

From 1965, however, the Vietnam War posed an insuperable obstacle to serious negotiations. US involvement in the war escalated because of many factors. Lessons from the experience of the French, persistently stressed by George Ball for as long as he remained in the administration, were all but ignored.[4] Escalation resulted from alliance and domestic politics, the dominance of certain historical analogies that blinded policy makers to realities[5] and Johnson's and his advisers' styles of decision making and leadership. These combined with a strong anti-communist impulse and blindness to local conditions to imbue what was a nationalist civil war with the attributes of a major Cold War confrontation. The USA was determined to stop what it perceived as Chinese-backed external aggression. As the domino theory still held sway, US credibility was held to be at stake. Johnson was determined that he would not be the first president to lose a war, or to abandon an ally to whom commitments had been made. He was not going to allow the right to ruin his presidency with charges that he was weak on communism: he would have a war on poverty at home and on communism abroad.

Chinese backing for Ho Chi Minh, the communist leader of North Vietnam, impacted on US and Soviet policy. The one saw only expansionist communist aggression pitched against efforts to build a democratic nation and bulwark against totalitarianism. The other saw a rival trying to steal a march within bloc politics.[6] Faced with a collapsing regime in South Vietnam, Johnson stepped up aid rather than pull back. After naval incidents in the Gulf of Tonkin in August 1964, the administration put forward long-prepared proposals for Congressional sanction for escalation. In February 1965 Johnson, having been elected as the peace candidate, decided to undertake a massive air war and send in US ground troops. By 1967 there were over half a million US troops in Vietnam. By 1973 US forces had dropped a heavier tonnage of bombs there than they had done during the entire Second World War.[7] With escalation, the pressure to ensure victory grew, as did the administration's promises of victory. So too did the Soviet and Chinese sense that they must aid an embattled ally – Soviet aid, for example, increased significantly only after the Tonkin Gulf Resolution of August 1964.[8]

As the war escalated, Ho played his allies off against one another to maximum advantage. Between 1965 and 1969, the Soviets and Chinese competed for influence through aid. With more than 320,000 Chinese troops serving in Vietnam, the massive military support and resupply operations freed northern forces to move south and aid the National Liberation Front (NLF) guerrillas, or Vietcong.

At the same time, the desire to prevent the war from escalating out of control operated on all sides. Lessons from the Korean War were internalised and no US troops crossed the 17th parallel. China's rhetoric stressed preparedness against nuclear attack, but Chinese behaviour tended to limit the risks of such a step. At the same time they discouraged North Vietnam from responding positively to US peace overtures or neutral mediation efforts between 1965 and 1968.[9] This contributed to US perceptions of a powerful Chinese challenge in the developing world, despite actual setbacks in 1965 and 1966 to China's allies. The USSR gently pressed Ho for moderation without ever formally becoming an intermediary. What is more, both the Johnson and Nixon administrations recognised that their efforts to extricate themselves would necessitate contact, if not assistance, from Moscow. Indeed, they tended to overestimate Soviet influence on Hanoi. US strategy consistently sought to have the Soviets use their influence to obtain a solution by compromise.

With the communist Tet Offensive of January–February 1968 the 'credibility gap' between Johnson's claims of progress and the reality as perceived by many Americans became unbridgeable. In March veteran establishment figures who, as late as the previous November, had backed the war came out against further escalation. Johnson fared badly in the New Hampshire presidential primary; on 31 March he announced that there would be no more escalation, that he would henceforth seek a negotiated settlement and that he was withdrawing from the election. Soon all major candidates had pronounced themselves in favour of seeking a negotiated peace. Although the war would continue until 1973, the way was open both to peace talks in Paris – Moscow and Beijing now pressed the North Vietnamese hard to attend – and to renewed efforts at détente. For the Americans, détente was partly a way to seek help in extricating themselves from Vietnam.

The thaw, 1968–69

In 1967–68 there were a number of crucial developments. Johnson's decision to seek compromise and Nixon's election pledges to withdraw US forces from Vietnam coincided with growing antagonism between China and the USSR after the Warsaw Pact invasion of Czechoslovakia. Domestic politics in all three major powers shifted to configurations that gave pragmatists the upper hand over crusaders. Economic concerns also played their part as did the development of ABM systems by both superpowers. During the 1967 Arab–Israeli War, the hot line had been used and Kosygin had warned Johnson, 'If you want war, you will get war.'[10] In this atmosphere of high tension, the two leaders met in Glassboro,

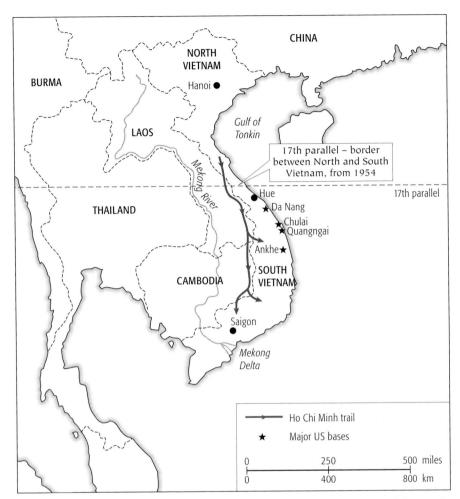

Vietnam and south-east Asia showing the major US bases in South Vietnam and the Ho Chi Minh trail, along which North Vietnam sent supplies to the Viet Cong.

New Jersey, later that year. Their talks were dominated by the need to limit ABMs due to their destabilising effect on nuclear deterrence. The resulting talks on the issue bore fruit in 1972 when the ABM Treaty was signed.

Yet détente was never amity, only the easing of tensions. In the aftermath of the 1968 invasion of Czechoslovakia, the Soviet Politburo adopted a policy that veered between traditional hostility and negotiations 'under certain conditions'. Ambassador Dobrynin summarised Soviet reasons for pursuing détente:

> Several factors made Brezhnev and highest officials of the party and state adjust their approach to foreign policy.

> First, a nuclear war was utterly unacceptable, as the Cuban crisis had clearly demonstrated. Second, there was the enormous burden of military expenditures

... Third, the process of improving relations between the Soviet Union and Western Europe, especially with the Federal Republic of Germany ... would become extremely complicated if the United States were to try to impede it. Fourth, there was a sharp aggravation in Soviet–Chinese relations ... Fifth, the improvement of relations with the United States would undoubtedly consolidate the prestige of Brezhnev's leadership within the Soviet Union.[11]

Soviet weakness seems clearer with hindsight than it did at the time. The need to respond to western European moves for détente was important in both Soviet and US calculations. To the former, it was clear that progress in Europe was not possible unless the USA was brought along, as the failure of the Rapacki plan of 1957–58 had shown. To the latter, any prospect of détente in Europe that left them behind posed a threat to the NATO system at a time when French policy and general unease over Vietnam were causing severe strains.

Ostpolitik

The most significant efforts at détente in Europe were in Germany. Under Adenauer, the Hallstein Doctrine held: West Germany would not have diplomatic relations with any state that recognised the DDR, except for the four victor powers of the Second World War. This intransigent attitude contributed to the crises over Berlin between 1958 and 1961. The sealing of the borders facilitated a period of long-term calm.

Domestic changes within the Federal Republic produced a rethink of how to deal with the division of the nation. As Adenauer's power waned, culminating with his departure from office in October 1963, so new leaders and ideas emerged. German politicians, while recognising the reality of the current situation, began suggesting new ways of normalising inner-German relations. Figures such as Egon Bahr, the top SPD specialist, went far beyond what Adenauer would have countenanced. He was especially responsible for popularising the notion of 'change through *rapprochement*', whereby the East would be transformed by gradually increased contact with the West. The scene was set for Germany to initiate détente under Erhard from 1963, still more under Kurt Kiesinger's grand coalition of 1966 and spectacularly once Willy Brandt became chancellor in 1969.[12]

Brandt's *Ostpolitik* marked a significant shift in the European Cold War. Claims to land were given up and the DDR was effectively recognised. Negotiations continued despite the events of August 1968 in Czechoslovakia. The aim was to accept the verdict of the war with regard to giving up old German lands, establish German status in negotiations on Germany and set in motion processes that might eventually reverse some Yalta decisions.[13] Autonomous German policies generated some suspicion in Washington that alliance solidarity might be under threat. Initially progress was held up by Ulbricht's reluctance to tolerate changes that undermined the DDR's claim to be the sole legitimate representative of German national aspirations. He could not, however, prevent the German–Soviet Friendship Treaty of August 1970 and, with Moscow's connivance, was eased out in 1971. Agreements that he had opposed soon followed. These included quadripartite measures settling Berlin's status and bilateral normalisation of inner-German relations. An irony of these developments was that the West Germans, changing through *rapprochement*, gradually found themselves defending the eastern European status quo. They did not allow the Soviet invasion of Czechoslovakia to derail détente. By the end of the 1970s their vision of slow progress to normalisation, economic subsidy in return for increased contacts and travel, and 'buying free' limited numbers of East Germans were well-established. They seemed to be threatened by movements like Solidarity in Poland which opened up the possibility of more rapid change. This risked provoking a clamp-down which would, in turn, deter the Western public and its governments from continuing to deal with the communist bloc.

Another important development in the 1960s was the foreign policy of Gaullist France. De Gaulle pursued an ambitious policy to restore French prestige, assert French independence from the Anglo-Saxon powers, limit German power in Europe and enhance his position as a statesman.[14] Most disconcertingly for the USA, he pulled France out of the military structure of NATO (though not the alliance) in 1966, ejecting NATO bases from France as part of the assertion of French independence. He also attempted détente with China, Romania and the USSR. These bids did not lead as far as *Ostpolitik* in changing the Cold War, but the Nixon administration felt that European progress towards détente played an important part in pushing the USA in the same direction, lest it be left behind by détente between the Western and Eastern powers.[15]

These were not the main tensions experienced in the two superpowers' alliance systems. For the USA, the war in Vietnam was the major point of friction. Intended to reassure allies of the steadfastness of US commitments, the escalation of the war produced mass demonstrations and condemnation in allied capitals against US policy as well as fracturing the Cold War consensus within the USA. France, Britain and most other allies refused to make even token contributions to the Vietnam War. France remained a presence in the area for some time, but played no role beyond hosting negotiations in the late 1960s and early 1970s.

Soviet bloc tensions

On the communist side, the Romanian government caused the Soviet leadership unease. Ceausescu's rise to power in 1965 was quickly followed by deviations from the Moscow line, such as his refusal to break off relations with Israel in 1967 and to participate in the Warsaw Pact invasion of Czechoslovakia the following year. Such prominent public gestures attracted attention in Washington, Beijing and Moscow. In the coming years the policy of differentia-tion (see p. 66) led to rewards for such displays of independence.

The USSR experienced major crises with its allies, in both the east and west. Romania's independence and renewed tensions with Yugoslavia (when Tito asserted his leading role in the non-aligned movement) were overshadowed by

German Chancellor Willy Brandt kneels at the memorial to the victims of the Warsaw Ghetto, 1970. This was a key moment in the diminution of historic fears of Germany during the détente years.

economic pressures. These produced widespread rioting in Poland in 1970 and led to the replacement of Gomulka with Gierek.

Even this was minor compared to events in Czechoslovakia. The replacement of older Stalinist leaders with reformers led by Dubček led to the 'Prague Spring' of 1968. Reforms included increased press freedom, tolerance of dissidence, legitimation of opposition groupings that challenged the leading role of the party, and greater parliamentary and other self-assertion. Throughout the early months of 1968 hardliners in the Czech Communist Party made common cause with like-minded communists in other Warsaw Pact countries. The likes of Zhivkov and Ulbricht pressed the Soviets for action and found allies within the Soviet leadership. Moscow tried to effect the sort of compromise that the Poles had found acceptable: a measure of discipline from outside, solidarity with the Warsaw Pact and limits placed on the national road to socialism. By the summer this was not working. As the Czech Communist Party prepared to legitimate its dissent through party structures, the Pact forces demanded greater concessions from Dubček; on 18 August they invaded. The Prague Spring was over and gradually 'normalisation' was imposed under Husak.

The invasion came about because the Soviet leadership decided it could not tolerate ideological deviations, especially challenges to the party's leading role.

They, and allied leaders, feared contagion across borders. They also regarded the Czech lands as a key strategic area for which the Red Army had fought in 1944–45 and they dared not risk losing them. A leader of the Prague Spring characterised Brezhnev's justification for the invasion of August 1968:

> Your country lies on territory where the Soviet soldier trod in the Second World War. We bought that territory at the cost of enormous sacrifices, and we shall never leave it . . . In the name of the dead of World War II who laid down their lives for your freedom as well, we are therefore fully justified in sending our soldiers into your country so that we can feel secure within our common borders. It is immaterial whether anyone is actually threatening.[16]

Their men on the spot advised them that the move was necessary. As in Hungary twelve years previously 'their' men comprised Czechoslovakians who wanted Dubček ousted and elements in the security apparatus and diplomatic corps who reported back to Moscow that things were running out of control. The KGB planting of US weapons for 'discovery' by the Czech authorities reveals much about Soviet reasoning.[17] It was as if the Soviet leaders could not bring themselves to conceive of an indigenous movement that threatened their control, but preferred to accept evidence they had fabricated in order to prove what they believed but could not back up.

The decision to invade was eased by indications from Western capitals that any response would be muted and that, just as the Soviets had restrained their reaction to escalation in Vietnam, so the West would limit its condemnations to little more than rhetoric. The Politburo considered US signals very carefully, and Gromyko reported on Rusk's and others' views at the key meetings in July.[18] One British evaluation, sent to Washington nearly a month before the invasion, talked of the need not to let the Soviets get away with intervention without making the most of it in propaganda terms, but:

> The West was not prepared to go to war to save the Hungarian Revolution. And it can be assumed that Western Governments would adopt a similar attitude in this case. In these circumstances military action would be useless and could be extremely dangerous. So would any statement that could be construed as a threat of such action.[19]

With little fear of escalation, the invasion went ahead. Outside Czechoslovakia, major repercussions were felt within the communist world. Romania's and Yugoslavia's leaders redoubled their efforts to distance themselves from Moscow and sought reinsurance with Washington and Beijing.[20] Tito found himself in agreement with the Chinese, who had previously berated him for his too-moderate views. There was widespread condemnation of the intervention among European communist parties, especially from the Italian leadership. This was, in fact, a formative moment that became known as Eurocommunism. Even within the USSR the invasion marked a watershed. Andrei Sakharov found that he could no longer continue his work as a nuclear physicist without speaking out against the system's abuses. Vassily Mitrokhin[21] testifies that this was the time when he decided to try to work against the system. Gorbachev-era reformers have borne similar witness to their disillusion after this enforcement of neo-Stalinism over 'socialism with a human face'.[22]

The China card

The invasion also worsened the USSR's already poor relations with China. The post-Khrushchev leadership had not resolved the ideological quarrels. Indeed, relations had worsened during the Cultural Revolution when Mao's Red Guards condemned Soviet and US 'imperialism' alike. Differences over Vietnam were clear, with China giving more aid and pushing against negotiations. The Brezhnev Doctrine, justifying Soviet intervention against internal or external threats to Moscow-defined socialist regimes, struck the Chinese leadership as especially threatening. In the late summer and autumn of 1968, the Chinese signalled a willingness to open lines of communication with the USA as well as with other dissident communist regimes. Once Ho Chi Minh's regime sided with the Soviets, the Chinese also increasingly distanced themselves from it. By early 1969 there were significant military clashes on the Sino-Soviet frontier.[23]

The emergence of China as a power that leant away from the Soviets transformed the context for USA–USSR relations. For Moscow, triangular diplomacy became more complex as the USSR could no longer assume Chinese passivity or support for its stance; for the USA it meant that they could play off the two great communist powers against one another; for the Chinese, triangular diplomacy created the chance of recognition of their status, a balance against growing Soviet power to their north and west, and access to Western money and technology. China moved to counterbalance the growth of Soviet power, which it considered dangerous. Nixon and Kissinger responded with an effort to redeem US status and domestic consensus through high-profile meetings in both major communist capitals. Détente was timely for all three powers.

Some allies, and some within each government, dissented. Ulbricht was removed, despite his pleas to Moscow to back him against those who accepted dialogue with the FRG. After attempts to prevent him from opening to the West had failed, Zhou Enlai emerged from struggles for influence with a decisive advantage over Lin Biao, who died fleeing to the USSR. The Ukranian leader, Shelest, a key hawk over the Prague Spring who feared contagion over the border, was ousted from the Politburo.[24] Elements in the US administration found themselves excluded from decision making by secretive methods, as did Congress. Kissinger journeyed secretly to Beijing to lay the groundwork for Nixon's visit after many months of back-channel diplomacy that had been kept from the Defense and State departments, lest they leak or otherwise derail the initiative.

For the Chinese, ideological and geopolitical calculations pushed in the direction of improving relations with the USA. So did the return to influence of pragmatists such as Zhou Enlai and Deng Xiaoping. Once the USA showed signs of pulling back from Vietnam and after Hanoi sided decisively with Moscow in communist infighting, the pieces were all in place for a decisive shift. This duly occurred in 1971–72. US efforts to end the war in Vietnam were bogged down in negotiations that illustrated the limits of outsiders' influence on Hanoi. Escalation of the ground war into Cambodia and Laos and major bombing offensives caused no lasting damage to US relations with North Vietnam's communist backers who, like the US administration, put geopolitics above ideology.

Symmetrical needs, not common aims

The symmetry of needs on all three sides dictated that efforts be made towards accommodation. Robert Gates recalls:

> Nixon's embrace of détente was not motivated primarily by the desire for a new kind of relationship with the Soviet Union. Rather it seems to have been a tactical response to (1) deal with the Soviet military buildup, (2) improve crisis management during a dangerous time, (3) manage pressures at home relating to Vietnam and the defense budget that threatened the President's ability to formulate and implement his foreign policy in Washington, and (4) counter pressures in Europe to kiss up to Moscow in a way that threatened the President's ability to maintain US leadership of the Atlantic alliance . . .

> [T]he other superpower had its own troubles . . . Above all, by 1969 the Kremlin's problem with China had become acute . . .

> The Soviet leadership simply could not allow the United States and China to develop a relationship independent of and hostile to the Soviet Union. Since reconciliation with Mao was out of the question, the Soviets found themselves compelled to reach out to Washington for a new kind of relationship . . . The second motive . . . was the sorry state of the Soviet economy.[25]

This account understates the extent to which domestic political concerns motivated Soviet decision makers. According to Anderson, during 1970 Brezhnev threw his weight behind the proponents of détente, while accommodating some of its opponents' preferences. He succeeded because he stressed the benefits of détente to Soviet security as well as its economic advantages and because he engaged in détente in ways that protected military budgets.[26] Détente was competitive, no attainable goals were sacrificed and Soviet weaknesses were glossed over by improved relations.[27] *Pravda* summed up the Soviet view at the height of détente:

> From the class and sociopolitical angle the implementation of the principles of peaceful coexistence means: securing the conditions for the peaceful development of the socialist countries; curbing the imperialist policy of aggression and the conquest and annexation of other people's territory; preventing imperialist interference in other countries' internal affairs, particularly for the purpose of suppressing the people's liberation struggle – that is, preventing imperialist 'export of counterrevolution'; and preventing the use of force to resolve conflict between states.[28]

At the heart of superpower détente was the attempt to limit the growth of nuclear arsenals. The SALT 1 Treaty, agreeing a limitation on launchers, was a significant step, though the advent of MIRV-ed missiles, which carried multiple warheads to multiple targets, meant that the arms race continued throughout these years. MIRV technology did, however, assist the passage of the ABM Treaty, as it greatly increased the difficulties facing anti-missile defences.

Given both sides' emphasis on domestic affairs, détente was prone to constant reinterpretation and challenge from within. Ambitious efforts that might have alienated strong internal lobbies (such as deep cuts to strategic or conventional arms or major cuts in aid to developing world clients) were avoided lest they stop the whole business of easing tensions. The vagueness of those arguing the benefits of détente and of specific agreements led to future misunderstandings. To obtain support for agreements in 1971 and 1972, Brezhnev had to move closer to the priorities of senior ideologist Suslov and Head of State Podgorny (who were sceptical about détente) than Kosygin (who favoured it).[29] Nixon avoided Congress or fudged issues, but oversold détente at times when he received the plaudits. US neglect of the significance of the declarations on the general principles underlying détente (1971) and avoidance of nuclear war (1972), to which the Soviets attached great importance, led to disagreements about the nature of détente. The compromises also meant that opponents of the process on both sides found opportunities to snipe at its perceived shortcomings.

Although détente changed the Cold War, it did not end it. Contrary to views widespread at the time, rivalry continued. Mistrust never disappeared from superpower relations. This manifested itself in the dealings of détente's proponents as well as its critics. The USA viewed détente very differently from its European allies for whom it was a deeper and a more far-reaching process:[30] European euphoria combined with extensive economic contacts and genuine hopes of changes to the security arrangements on the continent. Romanian, Yugoslavian and west European communists grew more assertive in differentiating themselves from Moscow. Comecon states queued to trade and borrow from capitalist sources. In German affairs, the small steps towards freedom, which included tourism, family reunions, emigration of ethnic Germans, the 'buying free' of East Germans, agreements on the ending of media jamming and other products of détente, caused concern among hardliners in the East that the process was undermining their rule and permitting subversion.

Détente meant different things for different states. In bilateral Soviet–US relations it produced four summits in as many years, a dozen joint commissions on various aspects of the superpower relationship and over 150 agreements on matters ranging from arms control to health care and transport. The USA tended to stress the importance of arms limitation talks, the ABM Treaty, talks on Mutual and Balanced Force Reductions,[31] bilateral links and summit talks with both communist powers. Although they conceded Soviet equality, their approach remained adversarial. For the USSR the key was acceptance of the European security order, recognition of parity with the USA and greater economic benefits. They never renounced their efforts to spread their influence in the developing world or the Brezhnev Doctrine in the second world. Having achieved parity, the Soviet's diplomatic goals were stabilising the arms race, winning acceptance of the post-1945 security order in Europe, facilitating East–West trade and technology transfer, and neutralising US–Chinese collusion.[32] The Chinese sought to balance Soviet power, aid their re-emergence as a major world force (as shown by their seat on the UN Security Council) and gain access to Western technology. To Brandt's West Germany, détente entailed a normalisation of relations with eastern and central Europe as well as the USSR and the DDR. To Egypt, détente entailed a rethink of allegiances as the Soviets seemed to put accommodation with the USA above old friends. The list could be extended, but the key to understanding détente is the variety of national interpretations.

The Middle East and south-east Asia were not the only parts of the developing world into which the Cold War extended in these years. In the Spanish-speaking Americas in 1973 the USA backed a coup to topple the elected Marxist government of Salvador Allende. It also consistently aided anti-communist governments against internal leftist opponents, as when US-trained and -led Bolivian Rangers killed Che Guevara. The Cuban government consistently sought to aid leftist movements in Africa, especially those fighting Portuguese rule. The superpowers each backed their proxies in the sporadic conflict between India and Pakistan, and Soviet backing for India in its 1962 border war with China was a factor in worsening Sino-Soviet relations.

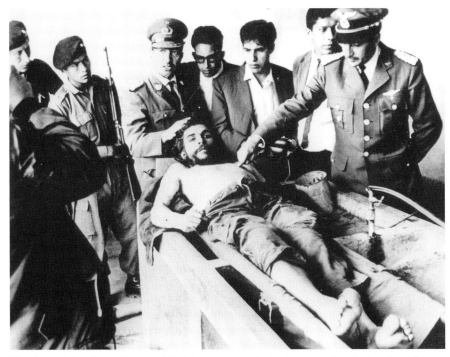

The Argentinian doctor Ernesto 'Che' Guevara was Castro's companion during the Cuban Revolution and a minister in his government. He became an icon of the revolutionary struggle in the developing world. He later joined in revolutionary activity in South America, and was captured and killed by US-trained Bolivian Rangers in 1967.

The Helsinki Accords

The Helsinki Conference on Security and Co-operation in Europe (CSCE), which ran from 1973 to 1975, was the fulfilment of an old Soviet ambition. After protracted negotiations, agreements emerged in three areas (or baskets): security, economic and other co-operation, and human rights. Even though no side felt easy about all three, they all made concessions to meet the requirement of unanimity. The USSR regarded the recognition of the post-1945 frontiers, including East Germany's right to exist and Poland's western border, as a major achievement – this was recognition of the USSR's status as a major power. The economic basket promised credits, contacts and technology transfers. There was far greater unease about the West's and neutrals' insistence that no agreement could be reached until there was recognition of human rights in the Helsinki Final Act. Brezhnev had to work hard to persuade allies and Kremlin hardliners to support internationally agreed standards and to open the system to scrutiny. Helsinki watch groups soon appeared and, to an extent, justified the fears of those who worried about the impact that more contacts and the pledge on human rights involved.

Critics of détente

The 1975 Helsinki Accords were regarded as a major breakthrough in west European and Warsaw Pact capitals. Their diplomatic and economic benefits seemed clear and there was the promise of advancement of human rights through the planned follow-up conferences. The accords were virtually ignored in the USA, except by critics who drew parallels with Munich and Yalta to damn them.[33] The Soviets welcomed the outcome although, as noted, some thought that too many concessions had been made.

The achievements of détente were questioned in many countries. Détente's Western critics seized on the human rights provisions of the accords and charged that Soviet failure to live up to them was in line with alleged breaches in SALT, ABM and other agreements. Soviet critics resented outside interference regarding human rights and blamed Egypt's 'loss' to the Soviet alliance system as the result of détente rather than the vagaries of local and regional politics. The Chinese were wary of US tendencies to play off the communist powers against one another. They were angry at the decision of President Gerald Ford and Brezhnev to meet in Vladivostok, a city they historically claimed, though Deng Xiaoping managed to joke with Kissinger about this.[34]

At best crisis management worked patchily during the October 1973 Yom Kippur/Ramadan War. Efforts to co-operate were made but, in the end, the Soviets felt that they had been shouldered out of the region by the USA. Both sides wished to control events, yet both strove to keep their allies and proxies resupplied and in existence (at one stage the USA felt that Israel's existence was under threat; the Soviets in turn came to believe that Egypt's was similarly in jeopardy). Egypt's appeal to both superpowers to prevent the total collapse of its armies was followed by an open move to DEFCON III nuclear alert status[35] by US forces in a signal to the Soviets not to act unilaterally. This was something that Kissinger, misinterpreting a Soviet démarche, had feared might happen.[36]

In negotiations, such as SALT II, both sides manoeuvred for tactical advantage. The MBFR talks in Vienna became bogged down. Recriminations began over Congress's moves to impose conditions (connected to Soviet emigration policy) on the grant of credits and MFN status. Nixon became embroiled in Watergate and, from 1974, Brezhnev's health began to deteriorate.[37] Critics of détente seized their chance. By the time of Ronald Reagan's challenge in the 1976 Republican primaries, Ford had stopped using the word and tried to harden his stance, demoting Kissinger. Cold War confrontations were reinvigorated in 1974–75 and it soon seemed that Helsinki marked the high point of détente, if not the beginning of its end. Western critics pointed to possible Soviet gains and NATO crises; Soviet ones to the USA rearming Iran, intervening in Chile and excluding them from the Middle East after the Yom Kippur War.

Document case study
Détente and confrontation

5.1 The major strategist of *Ostpolitik* lays out his vision at Tutzing, 1963

... the application of the strategy of peace to Germany ... Overcoming the status quo, by first not changing the status quo ... A process of many steps and stops ... The Zone [East Germany] must be transformed with the agreement of the Soviets ... The preconditions for reunification are only to be created with the USSR ... We have said that the Wall was a sign of weakness. One could also say, it was a sign of the communist regime's fear and urge for self-preservation. The question is whether there are not possibilities gradually to diminish the regime's quite justified fears, so that loosening up of the frontiers and the Wall will also become practicable, because the risk will be bearable. This is a policy which one could sum up in the formula: *Wandel durch Annäherung* (change through *rapprochement*).

Source: Egon Bahr quoted in T. Garton Ash, *In Europe's name: Germany and the divided continent*, London, 1994, pp. 65–66

5.2 Bulgarian leader Todor Zhivkov asserts the need for a hard line towards Czechoslovakia, August 1968

If the situation in the CSSR is to be changed and the communist party and socialist gains are to be preserved, we will have to use all possible and necessary means, including the armed forces of the Warsaw Pact if the situation so demands ... If we do not succeed in turning events around, this will be a catastrophe; it will be a blow against the Soviet Union, against our socialist countries, against the international communist movement, and against the development of our socialist countries ...

We cannot and must not give any further ground! ...

But if . . . Czechoslovakia leaves the Warsaw Pact or remains in it and behaves like Romania or some other revisionist state, the forces of the Warsaw Pact will be severely weakened, and this will pose a great threat to the GDR, Hungary, and Poland. In the event of war, the Soviet army will end up having to fight not along the Czechoslovak-German border, but along the Soviet-Czechoslovak border . . .

Our opinion is simple: Force them to capitulate. If they refuse, then we must resort to other, extreme measures.

Source: As reported by the Soviet ambassador in Bulgaria, 1 August 1968, in J. Navratil et al (eds.), *The Prague Spring of 1968*, Budapest, 1998, pp. 317–18

5.3 Gromyko's views, as approved by the Politburo, 16 September 1968

We should persist in our efforts at ensuring the most favourable conditions for the construction of communism. This should particularly include measures aimed at curbing the arms race etc.

Our aid to national liberation movements should be commensurate with our resources . . . There is growing awareness [in the USA] of the fact that the development of today's international life sets certain limits to the United States' potential, especially in the spheres where broad Soviet and US interests clash directly or indirectly.

The development of our relations with the United States calls therefore for combining the necessary firmness with flexibility in pursuing a policy of strength and for actively using means of diplomatic maneuver . . .

The Soviet–American dialogue of 1961–1963 was not, however, accidental; the reasons that gave rise to it are still in force today. That is why under certain conditions the dialogue can be resumed even on a broader range of issues. The preparations for this dialogue should be conducted systematically and purposefully even now.

Source: Quoted in A. Dobrynin, *In confidence. Moscow's ambassador to America's six Cold War presidents*, New York, 1995, p. 652

5.4 Ambassador Dobrynin's retrospective view of US priorities

[Nixon's opening to China] was even more than a breakthrough in Chinese–American relations . . . A third force had been added to the equation, offering the other two the challenges and risks of greater manuever. China was also altogether too willing to play this game. Nixon told Congressional leaders in private after he returned from his trip that he believed the Chinese leadership was motivated by two factors: first their eagerness to bring China to the level of a global power, and second, their unfriendly relations with the USSR . . .

Source: Dobrynin, *In confidence*, p. 246

5.5 Henry Kissinger recalls the priorities of the Nixon administration

The task at hand, as the Nixon administration saw it, was to get beyond Vietnam without suffering geopolitical losses, and to establish a policy toward the communists that was geared to the relevant battlefields. Nixon saw détente as a tactic in a long-run geopolitical struggle; his liberal critics treated it as an end in itself while conservatives and neoconservatives rejected the geopolitical approach as so much historical pessimism, preferring a policy of unremitting ideological confrontation.

Source: H. Kissinger, *Diplomacy*, New York, 1994, pp. 744–45

Document case-study questions

1 What light does extract 5.3 shed on Soviet motives for détente?

2 Compare the priorities expressed by Zhivkov in document 5.2 and Gromyko in document 5.3.

3 Explain the significance of the phrases 'national liberation movements' in document 5.3 and 'change through *rapprochement*' in document 5.1.

4 What do documents 5.4 and 5.5 reveal about US behaviour?

5 How far do these documents support the view that each major power had essentially selfish motives for détente?

Notes and references

1 Egon Bahr quoted in T. Garton Ash, *In Europe's name: Germany and the divided continent*, London, 1994, p. 57. J. L. Gaddis, 'Learning to live with transparency', in *The Long Peace*, Oxford, 1987. The first Corona satellite in 1960 produced more photographs of the USSR than all U-2 flights between 1955 and 1960, see R. M. Bissell et al, *Reflections of a Cold warrior: from Yalta to the Bay of Pigs*, New Haven, 1996, pp. 134–39.

2 A. Dobrynin, *In confidence. Moscow's ambassador to America's six Cold War presidents*, New York, 1995, p. 194.

3 R. Anderson, *Public politics in an authoritarian state. Making foreign policy during the Brezhnev years*, London, 1993, p. 201–03. Also R. Garthoff, *Détente and confrontation: American–Soviet relations from Nixon to Reagan*, revised edn, Washington, DC, 1994, pp. 113–22, 210.

4 George Ball was the leading 'dove' in the Johnson administration. He was in the US embassy in Paris in the 1950s and became under-secretary of state for European affairs under both Kennedy and Johnson. He resigned in 1966, disillusioned that his warnings were not being heeded.

5 Yuen Foong Khang, *Analogies at war: Korea, Munich, Dien Bien Phu, and the Vietnam decisions of 1965*, Princeton, 1992.

6 I. Gaiduk, *The Soviet Union and the Vietnam War*, Chicago, 1996, esp. pp. 6–10.

7 R. D. Schulzinger, *A time for war: the United States and Vietnam, 1941–1975*, Oxford, 1997; and G. Herring, *America's longest war*, London/New York, 1996, are the best accounts. See also P. Lowe (ed.), *The Vietnam War*, Manchester, 1998, for international perspectives.

8 Gaiduk, *Soviet Union and Vietnam*, p. 13; and Qiang Zhai, *China and the Vietnam wars, 1950–1975*, Chapel Hill, 2000, ch. 6.

9 Qiang Zhai, 'Beijing and the Vietnam peace talks, 1965–68', *CWIHP Working Paper*, no. 18 (1997).

10 Quoted in *Cold War*, programme 9, Turner/BBC, 1998.

11 Dobrynin, *In confidence*, p. 198. See also paper submitted by Gromyko and approved by the Politburo on 16 September 1968, p. 652.

12 W. R. Smyser, *From Yalta to Berlin: the Cold War struggle over Germany*, New York, 1999, pp. 210–72; Garton Ash, *In Europe's name*, pp. 48–83.

13 Smyser, *Yalta to Berlin*, p. 271. From the time of Yalta, the West had effectively accepted the changed boundaries of the USSR and Poland, even if it did not officially recognise them.

14 S. Hoffman, 'The foreign policy of Charles de Gaulle', in G. A. Craig and F. L. Loewenheim (eds.), *The diplomats, 1939–1979*, Princeton, 1994, pp. 228–54.

15 Garthoff, *Détente and confrontation*, pp. 11–13, 123–45. R.M. Gates, *From the shadows: the ultimate insider's story of five presidents and how they won the Cold War*, New York, 1996, pp. 39–47.

16 Zdenek Mylnar quoted in D. Oberdorfer, *From the Cold War to a new era: the United States and the Soviet Union, 1983–1991*, 2nd edn, Baltimore, 1998, p. 354. The best accounts of the Prague Spring are J. Navratil et al (eds.), *The Prague Spring of 1968*, Budapest, 1998; M. Kramer, 'The Czechoslovak Crisis and the Brezhnev Doctrine', in C. Fink et al (eds.), *1968: A world transformed*, Cambridge, 1998, pp. 111–72; and A. Dubček, *Hope dies last*, tr. J. Hochman, London, 1993. He too stresses the Soviet fixation on the Second World War (see p. 212).

17 C. M. Andrew and V. Mitrokhin, *The Mitrokhin archive. The KGB in Europe and the West*, London, 1999, pp. 326–41, esp. p. 333.

18 R. Pikhoia, '1968 vu de Moscou: comment l'invasion fut préparée', in F. Fejtö and J. Rupnik (eds.), *Le Printemps tchécoslovaque 1968*, Paris, 1999, esp. p. 149. On the weak US reaction, see Navratil, *Prague Spring*, p. 87.

19 FO to Washington embassy, 22 July 1968, PREM 13/1993, PRO, London.

20 The idea of reinsurance is a Bismarckian notion that you need belts and braces in world affairs if your trousers are to stay up. The two countries sought to distance themselves from Moscow in bilateral relations with the USSR and to cover their backs by building better relations with both Moscow's major rivals in case relations with the USSR deteriorated further.

21 Vassily Mitrokhin was a senior KGB employee, and latterly archivist, who copied hundreds of documents and eventually smuggled them out of the USSR in the early 1990s with the help of the British Secret Service. Some of the material has been published in *The Mitrokhin archive*.

22 Andrew and Mitrokhin, *Mitrokhin archive*, p. 8. See also the extract from V. Medvedev's memoirs in Navratil, *Prague Spring*, p. 571–75.

23 Garthoff, *Détente and confrontation*, pp. 228–42; and Navratil, *Prague Spring*, pp. 165–67.

24 Smyser, *Yalta to Berlin*, pp. 248–53; J. Mann, *About face: a history of America's curious relationship with China, from Nixon to Clinton*, New York, 2000, pp. 32–36; and Garthoff, *Détente and confrontation*, pp. 17, 254, 361.

25 Gates, *From the shadows*, pp. 29–36.

26 Garthoff, *Détente and confrontation*, pp. 16–18; Anderson, *Public politics*, pp. 14–15, 195 ff. A Soviet expert on the USA recalls Brezhnev's craven attitude towards the demands of the military–industrial complex, see G. Arbatov, *The system: an insider's life in Soviet politics*, New York, 1992, p. 201.

27 Neither superpower saw détente as an elimination of tensions or Cold War competition, rather they saw it as an easing of the rivalry that gave them benefits in a Cold War context. Sovietologists quickly developed the concept of competitive détente to describe Moscow's priorities.

28 *Pravda*, 22 August 1973, quoted in A. H. Cahn, *Killing détente: the right attacks the CIA*, University Park, Pa., 1998, p. 51.

29 Anderson, *Public politics*, p. 217.

30 Garthoff, *Détente and confrontation*, chs. 2–4.

31 Garthoff, *Détente and confrontation*, pp. 24–25, p. 533, note 15. The two sides could not agree even on the name of MBFR, with the Soviet side objecting to Western definitions of 'balanced'.

32 R. Craig Nation, *Black earth, red star. A history of Soviet security policy, 1917–91*, London, 1992, pp. 256–59.

33 Cahn, *Killing détente*, pp. 59–60.

34 Mann, *About face*, pp. 56–57.

35 See Garthoff, *Détente and confrontation*, p. 427: 'DEFCON III nuclear alert status is short of full readiness, but higher than the normal state of alert . . . involving American strategic nuclear forces as well as other field commands in Europe and around the world . . . the alert – which Kissinger had intended to be picked up promptly by Soviet intelligence and have an impact in the Kremlin – was headline news in the morning American newspapers.'

36 R. Ned Lebow and J. Gross Stein, *We all lost the Cold War*, Princeton, 1994, pp. 245–50.

37 Arbatov, *The system*, p. 191.

6 Renewed confrontation, 1975–85

1974 *June–July:* Portuguese Revolution

1975 *April:* Vietnam War ends; reunification under Hanoi's rule
      August: Helsinki Conference on Security and Co-operation in Europe produces Final Act

1976 *February:* MPLA government in Angola
      June: Strikes and sabotage in Poland

1977 *January:* Charter 77 formed in Prague

1978 *October:* Karol Wojtyla elected Pope John Paul II
      December: Vietnam invades Cambodia

1979 *February:* War breaks out between China and Vietnam
      June: Pope visits Poland; SALT II signed
      December: Soviets invade Afghanistan

1980 Persistent Polish unrest and rise of Solidarity

1981 *January:* Reagan inaugurated as president
      December: Jaruzelski declares martial law in Poland

1982 *November:* Brezhnev dies, replaced by Andropov

1983 *March:* Reagan announces SDI
      August: KAL 007 shot down

1984 *February:* Andropov dies, replaced by Chernenko

1985 *March:* Chernenko dies, replaced by Gorbachev

In the early 1980s books and articles appeared that discussed the idea of a 'second Cold War'. In retrospect this is a problematic concept. There was a great continuity in Cold War rivalry into the 1980s. Events after 1985 suggest that those who posited an end to the Cold War in the era of détente misunderstood the situation. The revitalisation of Cold War tensions from 1979 ended a period of détente and heralded a return to rhetoric and actions reminiscent of the late 1940s and early 1950s. In the USA there was a feeling of *déjà-vu* as a Democratic president was criticised by a renewed Committee on the Present Danger for softness on communism, among other things. He was succeeded by Republicans who pledged to unleash the CIA and challenge the Soviets globally. Soviet pressure on Poland involved threats of invasion. Western European economic problems and debates about greater military spending escalated into a NATO crisis. There were confrontations in Asia, Central America and Africa. By the time Soviet forces toppled the Afghan president and moved in to bolster their handpicked successor in December 1979, détente was over.

This renewed hostility was not a mirror image of previous times: inner-German relations, for example, continued smoothly. Within a few years it became plain that the pervasive Western sense of crisis and weakness had been exaggerated, as had communist strength. Trends (such as a renewed emphasis on NATO solidarity, modernisation of nuclear weapons and increases in defence spending as well as a more hardline attitude towards the USSR in Cold War matters), begun by Carter, Callaghan and Schmidt, continued and accelerated under their successors. Mitterand moved France closer to NATO.[1] Reagan's unfailing conviction that the West could prevail in peaceful competition and negotiate successfully from strength came to seem less far-fetched than it had when he had espoused it as a critic of Ford and Carter and as a presidential candidate. In the USSR, the rapid succession of elderly statesmen like Brezhnev, Andropov and Chernenko seemed to many in government to symbolise sclerotic weakness in their society and the fading allure of their system.

Détente and domestic politics

Critics of détente depicted the West as weak in the face of a mighty enemy. They sought less reliance on diplomacy until the West was stronger, a military build-up and active challenges to the Soviets wherever possible. The extent to which they wilfully exaggerated détente's failings is hard to gauge. On taking office, Secretary of Defense Weinberger reputedly refused to read a briefing on actual increases in spending that his predecessor had overseen. He increased spending on the basis of election campaign claims about what Carter was spending, ignoring the fact that these were gross underestimates of what was really being spent. Certainly there were few in Moscow who did not regard Reagan's and Thatcher's rhetoric as sincere.

Even before the Helsinki conference, strains within the superpowers as well as the international environment brought détente's prospects into question. In 1975 Ford and Brezhnev continued to speak of the process positively and to pursue it in bilateral relations. In Europe contacts and exchanges increased. Nevertheless, there were voices raised against the whole concept. In the USA, Cold warriors like Senator Henry Jackson and Secretary of Defense James Schlesinger campaigned against détente; in Congress efforts to accord MFN status to the USSR and vote trade credits were stalled by Jackson and Representative Charles Vanik's efforts to link economic concessions to emigration rights for Soviet Jewry.[2] This issue brought liberal advocates of human rights, anti-communist union leaders concerned about their members' interests, die-hard Cold warriors and other critics of Kissinger's policies into an alliance that derailed his plans, despite the fact that Soviet pledges, notably to repay lend–lease debts, were being honoured. Jackson, who seems to have cared more for his presidential prospects than for good superpower relations, acted in ways that prevented compromises that could have resolved the issue.

In the USSR in the mid 1970s Brezhnev had the authority to push ahead with détente, in which he had invested so much prestige. His domestic opponents were unable to make the use of the word 'détente' taboo. As his health declined after 1975 such figures as KGB head Andropov, Defence Minister Ustinov, Head of the Party International Department Ponomarev and Foreign Minister Gromyko gained ascendancy over foreign and military policy. Such was the relationship among them that no-one dared to challenge Ustinov and the military–industrial complex, leading to increases in military spending and challenges to détente. These were the five men who made the crucial move into Afghanistan in December 1979. In the mid 1970s the USSR also took the decision to deploy new intermediate range nuclear weapons in central Europe. This altered the balance of forces, but the demands of the army and military–industrial complex were hard to resist within Soviet politics.

Africa and Asia

Détente never involved an end to competition between the superpowers for global influence. The views of the top Soviet leaders were coloured, according to one well placed to observe them, by the seeming success of the USSR in the developing world, especially in Angola.[3] The origins of the USSR's involvement in that region lay in Portuguese decolonisation and revolution, local politics, intra-alliance relationships, especially between Cuba and the USSR, and the Cold War assumptions that continued to function. As Portugal's empire collapsed in 1974 it seemed, for a time, that communist influence would prevail in a NATO member. In Angola local factions jockeyed for position: each represented regional and ethnic groupings as well as ideological tendencies. The MPLA aligned with Cuba and the Eastern bloc, the FNLA with China, and UNITA with South Africa and the West. Cuban involvement reflected its decade-old commitment to Africa and showed how Moscow's allies could influence Soviet policy. In their books Dobrynin stresses the role of party structures in promoting greater involvement in the defence of fellow communists abroad, while Arbatov emphasises the role of the Cubans. The level of US support was constrained by Congressional concern, in the aftermath of Vietnam, that involvement in the developing world be strictly controlled.[4] US critics of détente and of Congressional limits on presidential freedom of action soon held that the seizure of the government in Angola by the MPLA resulted from the level of support it received from outside, compared with the support received by Jonas Savimbi's UNITA.

The MPLA government in Maputo received widespread recognition but faced determined resistance from UNITA in the south. Savimbi secured enough support to keep fighting. A bitter civil war eventually escalated into open conflict between Cuban and South African forces. In Arbatov's opinion, the success of the MPLA affected the judgement of Moscow's leaders. This was partly due to the weakness of US resistance to Cuban intervention. Although experts raised concerns about the wisdom of interventions in the Horn of Africa, Yemen and Afghanistan, Andropov, Gromyko and Brezhnev overruled them:

... that the Soviet Union became even more suspect and untrustworthy was hidden under the surface of what soon seemed to become business as usual. One could at first have thought that the Angola operation was a smashing success. This made the Americans even more angry. The MPLA came to power ... I began to worry that our government would remember only the success of the action and the absence of serious international complications ... We were unable to resist the temptation to become involved in the complex affairs of other countries. After Angola we went boldly down the path of intervention and expansion that we had beaten so assuredly. It led us through Ethiopia, Yemen, a series of African countries and, eventually, into Afghanistan.

Arbatov suggests an abiding ideological commitment to the 'anti-imperialist struggle' was important in blinding Soviet decision makers to the reality of interference in others' affairs and enmeshing them in local power struggles.[5] A pattern emerged of involvement in revolutionary politics: in Ethiopia, for example, the USSR abandoned one ideologically friendly regime, Somalia, for another during the 1975–77 Ogaden conflict.[6]

The fall of South Vietnam in the spring of 1975 and the subsequent expansion of Vietnamese influence into Cambodia provided détente's US critics with evidence of global expansionism by Soviet proxies. In Angola and Vietnam the proxies were especially unwelcome for the USA. The sight of Vietnamese in Phnom Penh, East Germans in the Ogaden, Cubans in Angola and Soviet advisers in Middle Eastern countries such as Yemen, Iraq and Syria suggested that détente did not favour US interests. In response Carter administration officials, some of whom were more anti-Soviet than anti-communist, sought solace in a closer relationship with Beijing. Years later Margaret Thatcher impressed on Gorbachev the extent to which these ventures had alienated the West.[7]

For the Soviet leadership the situation in south-east Asia gave no cause for pleasure. Brezhnev reviewed matters with Honecker, the East German leader, after the latter had visited Hanoi in 1978 and lamented Chinese pressure on the regime there. He stressed, 'We are taking measures in order to support energetically our Vietnamese friends ... we cannot desert Vietnam.' The exchange dwelt on US efforts to play the 'Chinese card'. For the USA, the issue was no longer simply to normalise relations between themselves and China, but *rapprochement* 'on an anti-Soviet, anti-Socialist basis'. This was seen as coinciding with Chinese efforts to use the 'American card' in their fight against the USSR and the other countries in the socialist community.[8]

Between 1968 and 1975 Hanoi persistently sided with Moscow, but the Soviets were concerned about its independent attitudes, especially its criticism of détente. Despite strained relations, a Friendship Treaty was concluded in 1978 and Vietnam joined Comecon. China's friends in Hanoi grew less influential (one defected in 1979) and relations also deteriorated over Vietnamese treatment of its ethnic Chinese minority. After Vietnam invaded Cambodia in December 1978 China decided to teach the Vietnamese a lesson and war broke out in February 1979.

Carter tacitly supported the very thing – Chinese military intervention in Vietnam – that the long US commitment in Indochina had tried to prevent.[9]

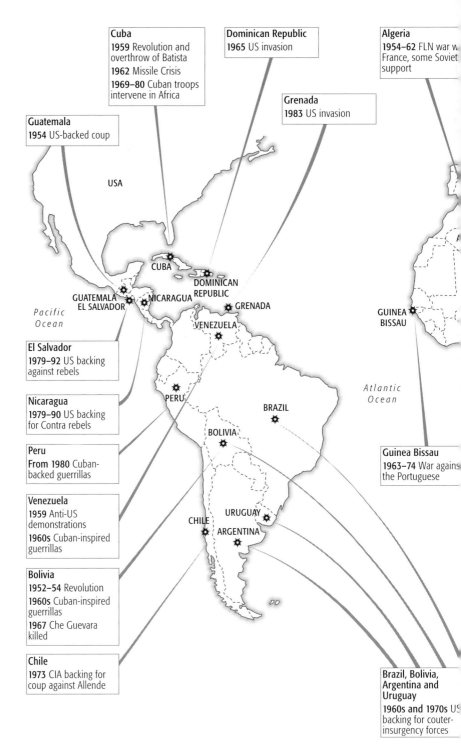

Cuba
1959 Revolution and overthrow of Batista
1962 Missile Crisis
1969–80 Cuban troops intervene in Africa

Dominican Republic
1965 US invasion

Algeria
1954–62 FLN war w France, some Soviet support

Grenada
1983 US invasion

Guatemala
1954 US-backed coup

USA

CUBA

DOMINICAN
REPUBLIC

GUATEMALA
EL SALVADOR

NICARAGUA

GRENADA

*Pacific
Ocean*

VENEZUELA

GUINEA
BISSAU

El Salvador
1979–92 US backing against rebels

Nicaragua
1979–90 US backing for Contra rebels

PERU

BRAZIL

*Atlantic
Ocean*

BOLIVIA

Peru
From 1980 Cuban-backed guerrillas

Venezuela
1959 Anti-US demonstrations
1960s Cuban-inspired guerrillas

Guinea Bissau
1963–74 War agains the Portuguese

Bolivia
1952–54 Revolution
1960s Cuban-inspired guerrillas
1967 Che Guevara killed

CHILE

URUGUAY

ARGENTINA

Chile
1973 CIA backing for coup against Allende

Brazil, Bolivia, Argentina and Uruguay
1960s and 1970s US backing for couter-insurgency forces

The Cold War in the developing world. The flashpoints indicate proxy conflicts and interventions by the superpowers or their allies.

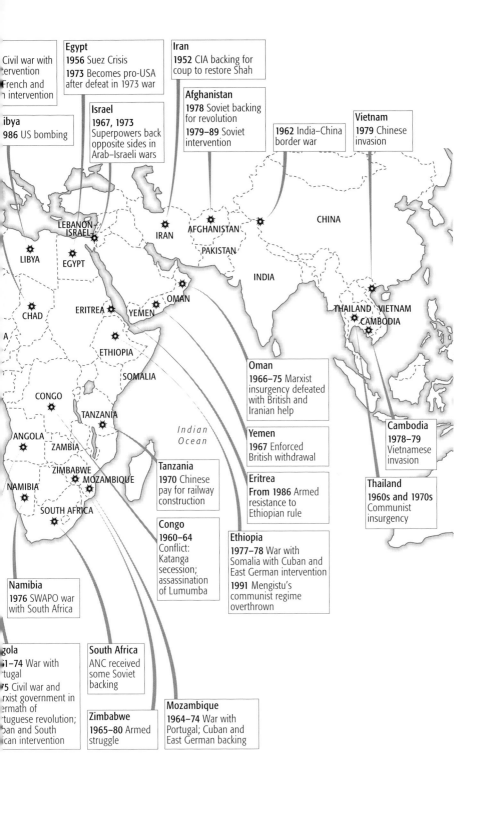

Civil war with ...tervention

▶**French and ... intervention**

Egypt
1956 Suez Crisis
1973 Becomes pro-USA after defeat in 1973 war

Iran
1952 CIA backing for coup to restore Shah

...ibya
...986 US bombing

Israel
1967, 1973 Superpowers back opposite sides in Arab–Israeli wars

Afghanistan
1978 Soviet backing for revolution
1979–89 Soviet intervention

1962 India–China border war

Vietnam
1979 Chinese invasion

Oman
1966–75 Marxist insurgency defeated with British and Iranian help

Cambodia
1978–79 Vietnamese invasion

Yemen
1967 Enforced British withdrawal

Tanzania
1970 Chinese pay for railway construction

Eritrea
From 1986 Armed resistance to Ethiopian rule

Thailand
1960s and 1970s Communist insurgency

Congo
1960–64 Conflict: Katanga secession; assassination of Lumumba

Ethiopia
1977–78 War with Somalia with Cuban and East German intervention
1991 Mengistu's communist regime overthrown

Namibia
1976 SWAPO war with South Africa

...gola
...1–74 War with ...rtugal
...75 Civil war and ...rxist government in ...ermath of ...rtuguese revolution; ...ban and South ...ican intervention

South Africa
ANC received some Soviet backing

Zimbabwe
1965–80 Armed struggle

Mozambique
1964–74 War with Portugal; Cuban and East German backing

Military and intelligence co-operation between China and the USA grew markedly under Carter and Reagan, much to the dismay of the Soviet leadership.

Western malaise

Cambodia, Angola and Ethiopia featured prominently in critical Western appraisals of détente which presented it as overwhelmingly biased in Moscow's favour and detrimental to Western interests. In the mid to late 1970s developments elsewhere accentuated such perceptions. In Central America, the Sandinista challenge to the Somoza dictatorship brought down Nicaragua, a US client, in 1979, apparently with Cuban support. Radical regimes in Grenada and Guyana seemed further evidence of communist success. In Europe Soviet moves to deploy new missiles seemed provocative. Helsinki watch groups in the USSR and other groups, such as Charter 77 in Czechoslovakia, suffered repression in violation of the accords. Both sides complained that the other was violating arms limitation agreements. Communist parties in European countries made electoral gains. All this took place against a background of economic crisis for the West and weak efforts at co-operation in order to deal with the problems. In NATO, economic tensions exacerbated divisions over strategy and policy. If anyone was winning the Cold War, it appeared to many to be the USSR.

Critics of détente in the USA questioned the reliability of the CIA's judgements on the Soviet threat. In 1975 Ford allowed CIA chief George Bush to establish the 'Team A, Team B' exercise. Intelligence material was made available to sceptics from inside and outside the intelligence community who then second-guessed the CIA's estimates. Although the CIA view was eventually vindicated, leaks at the time deepened concerns in the USA that the threat had been underestimated. As its critics strove to kill détente, leaked aspects of the Team B evaluation contributed to notions that the communists were cheating on their agreements.[10]

Mistrust was fostered in many ways. President Carter's emphasis on human rights and public gestures of support for dissidents did much to sour the mood of relations with Moscow in 1977, as did a ham-fisted attempt to alter the terms of the SALT II agreement before he met with Soviet leaders. Carter tried hard to repair relations with the USSR, but domestic politics made it increasingly difficult for him to pursue détente. Within his administration there was persistent warfare between anti-Soviet hawks and dove-ish elements. The 'discovery' of a Soviet combat brigade in Cuba in 1977 did little to help matters. In fact, there had been a force of that size there since 1962 but US intelligence had lost it from view. Bad handling on the administration's part and political posturing by Carter's opponents turned this into further evidence of Soviet expansionism in the opinion of many Americans. As so often in the Cold War, what was most important was how things seemed.

Negative appraisals by Team B and worst-case-scenario analysis of Soviet actions and intentions were prominent in the propaganda produced by the bipartisan Committee on the Present Danger, one of whose most prominent spokesmen was former Governor of California, Ronald Reagan. As he began his run for the presidency he lamented US weaknesses and castigated the administration for persisting in failed policies.

Ratification of the SALT II agreement languished as Carter used his limited influence to secure support for the Panama Canal Treaty and on positive gestures to China such as granting MFN status and full diplomatic recognition at the end of 1978. Soviet MFN status was not approved. Although Soviet disillusion grew, the USSR remained committed to its version of détente. It was also tempted to push at the limits of the permissible by domestic pressures, alliance politics, ideology, overconfidence and a misreading of US reactions.

In 1979–80 matters came to a head. The fall of the Shah's regime in Iran, one of the USA's closest allies in a key region, accentuated fears for the oil-rich area. US weakness was epitomised by its impotence in the hostage crisis that lasted into January 1981. National Security Adviser Zbigniew Brzezinski discerned an 'arc of crisis' that ran from the Horn of Africa, through the Middle East and beyond. President Carter approved the creation of a rapid reaction force for the Gulf region. The mood was caught by Carter's increases in defence spending, the decisions to go ahead with new NATO Euromissile deployments and lack of progress in bilateral talks. Reagan's rhetoric of unleashing the CIA, increasing defence expenditure, restoring such projects as the B1-bomber, the neutron bomb and the MX missile systems appealed to patriotic sentiments. He expressed a desire to put the humiliations of Vietnam behind the nation, stand tall in the saddle and defend freedom. Reagan defeated Carter comfortably in the 1980 election.

The invasion of Afghanistan

Proponents of détente, many of whom were still to be found in Moscow, were dismayed by this turn of events. Problems on their borders, however, provoked decisions and actions that hastened the turn from détente to confrontation. Although the Soviet intervention in Afghanistan in December 1979 capped the decline of détente, it may have helped – indirectly – to prevent the concurrent Polish crisis from being resolved by an invasion that would have entailed very grave risks of escalation. The strength of the West's response to Afghanistan contributed to a sense of caution on the part of the Warsaw Pact countries when their forces were poised to invade Poland in December 1980 (see p. 121).[11]

A very small group took the key decisions about the invasion: highly placed Soviet experts, including Arbatov, Ambassador Dobrynin and Politburo members, first heard of the invasion over the radio. The decision to invade resulted from Soviet disillusion with Hafizullah Amin's regime. When he came to power in a coup in September 1979 they had initially hoped that he would be as friendly as his predecessor, Nur Mohammad Taraki, who had come to power after a revolution in April 1978. When Amin appeared to be trying to distance himself from Moscow and making overtures to Washington, rumours began to circulate that he had been recruited by the CIA when a student in the

USA. Brezhnev, Andropov, Gromyko and Ustinov grew fearful of losing a friendly government committed to policies that met Moscow's approval. Having listened to the pro-Soviet Babrak Karmal, and taking his optimistic claims of support for granted, the Soviet leadership decided to move to depose Amin. One member of the top decision-making elite commented that he would not tolerate 'another Sadat'. Fears of Islamic or pro-Western strength close to the central Asian republics may also have played a part. Dobrynin recalls how lessons learnt from the moderate Western response to the invasion of Czechoslovakia in 1968 (mistakenly as it turned out) encouraged those who wanted intervention in Afghanistan in 1979.[12]

Brezhnev was ailing and inattentive, and Gromyko was keen to go along with the majority. The key actors were Ustinov and Andropov. The KGB provided troops to seize the presidential palace and assassinate Amin. Karmal then invited the Soviet forces to assist his hastily recognised government and Soviet troops moved in.[13] The Politburo ratified the decision after the event. Fear of losing a friendly regime and the ensuing loss of prestige seems to have outweighed risks to détente. In any event, Ustinov was not a proponent of that policy. Andropov may have been swayed by memories of his experience in Hungary in 1956. Certainly he followed the same line in 1979 as he had done in 1956 and 1968. There is evidence that some in the uniformed military were sceptical, but nonetheless the USSR sustained a friendly government in power by force of arms.

Chernenko summarised the attitude of the leadership:

> . . . outside aggression against the revolutionary Afghanistan perpetuated by counter-revolutionary bands, which were organized and are armed and encouraged by American special services joined with the Peking militarists, made Soviet assistance necessary in defending the Afghan people's gains. In fact Washington, with the assistance of Peking, provoked the 'Afghan crisis' in order to finally gain a free hand in the policy of anti-détente.[14]

The US reaction was far stronger than the Soviets had expected. Carter's National Security team perceived a threat to the Gulf in the Soviet move into the 'arc of crisis'. They decided to resist the Soviet invasion by proxy. The CIA provided support to the Mujahideen rebels who were fighting the invading troops and their Afghan army allies. Pakistan, a long-standing ally of the USA and China, provided the advantage of a secure rear. The fighters received Chinese weapons, Israeli stocks of captured Warsaw Pact arms and other weapons carried on Chinese mules, bought with US money.[15] Carter also initiated a range of sanctions, including pulling SALT II from the Senate's consideration, boycotting the 1980 Moscow Olympics (which the Soviet leadership had hoped would reconfirm their status as an accepted world power), embargoing trade and cutting off diplomatic contacts. The ensuing election year saw heightened Cold War rhetoric from all candidates. Reagan stepped up levels of aid, but it was only in the mid 1980s that direct US arms supplies began. The confrontation returned to a bitterness not seen since the early 1960s and a lack of communication absent since 1953.

Carter also committed resources to helping groups resisting the Sandinista regime in Nicaragua. Again, aid was not on the scale later offered by Reagan, but the commitment to the Contra rebels began before January 1981. The cycle of alienation resembled that over Cuba in 1959–60. The actions of the USA, as seen from the Nicaraguan side, pushed Daniel Ortega's government closer to the Cubans and their allies. Nicaragua's friends and its activities, as seen from the US side, increased a sense of threat and justified actions that made this confrontation less amenable to compromise.[16]

Poland in crisis

Renewed confrontation also emerged over Poland. The Gierek government had never been entirely stable. Substantial assistance from the USSR and heavy borrowing from the West kept the economy viable, but resentment surfaced whenever prices had to be raised on such articles as bread or meat, as in 1976 where strikes were followed by the formation of the opposition grouping KSS-KOR. This unstable situation grew more complex with the election of Karol Wojtyla as Pope in September 1978 and his desire to visit his native Poland. Although Wojtyla had been a thorn in the side of the regime, even Communist Party members filled with pride at their countryman's election. His visit took place in June 1979 and the crowds were spontaneous, massive and enthusiastic. This was a total contrast to state parades and holidays.[17] When economic resentments spawned strikes in Gdansk and Gdynia later in the year a number of strands converged. By the summer of 1980 the slogan 'Solidarity' surfaced. Demands from the striking workers led by Lech Walesa included the erection of a memorial to those killed in previous unrest of 1970 and the recognition of rights for the new movement – known as Solidarity – that the strikes had spawned. The movement received backing from Western trade unions, the CIA and other sources. The Polish authorities were desperate to deal with the problem themselves and stave off intervention from outside. For over 18 months there were increasingly difficult meetings between Warsaw Pact and Soviet leaders.[18]

Hardliners, including Brezhnev, Ulbricht, Zhivkov (the Bulgarian leader) and Husak, sought a military solution. There are signs that Andropov and Ustinov had been sobered by the Soviet experience in Afghanistan and were more cautious. Mikhail Suslov, whose responsibilities included ideology and doctrine, was equally reticent about using force against workers, as was Gromyko. All agreed that they could not afford to 'lose' Poland. Plans were drawn up for an invasion by Soviet, Czech and East German troops in December 1980 and the Polish leader, Stanislav Kania (who had replaced Gierek in September), was exhorted to do more to restore order while he strove to dissuade his allies from intervening. The Americans knew of these details as they had an agent – Colonel Kuklinski of the Polish General Staff – who kept them fully informed. Carter's administration sent signals about how negatively any invasion would be viewed, disclosed details of the military build-up, and used the hot line to hammer the message home. At the last minute the Soviet leadership allowed Kania one more chance to effect a political, Polish solution and the invasion was postponed.

General Jaruzelski and the Polish military now had the responsibility to impose a solution acceptable to the Warsaw Pact. Pressure on the Poles took the form of political exhortation and military manoeuvres in early 1981, while Jaruzelski went ahead with plans for military rule. Pact manoeuvres in March did not, however, result in martial law because of Polish concern after the powerful Solidarity reaction to an incident in Bydgoszcz where some of their activists were beaten up. Poland's allies were furious at yet another delay. The military option receded because the Poles were not prepared to go along with it, and Brezhnev accepted that 'it is very important that we keep the relations with our friends in the right mode. We shouldn't pester them without need . . . On the other hand we should keep them constantly under pressure while patiently reminding them of their mistakes and the deficiencies of their policy.' Honecker was less circumspect: 'Convene the leaders of the fraternal parties in Moscow, invite comrade Kania, and then tell him that he had agreed to resign; then recommend [hardliner] comrade Olszowski to succeed him.'[19] Recognising that Olszowski was not acceptable to the Poles, the Soviets approved the less-unpopular Jaruzelski for the top party post in October. He soon moved to impose martial law. At the 5 December 1980 meeting of Warsaw Pact leaders, the Hungarians and Romanians had insisted that any solution must come from the Poles themselves. They effectively blocked the DDR, Czech and Bulgarian hardline that the Poles must do as they were told by their allies. The two countries took a similar line a year later, thus robbing Jaruzelski of his excuse (to pre-empt external intervention) for a clampdown. From his perspective he was protecting his country. To his opponents the repression of military rule was more important than the threat of Pact intervention, though since 1989 the former leaders of Poland have experienced an easier time than many of their bloc counterparts and the plausibility of Jaruzelski's claims has been recognised.[20]

Soviet leaders feared that outside intervention would provoke Western sanctions. Washington's reaction to the preparations for martial law was actually indecisive, but the Soviets were cautious about world as well as US opinion. The clampdown was to be an entirely Polish affair. It came on 13 December and reactions were muted. After a meeting with Honecker, Helmut Schmidt, who significantly did not cancel his meetings in the DDR, expressed his and Honecker's shared disappointment that the step had proved necessary. Détente had seen a massive expansion of German–German contacts, trade and travel. Emigration to the West and the buying free (at about DM 50,000 each) of dissidents had also continued throughout the decade.[21] As they prized stability, the West German reaction was rather sympathetic to Jaruzelski; they were relieved that the status quo had been preserved rather than risk instability.[22] Although the main concern of the USA was to forestall outside intervention, Reagan did insist on sanctions against Poland and the USSR.

The clampdown was, however, a propaganda boon for the West and various steps followed that backed Reagan's line. In September 1982 National Security Decision Directive (NSDD) 54 summarised policy toward eastern Europe and restated the long-term goal of reintegration of the region into 'the European community of nations'. The policy of differentiation was the key to success. While some sections remain classified, the document shows the emerging emphasis on communist economic vulnerability. The ways to secure greater human rights and liberalisation of their systems were primarily 'commercial, financial, exchange, informational and diplomatic instruments'. MFN status, credit policy, IMF membership and debt rescheduling were the main means identified.[23] Covert help to the underground Solidarity also continued as did other efforts to foster opposition.

Crisis and confrontation

The extreme rhetorical antagonism of the early 1980s culminated with a crisis in the autumn of 1983. Plenty of highly public issues agitated opinion. US generals talked of winning a limited nuclear war which brought strong European reactions, especially in Germany. Bitter debates on rising military budgets included the new generation of nuclear weapons that both sides were planning to deploy. The Euromissiles became the subject of prolonged inter-alliance and intra-alliance polemics. Mass demonstrations against Pershing II and other weapons convulsed European capitals. Reagan's denunciations of the USSR as the source of evil in the world alarmed both Soviet leaders and Western opinion. A nuclear freeze movement flourished in the USA. There were no negotiations in Carter's last year in office. Reagan and Secretary of State Haig continued to avoid meetings. Only when George Shultz succeeded Haig in 1982 were contacts resumed. By this time the USSR had deployed its missiles and the USA was preparing to do the same. The resumed talks made no progress.

Tensions rose with Reagan's denunciation of the 'evil empire' to US Evangelicals in March 1983. A few days later he announced the Strategic Defense Initiative (SDI). By late 1983 Soviet fears had reached fever pitch. Politicians schooled in a closed system, where the official party line counted for all and dissent was frowned upon, had little understanding of the world of Western politics. They struggled to disentangle rhetoric aimed at specific domestic audiences from policy plans, or Congressional hawkishness from administration policies, and reacted with alarm that was sharpened by their ideological blinkers.[24] Such was the alarm that there was a real fear of a US first strike. From 1981 the Soviet leadership initiated Operation Ryan.[25] It involved extensive monitoring of Western capitals for anything that might indicate that a first nuclear strike was about to be launched or that the West was on the path to war. Contrary evidence and sceptical reports were discouraged. Only alarmist evidence found its way through, as when British resident and KGB agent Oleg Gordievsky was told to monitor the price of blood in Britain despite his rejoinder that blood was not sold. Ryan was evidence of the high state of alarm among the leadership in Moscow.

The shooting down of Korean Airlines flight 007 when it strayed into Soviet airspace in August 1983 brought a new crisis. The Soviets first denied any knowledge of this event and assumed that the flight had deliberately tested their radar defences. This excuse was being given even as Andropov privately berated the military for bringing relations with the USA to the verge of a complete breakdown. Only four days into the crisis did the USSR acknowledge it had shot down the plane. Reagan's rhetoric reached new heights of denunciation. The Conference on Security and Co-operation in Europe talks in Madrid were the scene of bitter US condemnations. In the words of Dobrynin, both sides seemed to have gone slightly crazy.[26]

The strong words were, to some extent, a deliberate strategy designed to place the Soviets on the defensive and convince them that Reagan could not be intimidated. It may be significant that Reagan's advisers at first dismissed contemporary Soviet talk of the danger of war as a scare tactic aimed to intimidate the USA and NATO.[27] His rhetoric accompanied a massive military build-up, similar moves and words from Margaret Thatcher, Britain's 'Iron Lady', the advent of a Christian Democrat government in Germany under Helmut Kohl, and a socialist government in France that went out of its way to demonstrate its solidarity with the USA and NATO. It added up to a major challenge.

The Warsaw Pact invasions of Hungary and Czechoslovakia, like threats to Poland in 1981–82, used military exercises as cover for the build-up of troops. The coincidence of a major NATO exercise in Norway and Operation Able Archer, a nuclear war-gaming exercise, in November 1983 further frightened the Soviet leadership. Some Soviet forces were in a heightened state of readiness and a special KGB signal asked for evidence of a surprise attack. From 1984 the tone and content of Western rhetoric calmed down. Shultz's efforts to resume negotiations met with a more receptive presidential response and the secretary of state began to gain the upper hand in his struggle with Perle, Weinberger and the hawks for control of national security policy.[28] There were still moments, such as the retaliatory raid on Libya after a Berlin terrorist attack killed US servicemen or crises in southern Africa or Central America, when the administration appeared hawkish. The deployments of Euromissiles went ahead. The US administration and Mrs Thatcher's government, however, reacted to information from Gordievsky about just how jittery their stance was making the Soviet leadership. What seemed at the time like mere election-year language of moderation was, in fact, more complex. Signals were being sent to Chernenko's Politburo of readiness for talks. The West felt strong enough, and NATO was sufficiently united, to allow negotiations.[29]

A changing world

Once meaningful negotiations got under way they took place in a radically different context from that in which détente had developed. In the mid 1980s the sense of Western weakness had been replaced by the strength fostered by booming economies. Firm Cold War priorities in foreign policy saw the implementation of the Reagan Doctrine, not least through the National Endowment for Democracy's channels for funds and ideas to those resisting communist rule. Shultz and Robert Gates claim to have been conscious of the growing weakness of the USSR by this time.[30] Not all Western leaders were as alive to the prospects for change. Garton Ash has stressed how West German leaders drew lessons from their *Ostpolitik* of the 1970s that blinded them to possibilities for change in the 1980s and hampered the development of policies they feared might destabilise the DDR.[31]

In March 1985 a new leader, Mikhail Gorbachev, succeeded Chernenko and Andropov. He had visited the West as the man responsible for Soviet agriculture and been impressed with the productivity of Canadian farms. He met Mrs Thatcher, who memorably deemed him a man with whom she could do business. He assumed power in a country whose bloated military budget was one of many issues facing him. The war in Afghanistan was going badly and showed no signs of ending. China had been co-operating closely with the USA there for some years, as well as in the intelligence and military fields. Experts believed that Soviet alliances were extremely costly and should perhaps be reassessed and there were systemic economic problems in eastern Europe.[32] Dissident movements could not be made to disappear. The economy was in some disarray and the only way that the system could even slightly keep up with the exponential pace of Western technological development was through the strenuous efforts of the KGB and fraternal services' Scientific and Technical lines responsible for collecting technological material, often from private sector sources.[33]

A particular worry for the new leadership was the Strategic Defense Initiative, commonly referred to as 'Star Wars'. This combined Western opulence, technological sophistication, aggressiveness in bipolar competition, the threat of increased Soviet vulnerability to a first strike and US renunciation of a détente era agreement (in this case unilateral expression of redefinition of the ABM Treaty). If the Americans could develop SDI, all the worst-case scenarios of Soviet planning would come together, yet to try to match it would impose a ruinous strain on the system.

Since the 1970s some Western analysts had claimed that the Soviet economic and technological weakness would lead to stagnation and perhaps crisis for the system. So had some Soviet writers. Shultz claimed in 1985 that 'we have reason to be confident that the correlation of forces is shifting back in our favour'.[34] The cycle of détente and confrontation now turned back towards détente. None in the US administration dared use such a taboo word, but the pattern of events and rhetoric moved again toward greater cordiality and negotiation. Although Reagan had been the first US president since Truman to go an entire term without meeting his Soviet counterpart, in his second term he met Gorbachev for four full summits and one mini-summit. He did so after a period of high tension in which the alliance that he led had overcome its problems, whereas his opponents were only beginning to discern the magnitude of theirs.

The 'second Cold War'

6.1 Brezhnev's views on the world situation, 1978

Brezhnev: The defense of the country is important. The strengthening of the country's defensive capabilities still requires our continual attention. Unfortunately, it is not possible to reduce military expenses significantly for now. NATO, especially the USA, is heating up the arms race. We must take care of our security and the security of our allies. The production of modern weapons is a heavy burden on the economy. But we view the strengthening of our defenses as a national as well as an international duty . . . The situation in the world has not developed badly in the last one to two years. On the one hand important results have been achieved under the conditions of détente, on the other hand we are experiencing an open activation of imperialist forces in their attempts to roll back the position of socialism in the various regions.

. . . there is no reason to assume that [Carter] is willing to eliminate the principal matter which has caused the turn for the worse in our relations. I am speaking above all of the arms race heightened by Washington which is at the same time delaying the negotiations on arms control, and the continuing campaign for the so-called 'human rights.' . . .

Source: Transcript of a meeting between Erich Honecker and Leonid Brezhnev, 25 July 1978, *CWIHP Bulletin*, no. 8–9, 1996–97, tr. C. F. Ostermann

6.2 Top Soviet leaders explain the Afghan intervention

By direct order of H. Amin, fabricated rumors were deliberately spread throughout the DRA [Democratic Republic of Afghanistan], smearing the Soviet Union and casting a shadow on the activities of Soviet personnel in Afghanistan . . . At the same time, efforts were made to mend relations with America . . . DRA special services have ceased operations against the American embassy.

H. Amin attempted to buttress his position by reaching a compromise with leaders of internal counter-revolution . . . In effect, the objective was to liquidate the party . . . In this extremely difficult situation, which has threatened the gains of the April revolution and the interests of maintaining our national security, it has become necessary to render additional military assistance to Afghanistan, especially since such requests had been made by the previous administration in DRA. In accordance with the provisions of the Soviet–Afghan treaty of 1978, a decision has been made to send the necessary contingent of the Soviet Army to Afghanistan . . .

Source: Andropov-Gromyko-Ustinov-Ponomarev Report to the Central Committee on Events in Afghanistan on 27–28 December 1979, dated 31 December 1979, *CWIHP Bulletin*, no. 8–9, 1996–97, tr. D. Rozas.

6.3 CIA director Stansfield Turner sums up the US view of Soviet behaviour in the developing world, March 1980

I agree we do not have evidence that the Soviets are firmly committed to continuing as aggressive a policy in the third world as was this Afghan example. Yet I do believe that the Soviet track record over the past five or six years indicates a definitely greater willingness to probe the limits of our tolerance. 'Detente' was not a bar to this greater assertiveness in Angola, Ethiopia, Kampuchea and Yemen. It need not be so again, even if we return to détente. As the paper concludes, how assertive the Soviets will be in future will very likely depend upon how 'successful' the Soviet leadership views their intervention in Afghanistan to have been.

Source: A CIA document that was forwarded to Brzezinski, March 1980, quoted in R. Gates, *From the shadows: the ultimate insider's story of five presidents and how they won the Cold War*, New York, 1996, p. 148

6.4 A senior CIA figure recalls US policies

The imposition of martial law [in Poland] resulted in CIA and American covert action being targeted against Soviet domination in Eastern Europe in a significant way for the first time since the early years of the cold war . . . Most of what flowed out of CIA and through the intermediaries to Solidarity was printing materials, communications equipment, and other supplies for waging underground political warfare . . . [Kuklinski] provided us with over thirty thousand Soviet documents over a ten year period . . . his efforts . . . allowed the United States and its allies to help deter a Soviet invasion of Poland in December 1980 . . . Casey [from 1982] would remain obsessed with Soviet and proxy subversion . . . By the end of 1982 the Reagan administration's covert offensive against the Soviet Union was beginning to take shape. In Central America, Afghanistan, Chad, and elsewhere, often building on programs started by Carter, they confronted Soviet clients with resistance forces now funded and often armed by the United States. In Poland, Cambodia, the Caribbean, Libya, the Middle East, Africa, Central America, and elsewhere, the Soviets and their satellites and proxies faced opposition now supported by the United States . . . SDI was a Soviet nightmare come to life. America's industrial base, coupled with American technology, wealth, and managerial skill . . . would require an expensive Soviet response at a time of deep economic crisis.

Source: Gates, *From the shadows*, pp. 236–64

Document case-study questions

1 What do documents 6.1 and 6.2 contribute to an evaluation of the significance of the claims about Soviet attitudes in document 6.3?
2 Compare the attitudes to détente revealed in the four documents.
3 Explain the terms 'continuing campaign for so-called "human rights"' in document 6.1 and 'Solidarity' and 'covert action' in document 6.4.

4 What do the documents contribute to any comparison of the policies of the Carter and Reagan administrations?

5 Using the documents and your wider knowledge, assess the view that the period 1979–85 saw a transformation of the correlation of forces in world politics.

Notes and references

1 T. Wolton, *Le KGB en France*, Paris, 1986, pp. 403–04, stresses Mitterand's efforts to reassure Reagan of his priorities, even though he had ministers from the French Communist Party in his left coalition cabinet.

2 Representative Charles Vanik, a third generation Czech, was a Democrat from Ohio whose district had approximately 11 per cent Jewish voters, and many from east European ethnic backgrounds. He co-sponsored the resolution on Jewish emigration being linked to MFN status.

3 G. Arbatov, *The system: an insider's life in Soviet politics*, New York, 1992, p. 196.

4 I. Belikov, 'Soviet–Angolan relations', in M. Light (ed.), *Troubled friendships. Moscow's third world ventures*, London, 1993; A. Dobrynin, *In confidence. Moscow's ambassador to America's six Cold War presidents*, New York, 1995, p. 367; and Arbatov, *The system*, p. 193. See also K. Mokoena (ed.), *South Africa and the United States: the declassified history*, Washington, DC, 1993, part IV; and R. Garthoff, *Détente and confrontation: American–Soviet relations from Nixon to Reagan*, revised edn, Washington, DC, 1994, ch. 15.

5 Arbatov, *The system*, pp.195–96.

6 Somalia and Ethiopia both claimed the Ogaden region on their border. As long as Ethiopia was pro-Western, Moscow backed Somalia. After the revolution in Ethiopia and the rise of Mengistu Haile Mariam, they switched to backing Ethiopia and the USA to backing Said Barre and the Somalis. A similar *volte-face* happened over the Eritrean war for secession from Ethiopia.

7 J. Mann, *About face: a history of America's curious relationship with China, from Nixon to Clinton*, New York, 2000, pp. 86–97; A. Chernyaev, *My six years with Gorbachev*, tr. and ed. R. English and E. Tucker, University Park, Pa., 2000, p. 104.

8 Transcript of a meeting between Erich Honecker and Leonid Brezhnev, 25 July 1978, tr. C. F. Ostermann, *CWIHP Bulletin*, no. 8–9, n.d.

9 Mann, *About face*, p. 100. See also S. J. Morris, 'Soviet–Chinese–Vietnamese triangle in the 1970s', *CWIHP Working Paper*, no. 25 (1999).

10 A. H. Cahn, *Killing détente: the right attacks the CIA*, University Park, Pa., 1998, esp. chs. 7–9.

11 Arbatov, *The system*, p. 200.

12 Andropov might initially have been more reluctant than the others, Ustinov was most committed, and Ponomarev was absent from the crucial 12 December meeting. Arbatov, *The system*, pp. 196–201; S. Mendelson, *Changing course: ideas, politics and the Soviet withdrawal from Afghanistan*, Princeton, 1998, pp. 52–64; Garthoff, *Détente and confrontation*, pp. 998–1046; and Dobrynin, *In confidence*, p. 189.

13 Soviet documents on the Afghan Crisis, *CWIHP Bulletin*, no. 8–9 (1996–97); also Garthoff, *Détente and confrontation*, pp. 1012–46.

14 Quoted in Mendelson, *Changing course*, p. 76.

15 Mann, *About face*, pp. 136–37.

16 W. L. Leogrande, *Our own backyard: the United States in Central America, 1977–1992*, Chapel Hill, 1998, part III; and T. Smith, *America's mission. The United States and the worldwide struggle for democracy in the twentieth century*, Princeton, 1994, ch. 9.

17 R. Sikorski, *The Polish house*, London, 1998, pp. 44–56, describes both how families, doctors and friends covered up Sikorski's May Day rally truancy and the Pope's impact.

18 See V. Mastny, 'The Soviet non-invasion of Poland in 1980/81 and the end of the Cold War', *CWIHP Working Paper*, no. 23, (1996), on which this section draws heavily. M. Kramer, 'Soviet deliberations during the Polish Crisis, 1980–81', *CWIHP Special Working Paper*, no. 1 (1999); and his 'Poland 1980–81', *CWIHP Bulletin*, no. 5 (1995), bring together key documents on the crisis.

19 Quoted in Mastny, 'Soviet non-invasion', p. 23–24.

20 Mastny is highly critical of Jaruzelski, but compare Sikorski, *Polish house*, on his later experience as a defence minister and his ambivalent feelings about meeting Jaruzelski's daughter at a North Korean reception, pp. 209–11.

21 W. R. Smyser, *From Yalta to Berlin: the Cold War struggle over Germany*, New York, 1999, p. 275.

22 T. Garton Ash, *In Europe's name: Germany and the divided continent*, London, 1994, pp. 289–91.

23 NSDD 54, 2 September 1982, document 109, Polish Crisis Reader, National Security Archive, Washington, DC.

24 D. Oberdorfer, *From the Cold War to a new era: the United States and the Soviet Union, 1983–1991*, 2nd edn, Baltimore, 1997, p. 66.

25 C. Andrew and O. Gordievsky, *Instructions from the centre*, London, 1993, pp. 111–40.

26 Dobrynin, *In confidence*, pp. 541–46; and G. Shultz, *Turmoil and triumph*, New York, 1993, pp. 361–71.

27 Oberdorfer, *Cold War to new era*, p. 67.

28 Perle was a former staffer for Senator Jackson who served at the Pentagon under Weinberger, though he eventually left the administration before 1988. He was noted as a critic of détente and opponent of anything that smacked of compromise with the Soviets.

29 Shultz, *Turmoil and triumph*, ch. 25; C. M. Andrew and O. Gordievsky, *KGB. The inside story of its foreign operations from Lenin to Gorbachev*, London, 1990, pp. 487–507; and R. M. Gates, *From the shadows: the ultimate insider's story of five presidents and how they won the Cold War*, New York, 1996, pp. 258–92.

30 G. Shultz, 'New realities and new ways of thinking', *Foreign Affairs*, vol. 63 (1985), catches the mood. Gates, *From the shadows*, pp. 317–26.

31 Garton Ash, *In Europe's name*, pp. 362–71 and *passim*.

32 Light, *Troubled friendships*, ch. 5; D. Paszyn, *The Soviet attitude to social and political change in Latin America, 1979–1990*, London, 2000, pp. 12–21, 192–203.

33 C. M. Andrew and V. Mitrokhin, *The Mitrokhin archive. The KGB in Europe and the West*, London, 1999, pp. 280–87. Brzezinski had noted this technological lag as early as 1970, see 'What future for Soviet power?', *Encounter*, vol. XXIV, no. 3 (1970). So had Khrushchev in the same year, though his veiled comment that Soviet science was 'propped up' by the West was not published until *glasnost*, see N. Khrushchev, *Khrushchev remembers. The glasnost tapes*, tr. J. Schechter, London, 1990, p. 94.

34 Cahn, *Killing détente*, pp. 193–94. G. Ball, *The past has another pattern. Memoirs*, London, 1982, pp. 481–85, made prescient predictions. Shultz, 'New realities', p. 707.

7 The end of the Cold War

1985 *March:* Chernenko dies, replaced by Gorbachev

1986 *February–March:* CPSU Congress and announcement of reforms

1987 *December:* INF Treaty signed at Washington summit

1988 *May:* Strikes and unrest in Poland; Moscow summit
December: Gorbachev speech at the UNO on de-ideologisation of foreign policy; Soviet troops begin to withdraw from Afghanistan

1989 *February:* Round table discussions in Poland
June: Polish elections
Summer: Exodus of East Germans after opening of Hungarian border
12 September: Mazowiecki becomes prime minister of Poland
October: Fundamental changes in Hungary
9 November: Berlin Wall opens
November: Velvet Revolution in Czechoslovakia
December: Malta summit and Romanian Revolution

1990 *March:* Talks on Germany
May: Kohl and Gorbachev meet in the Caucasus to discuss aid and reunification
3 October: Germany reunified
November: CFE Treaty signed and CSCE reforms take place

1991 *August:* Coup against Gorbachev
25 December: Final collapse of USSR

In 1970 Brzezinski suggested five possible futures for the USSR: petrification, evolution, adaptation, fundamentalism or disintegration. Like most Western commentators, then and later, he did not think the last the most likely to occur, believing a combination of the first and third to be more probable. Between 1989 and 1991, however, with the end of Soviet domination in eastern Europe, the USSR disintegrated. Just a few years previously this had been unthinkable. Respected authorities on international politics suggested the division of Europe was permanent, that the Cold War was the best possible solution, and that issues such as the reunification of Germany had been removed from the realm of practical politics. Even as the events of 1989 unfolded, leading Germans and senior figures in both alliances continued to assume the prolonged existence of two Germanies.[1]

Such views epitomised a conventional wisdom with which few disagreed. More importantly, the collapse of Soviet power was as rapid as it was unforeseen. Soviet reformers did not envisage the reunification of Germany and the collapse of a Russian/Soviet empire which had been built up from the time of Peter the Great to that of Stalin. Gorbachev did not foresee that his state would collapse, that by 1999 NATO would embrace former members of the Warsaw Pact or that a reunited Germany would be called upon to subsidise the costs of rehousing 300,000 Soviet troops as they withdrew from East Germany.[2]

US pressure

The external policies of 'the imperium'[3] were profoundly affected by its internal crisis. Outside pressures were also significant. US leaders drove hard bargains. The policy of differentiation towards the countries of eastern Europe continued: deviations from the Moscow line were rewarded and its enforcers punished, as the Poles found from 1982. Soviet weaknesses were exploited to extract concessions. The Americans were not prepared to co-exist – they moved 'beyond containment' to demand fundamental change, even in the USSR.[4] Until Soviet behaviour changed and Soviet power collapsed, the Cold War continued.

Ronald Reagan and Mikhail Gorbachev walked through Red Square during the May 1988 summit. Gorbachev told a Russian child to shake hands with 'Grandfather Reagan' and the president responded to press questions about the 'evil empire' by saying that that phrase belonged to 'another time, another era'.

After his walkabout in Red Square in 1988 Reagan was asked whether he still considered the USSR to be an 'evil empire'; he responded by saying that the phrase belonged to 'another time, another era'. Vice-president Bush's remark, however, was 'The Cold War's not over'.[5] Between then and Gorbachev handing over the *chemodanchik* (the Soviet nuclear code briefcase) to Boris Yeltsin on Christmas Day 1991 and the Red Flag no longer flying high over the Kremlin, the Cold War ended.[6]

When in June 1991 Secretary of State James Baker welcomed Albania to the community of democratic nations, he stressed how policies characteristic of the old regimes had to change: 'You have joined the nations that have pledged to uphold the standards of the CSCE – standards that govern a state's behaviour towards other nations and towards its own people . . . Pursuing democratization at every level of government and society . . . '.[7] He then outlined what had to happen within the country as well as in its external relations. Baker's vision demonstrates a continuity of aims and values with Truman's justification for aiding Greece and Turkey. The vision of containment elaborated by Kennan, Marshall and Acheson had endured and triumphed. Baker's view combined changed international relations with the triumph of democracy in a Europe whole and free, just as his predecessors' had done.

The beginning of the end

With hindsight the mid 1980s can be seen as the beginning of the end. It did not seem that way at the time, but the deployment of Euromissiles, SDI, the US invasion of Grenada, aid to the Contras and Mujahideen, and other initiatives of the first Reagan administration laid the basis for two interconnected developments. First, they created the position of strength from which Western leaders felt they could now negotiate. Second, they increased the pressure on the new Soviet leadership to seek a breathing space in foreign affairs so that domestic reforms could be given a chance to take hold. Fear of the costs of matching SDI and the destabilising effect it would have on deterrence and parity played a crucial part. Trying to persuade the Americans to abandon this project became something of a fixation for Gorbachev.[8] SDI was the sticking point that resulted in the failure of the October 1986 Reykjavik summit, and Soviet antagonism to the project surfaced repeatedly. At the time some joked that only two groups of people actually believed it could ever work but that, as one was in the White House and the other in the Kremlin, that was all that mattered.

As the 1980s progressed it became ever clearer that Soviet and other communist leaders were facing a crisis that their rhetoric belied. Their Western counterparts, who enjoyed excellent intelligence, knew better than they did how bad things were. George Shultz recalls trying to educate the new Soviet leader about the realities of economic and political life in the 'information age'.[9] High levels of hard currency debt plagued most Comecon countries. East Germany's apparent success was, in fact, due to huge subsidies from Moscow and massive infusions of cash from Bonn – the country was actually close to bankruptcy. As Ulbricht and other hardliners had predicted, economic contacts had created a dependence on the West. This was most true of Germany, but the economic leverage of aid greatly facilitated the policy of differentiation in the 1980s and gave Kohl and Bush a crucial advantage over Gorbachev in 1990.[10] At the end of the Cold War conditions were accepted that had been rejected by Stalin in 1947. The Soviet satellites had not modernised or rationalised their economies. The knowledge- and skills-based global economy of the G-7 countries put a premium on high technology and effective flows of information that were bewildering to those who had risen through the Soviet apparatus.

New thinking

As the Soviet system changed, the Cold War began to change. Gromyko's replacement by Eduard Shevardnadze was a harbinger of new views. The new foreign minister sought to create international conditions that would promote the cause of reform at home.[11] Throughout 1986 the signals emanating from Moscow were mixed, but it was clear that new ideas were circulating in Moscow's highest policy-making circles. The November 1985 summit in Geneva produced a stated intention to keep talking and established a good personal relationship between Reagan and Gorbachev. In Moscow reform-minded and pragmatic advisers rose to prominence. From early on Gorbachev regarded withdrawal from Afghanistan as his 'highest priority issue' and one of his close advisers is convinced that only domestic politics prevented him pulling out before 1989.[12] Simultaneously Shultz won bureaucratic political battles in Washington. In 1986 and 1987 tangible progress was made towards an INF treaty and on regional affairs. The establishment of new ideas in Moscow was crucial to this process, but so was competition between the superpowers to win European public opinion and the shift in the balance of power in Washington.

The new political thinking encompassed a major rethink of Soviet priorities and eventually the removal of Marxist-Leninist ideology as a major force in shaping Soviet foreign policy. This process culminated in Gorbachev's December 1988 speech to the UN General Assembly. It could be regarded as systematic appeasement by a weak power, dressed up as a bid to court world opinion. Old thinkers at home hoped it was merely cosmetic, revealing something of their views of détente. Chernyaev quotes Ponomarev, a leading figure under Brezhnev, as deprecating the concept: 'Our thinking is right. Let the Americans change their thinking. What Gorbachev says abroad is meant exclusively for them, for the West.'[13]

Gorbachev had few ties to the military and had grown close to reform-minded experts during his time in charge of agriculture. They were sceptical of the merits of costly foreign interventions and wanted to concentrate on domestic reform.[14] During 1986 Gorbachev espoused other elements of new political thinking. One of his closest aides dates his changed views of international affairs to the start of that year:

Before this, a roundabout tactic prevailed – that of influencing Western Europe by encouraging contradictions in the Atlantic alliance, through propagandistic pressure . . . our traditional strategy albeit with the new goal of achieving real disarmament. But by April or May, Gorbachev was already thinking . . . about a new meeting with Reagan and counting on real progress in disarmament.[15]

The problem was to match behaviour to rhetoric. The Twenty-Seventh Congress of the CPSU held in February–March was a key moment. It followed high-profile Soviet offers on nuclear arms cuts in Europe that had been made in January. At the Congress the new thinking was elaborated and strengthened by personnel changes, notably the replacement of Ponomarev by Dobrynin. New thinking encompassed a sense that, given the nuclear arms race, security should be redefined in national terms and should encompass notions of interdependence and mutual security rather than military competition, 'proletarian internationalism' and eternal ideological struggle. It also envisaged a reduction in the economic burdens of the old alliance system: if foreign policy was going to enhance the country's wellbeing and old notions of internationalist duty were jettisoned, the value of friendship treaties would be called into question.[16] By December 1988 Gorbachev's aides were telling him that old ideological friends were getting in the way of convincing the world that he meant what he had said at the UNO. The cancellation of a visit to Cuba due to the Armenian earthquake seemed fortunate.[17]

In the short term, the hardliners benefited from the atmosphere of the Cold War in the mid 1980s and were able to thwart significant shifts in foreign policy by depicting a besieged USSR struggling against aggressive imperialists. There was resistance in the policy elite to new ideas, especially when the USA escalated its aid to the rebel forces in Afghanistan in 1985. For the armed forces the new thinking was at least partially welcome as, by 1985, the commitment to Afghanistan had become more unpopular in the upper reaches of the army.[18] Gorbachev's way forward became easier when, following the landing of a light aircraft in Red Square piloted by a teenage German, Mathias Rust, he sacked many opponents. In addition, he brought in experts who stressed local factors and politics over global ideological considerations; they added legitimacy to departures from old thinking. As they gained more access to policy makers, so policy began to shift. The top leaders worked on educating public opinion and increased the role of professional diplomats who were more pragmatic. Pragmatists initiated debates about where policy should be changed and soon domestic reforms and changes in foreign policy became mutually reinforcing. This new discussion about Soviet diplomacy was not limited to Afghanistan, but had most impact there.[19] With qualified support from military and diplomatic figures such as Akhromeyev and Vorontsov, who had been promoted by Gorbachev, policy shifted. By the end of 1987 Gorbachev and Shevardnadze declared an intention to withdraw troops. By 1988 they did so and by February 1989 they were gone. Actions had matched words and a Cold War confrontation had been resolved to the West's satisfaction, even if the situation within Afghanistan remained unresolved and dangerous.[20]

Agreements, 1987–88

At the December 1987 Washington summit the INF Treaty – the first major arms *reduction* treaty of the Cold War – was signed. It marked the occasion for serious work to begin on a more comprehensive START agreement, as the agenda shifted from limitations to reductions. Although it proved impossible to finalise this during Reagan's term in office, momentum was established and, not long before the collapse of the USSR, President Bush oversaw its successful conclusion.[21]

Such developments did not immediately persuade the Americans that the Cold War was over. A leading US policy maker, who was intimately involved in these events, has offered his evaluation of their significance:

> The Cold War began in, and because of, Eastern Europe, and it was there that it had to end. Eastern Europe, therefore, was the key 'test' of whether Soviet 'new thinking' would lead to a fundamental amelioration of the Cold War division of Europe . . .[22]

As on previous occasions, change in the USSR quickly impacted upon alliance relationships. The new thinking in the USSR borrowed extensively from Hungarian and Czech ideas of the 1960s and 1970s. The de-emphasis on ideology and the distancing of the USSR from armed struggle impacted on the Warsaw Pact allies and others. Castro, Honecker and other hardline leaders agreed with Ponomarev on the new thinking (see p. 133). During *glasnost* the East Germans took to censoring Soviet publications as they contained material that the government preferred to keep from the public. The USSR's European allies, however, came under domestic pressure to emulate what was happening in the USSR. This was never clearer than when Gorbachev visited Czechoslovakia or

Thousands of warheads/bombs

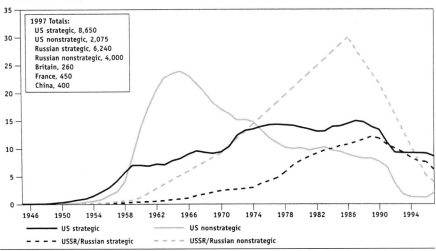

Global nuclear stockpiles, 1945–97, shown as thousands of warheads/bombs. The graph illustrates the dramatic impact of the agreements of 1987–91. Adapted from Schwartz et al., *Atomic audit*, Washington, DC, 1998, p. 46.

when Hungary sought to push on with reforms in 1987 and 1988. Plans for change in Poland were, however, blocked that year.

Europe transformed, 1989

In the months following Gorbachev's December 1988 declaration at the UNO that ideology should play a smaller part in foreign affairs and the announcement of major reductions of force in Europe, Poland and Hungary tested the limits of Soviet tolerance. From February 1989 the former moved slowly towards a multiparty system and no serious repercussions ensued. There was an opportunity for Jaruzelski to respond to demands to renegotiate the compromises made in the 1980s. On 6 February round table talks led to accords in early April for partly free elections. On 4 June the Solidarity opposition scored a massive victory. In September Tadeusz Mazowiecki became the first non-communist prime minister in the region since 1948. The leading role of the communists was overturned and nothing happened. All that was heard from Moscow was the sound of Gorbachev's press spokesman, Gennady Gerasimov, announcing a Frank Sinatra doctrine: they could all do it their way.

Poland was not alone in testing Moscow's new tolerance. Following intimations of liberalisation, the Hungarian government permitted a rush of nationalist sentiment on the occasion of the obsequies for the reformer Imre Nagy on 16 June. It also opened its border with Austria in May. This produced a flood of East Germans seeking to leave through that country in order to make their way to the West in July and August. The DDR then demanded unprecedented restrictions on travel from one bloc state to another, with the result that Hungary eventually imposed some border controls. When these restrictions were imposed, the West German embassies in Budapest and Prague were overwhelmed by would-be exiles, hoping to find a way out. By August 1989, a crisis had developed with embassy grounds being used by people camping out and refusing to go home. As face-saving deal was arranged whereby the trains carrying these exiles to the West had to travel through the DDR. Thus, technically, the refugees had left East Germany according to East German decisions and policies, rather than fleeing.

When Gorbachev attended the DDR's fortieth anniversary celebrations in early October his welcome by the people and his attitude towards Honecker spelled doom for the system. Demonstrations in favour of reform broke out in many cities and the authorities debated over whether to adopt the Chinese response (seen in Tienanmen Square in June) or to allow greater liberty. Backed by Moscow, the reformers won and changes of personnel were made. More demands followed, culminating in the opening of the Berlin Wall and its being torn down on 9 November. From there the whole structure of Soviet domination crumbled. The Velvet Revolution in Prague and similar events in Hungary ushered the communist regimes there into oblivion.

Three things were noteworthy about these events. First, local Moscow loyalists experienced political paralysis because of their ally's failure to aid them. Even though they led bankrupt states, their will to hold on to power was strong for as long as Soviet power backed them. Second, some hardliners in all the countries of the Warsaw Pact were prepared to countenance a repeat of previous repression. Even their will failed when they lost the certainty that they could bank on Moscow's armed support, without which they were unable to impose the sort of solution that the Chinese had sought. Third, their previous use of nationalism to bolster their legitimacy backfired when it was seized by their critics to move beyond the reforms proposed by Gorbachev's preferred

Germany
Exodus via Hungary:
Summer 1989
Berlin Wall falls:
October 1989
Elections:
March 1990
Reunification:
3 October 1990

Poland
Following partly free elections, Solidarity-led government takes office:
September 1989

Estonia, Latvia and Lithuania
Independence recognised by USSR:
September 1991

Belorussia
Declares independence:
August 1991

Former USSR
USSR ends:
25 December 1991

Czech Republic/Slovakia
Mass demonstrations spread from Prague, leading to the collapse of communist rule:
November 1989
Split into two countries:
1 January 1993

Ukraine
Votes for independence:
1 December 1991

Moldova
Declares independence:
27 August 1991

Hungary
Communist rule ends peacefully:
October 1989

Former Yugoslavia
(Slovenia, Bosnia, Croatia, Yugoslavia, Macedonia)
Croatia and Slovenia declare independence:
25 June 1991
This leads to civil war, spreading to Bosnia after it declares independence:
April 1992

Romania
Mass demonstrations lead to Ceaucescu's overthrow:
December 1989

Albania
Free elections take place:
March 1991

Bulgaria
Zhivkhov removed from office:
November 1989

Border of former USSR

German reunification and the collapse of communism in eastern and central Europe.

successors. In Leipzig and Prague there was some effort at repression, but more moderate voices demanded compromise. Gorbachev held his own counsel. By the end of November it was nearly over. The DDR still existed, as did the Warsaw Pact, but the world had changed.[23]

In December Romania was convulsed by its own 'refolution'.[24] This gave rise to an exchange that demonstrated that the Cold War was over. On Christmas Eve the US ambassador in Moscow suggested that the USSR might intervene militarily to support the National Salvation Front's efforts at change. The Soviets turned the idea down:

... we did not visualize, even theoretically, such a scenario. We stand against any interference in the domestic affairs of other states and we intend to pursue this line firmly and without deviations. Thus, the American side may consider that 'the Brezhnev doctrine' is now theirs as our gift.

... both sides confirmed the positive evaluation of the exchange of opinions that took place. They expressed support of continuing contacts with regard to the rapidly changing situation in Romania.[25]

The Americans now viewed the USSR as an ally in eastern-central Europe and had encouraged it to intervene in a neighbouring country. Ideology, mistrust, historical analogies and the other forces that had produced the Cold War antagonism were replaced by co-operation between Western and Soviet leaders. By early 1990 Mrs Thatcher and the Polish post-communist leadership both advanced the view that Soviet troops should stay in Germany for fear that Germany would be unified too quickly and emerge too independent. They, and Mitterand, looked to Gorbachev to rein in Bush and Kohl over the fate of the DDR.[26] In the space of two years Gorbachev had transformed his country's German alliance. He worked with Kohl and against Honecker more and more, from his first halting hints of flexibility in 1987 to his close working relationship with Kohl in 1989 and 1990.

The post Cold War world

The tendency to co-operation increasingly manifested itself as Shevardnadze built good relations first with Shultz and then with Baker. He and Gorbachev also built strong ties with Thatcher and Kohl. Among the Western bloc Japan remained the least affected by 'Gorby-mania', owing largely to unresolved disputes with the USSR over islands both countries claimed after the wars of 1905 and 1945. At a series of summits, Gorbachev and the USA moved towards common ground on a range of regional disputes. Cuts in Moscow's aid in these struggles facilitated superpower disengagement and peace accords in central America, southern Africa, Cambodia and the Horn of Africa. In March 1990 Soviet and Western leaders came together in Windhoek to celebrate Namibia's independence. Western-style democracy flourished and armed struggles ended, though some wars took longer than others to end. Eritrea finally won independence from Ethiopia and Mengistu's regime fell. Somalia descended into chaos and anarchy. Angola and Mozambique's civil wars had very different outcomes. The latter began a slow and painful transition to democracy. The former remains plagued by conflicts and fighting. Similarly, it took years for elections in Cambodia to produce stable government and a semblance of peace. In all these regions mines and bombs continue to exact Cold War casualties long after the confrontation itself has ended.

As the superpowers learned to talk about these issues, they also co-operated in the regeneration of the United Nations. The Iran–Iraq war was brought to an end once Soviet backing for Iraq waned. When Saddam Hussein invaded Kuwait in August 1990 the Soviet government gave strong backing to the USA and did little or nothing to hamper efforts to pass UN resolutions that formed the basis of the US-led coalition's mandate to fight the Iraqis. A Cold War proxy was abandoned, with only a few diplomatic efforts to show for the traditional ties and their friendship treaty.

Germany, trust and history

That this co-operation spread was due not only to the mutual trust that built up between the leaders. Bush and Kohl had the added lever of financial muscle that allowed them to drive hard bargains with Gorbachev. The parlous state of the Soviet economy and Gorbachev's need to demonstrate that his reforms did pay dividends made him ever more desperate for successful foreign policy coups. This bred appeasement of the West, troop reductions, agreements on bilateral and regional matters and co-operative gestures that angered conservatives at home.

The leverage was clearest in the 1990 negotiations over German reunification. As early as mid 1987 Gorbachev hinted at flexibility over German affairs.[27] In the end he tried to resist the reunification of Germany within NATO, but was powerless to prevent it when Kohl visited him in May 1990 and brokered a deal.

German economic assistance to the USSR, acceptance of Poland's western border by Germany and security guarantees for Poland (and, less formally, for the USSR) could not mask the fact that the Cold War contest was resolved entirely to the satisfaction of the West. Those for whom the lessons of the past remained fixed around the 1940s worried, but Bush trusted Kohl and worked hard to convince European sceptics that they should follow suit. When Ligachev, a conservative Politburo member, strove for a hard line, one of Gorbachev's advisers characterised his views as '1945-thinking'. On another occasion Kohl commented to Thatcher that the difference between them was that he lived in the post-Churchill era.[28]

The process of German reunification was marked by competing analogies. Mitterand feared a return to 1913; others worried about a repeat of the mistakes of Versailles, while Thatcher and Ligachev saw possibilities of a new Munich. Shevardnadze (who had lost a brother in 1941) and other Soviet leaders recalled the Second World War and initially sought to ensure the permanence of 'the decision of history' that there be two Germanies. Mazowiecki feared that Poland would be ignored as had happened at Yalta. Kohl and Bush were less restrained by what one participant called 'mind-closing axioms' from history. On the Soviet side, Chernyaev saw Baker's point that NATO membership would guarantee that Germany would be restrained. Shevardnadze overcame his sense that Kohl's rhetoric was reminiscent of the 1930s to persuade domestic critics that lessons from Afghanistan contradicted their policy of military strength and intransigent refusal to abandon old alliances.[29]

Domestic politics, alliance politics and Western economic strength all affected the process by which timetables for a united Germany were accelerated from decades to months during late 1989 and early 1990. Kohl's position was affected by up-coming elections as well as by his sense of history and the fact that the collapse of the DDR demanded a solution. Economic and monetary union preceded the incorporation of the eastern *Länder* into the Federal Republic.

Soviet policy vacillated between conciliation and a hard line. Economic weakness repeatedly forced both Gorbachev and the new leaders in East Berlin to make concessions they had previously ruled out. Red Army leaders in East Germany were dismayed at the loss of the old *cordon sanitaire*, but accepted the decision. Events closer to home demanded priority. The DDR's economy needed US and Soviet aid for credits, trade and food, and would be bankrupt without West German assistance. The USSR could not afford to help. Thatcher and Mazowiecki proved at least as difficult for Bush to handle as the Soviet leaders, who came to accept that a single Germany in NATO and in a deepened EU would be contained by those structures. Poland came to accept a border treaty that immediately followed reunification in October 1990. Germany subsidised the withdrawal of 300,000 Soviet troops from its soil.[30] This was packaged along with major multilateral troop reductions in the CFE (Conventional Forces in Europe) Treaty signed at the CSCE summit in November.

The end

The USSR was brought into the international capitalist economy during the very late 1980s and early 1990s. The economic Cold War can be seen to have ended at the Malta summit in December 1989. Aid with strings was made available in the form of political concessions and moves towards a market economy. It was perhaps no coincidence that just as these steps were taken historians and commentators in the USSR debated whether the refusal to participate in the Marshall Plan had been a mistake. This encompassed the third leg of the West's triumph. The ideological Cold War was ended at the UNO in December 1988. The military Cold War was brought to an end in November 1990 at the CSCE talks in Paris. There Bush, Gorbachev and European leaders signed the CFE Treaty and Soviet and general European support was gained for resolutions mandating military action against Iraq. Now the economic confrontation of the two rival systems had been decided too. In January 1990 the *Bulletin of the Atomic Scientists* reset its Doomsday Clock back by four minutes,[31] and declared the Cold War over.

The end brought new historical models and analogies that affected politicians' judgement, but old ones died hard. The memory of détente strengthened the

Munich analogy (see p. 7) for Thatcher, Reagan and their advisers. At the same time, the lessons of Afghanistan made the Soviet leaders rethink their global strategy and made the West more confident. The key, however, was that a weak USSR sent clear signals that the lessons of 1953, 1956 and 1968 no longer held. After the non-intervention in Poland in 1980 there were hints that the USSR would not fight for its client states in eastern Europe. In 1988–89 Gorbachev and Shevardnadze made it clear that they would not act as their predecessors had done in the face of nationalist pressure in eastern Europe. A bankrupt system, morally as well as economically, could not hold once that prop was withdrawn. And so the Cold War ended, with the sound of joyful crowds on the streets rather than gunfire and rockets in the air.

The end of the Cold War

7.1 A Gorbachev adviser describes the relationship between domestic and foreign policies

. . . efforts toward disarmament and new relations with the West – originally meant 'to create favorable external conditions for *perestroika*' – in fact became its locomotive. At least this was the case in the ideological sphere, and ideology was the chief obstacle to reforms. To succeed with the new foreign policy we had to demolish the myths and dogmas of a confrontational ideology . . . Our contacts with Western Europe had a similar impact on the democratization process. But our relations with socialist countries, especially China and Cuba, were holding back de-ideologization . . . One example concerned Ethiopia, from early April of 1988. Mengistu was sending secret messages one after the other: Send more arms, money, transport, food, etc . . . The Ethiopia issue was raised [at the Politburo]. Akhromeyev . . . described the hopelessness of Mengistu's attempt at military victory. He had been fighting for Eritrea for fourteen years, but was doing worse and worse. 'And we,' the marshal said, 'are supporting his policies in Ethiopia instead of having one of our own.'

Source: A. Chernyaev, *My six years with Gorbachev*, tr. and ed. R. English and E. Tucker, University Park, Pa., 2000, pp. 144–45

7.2 A Soviet diplomat reports new US attitudes, December 1989

Ambassador J. Matlock . . . referred to the positive significance of the fact that the opinions of the Soviet Union and the United States coincided to the effect that there should be support given to the group that is trying to govern Romania and to fulfill the will of the Romanian people . . .

Then Matlock touched on the issue that, apparently, he wanted to raise from the very beginning of the conversation. The Administration, he said, is very interested in knowing if the possibility of military assistance by the Soviet Union to the Romanian National Salvation Front is totally out of question.

. . . under the present circumstances the military involvement of the Soviet Union in Romanian affairs might not be regarded in the context of 'the Brezhnev doctrine.' . . . I gave the entirely clear and unequivocal answer, presenting our principled position. I declared that we did not visualize, even theoretically, such a scenario. We stand against any interference in the domestic affairs of other states and we intend to pursue this line firmly and without deviations. Thus, the American side may consider that 'the Brezhnev doctrine' is now theirs as our gift.

Source: Record of conversation by Deputy Minister of Foreign Affairs I. Aboimov, 24 December 1989, *CWIHP Bulletin*, no. 10 (1998), pp. 189–91, tr. by V. Zubok

7.3 A US policy maker describes the Bush administration's priorities

American grand strategy for ending the Cold War was elaborated in five major speeches delivered by President Bush in April and May of 1989 . . . The first, delivered in Hamtramck, Michigan, on April 17, elevated Eastern Europe to the top of the agenda . . . The second speech, delivered at Texas A&M's commencement on May 12, called for moving 'beyond containment' in US–Soviet relations . . . This was a conceptually new idea. The containment strategy had assumed that the US–Soviet relationship was essentially conflictual. So did the policy of détente, which sought to carve out areas of co-operation and ease tensions, but within what was still a basically conflictual relationship. If the notion of containing Soviet power no longer carried the same weight as in the early days of the Cold War, the other premise of containment remained – namely, that the nature of the Soviet system had to change for the relationship to change fundamentally . . . The kind of European future the United States was proposing contrasted starkly with the Soviet vision outlined by President Gorbachev in his speech to the Council of Europe in Strasbourg a few weeks later . . . [The nub of the matter was] a Europe 'whole and free' or a Europe based on the permanence of the 'two social systems'; an end to the division of Europe or an East-West accommodation based on Western acceptance of 'political realities' in the East.

Source: R. Hutchings, *American diplomacy and the end of the Cold War*, Baltimore, 1997, pp. 36–45

7.4 American policy makers reflect on the threat new political thinking posed to East German existence

Even if the East German government seemed invincible, it was not at ease. The theoretical implications of Gorbachev's new policies were profoundly unsettling. Otto Reinhold, a top social scientist in the East German Communist party, posed the dilemma for his country: 'What right to exist would a capitalist GDR have alongside a capitalist Federal Republic? In other words, what justification would there be for two German states once ideology no longer separated them?' . . . Soon it would become clear that socialism could be defended only to the extent that capitalism could be attacked. The Cold War was rooted in that conflict, and it in turn sustained the socialist myth at home and abroad. Class struggle was at the root of the myth that, together with Moscow's coercive power, held the Soviet bloc intact. It was the rationale by which Eastern European leaders oppressed their people, confident that the Soviet army would help if things got out of hand . . . without it, [there] was nothing more than an empire waiting to collapse.

Source: P. Zelikow and C. Rice, *Germany unified and Europe transformed. A study in statecraft*, Cambridge, Mass., 1997, pp. 37–38

7.5 A British historian appraises *Ostpolitik* and the events of 1990 in Germany

The Federal Republic succeeded in . . . establish[ing] a good relationship with the 'Eastern leading power' while at the same time retaining the protection and support of the leading Western power. The achievement . . . is clearly reflected in an internal memorandum drafted by the Bogomolov Institute in Moscow for one of Gorbachev's key foreign-policy advisers, Georgi Shaknazarov, in January 1990. 'In principle,' said this memorandum, 'the reunification of Germany does not contradict the interests of the Soviet Union. A military threat is not very likely, if one considers the radical fracture in the consciousness of the German nation that occurred with the national catastrophe of the past war. In the economic sphere, the Soviet Union can obtain tremendous gains from co-operation and interaction with Germany.'

. . . Forty-five years after the end of the war, Germany (West) had convinced key Soviet policymakers that it was no longer a threat, and that it was the Soviet Union's most promising and important economic partner in the West . . . Gorbachev and Kohl were the first Soviet and German leaders since 1945 not to have experienced the war as adults . . . But the contribution of conscious German policy is nonetheless very significant.

Source: T. Garton Ash, *In Europe's name: Germany and the divided continent*, London, 1994, pp. 364–65

Document case-study questions

1 Explain the terms 'the Brezhnev Doctrine' in document 7.2 and 'beyond containment' in document 7.3.

2 What do documents 7.1, 7.3 and 7.4 tell us about the role of ideas in US and Soviet Cold War policies?

3 What does the evidence in documents 7.2, 7.4 and 7.5 reveal about the US strategy outlined in document 7.3?

4 To what extent do these extracts support the view that the end of the Cold War was accompanied by a shift in the historical parallels through which international relations were understood by participants?

5 Using the documents and your wider knowledge, assess the view that by the end of 1989 the Cold War had ended.

Notes and references

1 Z. Brzezinski, 'What future for Soviet power?', *Encounter*, vol. XXIV, no. 3 (1970). One example of many appraisals of the stability of the Cold War system is A. DePorte, *Europe between the superpowers: the enduring balance*, 2nd edn, New Haven, 1986, pp. xi, xiii, with the preface from the 1979 edition, which contains the ideas summarised above. P. Zelikow and C. Rice, *Germany unified and Europe transformed. A study in statecraft*, Cambridge, Mass., 1997, pp. 34–35, stress that Germans from Kohl and Honecker downwards were taken by surprise by the events of 1989–90.

2 The quid pro quo for withdrawal on Germany's timetable at the time of reunification was massive German subsidy, most of which covered the costs of building enough housing for the 300,000 plus troops who had been stationed in the DDR.

3 R. Kapuczinski, *Imperium*, tr. K. Glowczewska, London, 1994, relates his journalistic travels around the USSR.

4 G. Shultz, *Turmoil and triumph*, New York, 1993, gives a full account of the Reagan administration's approaches. D. Oberdorfer, *From the Cold War to a new era: the United States and the Soviet Union, 1983–1991*, 2nd edn, Baltimore, 1998. See also G. Bush and B. Scowcroft, *A world transformed*, New York, 1998, pp. 37–56; and R. Hutchings, *American diplomacy and the end of the Cold War*, Baltimore, 1997, pp. 6–47 for analysis of 'beyond containment'.

5 Oberdorfer, *Cold War to new era*, p. 299; M. Beschloss and S. Talbott, *At the highest levels: the inside story of the end of the Cold War*, London, 1993, p. 9.

6 T. Blanton, 'When did the Cold War end?', *CWIHP Bulletin*, no. 10 (1998), pp. 184–88.

7 Quoted in Hutchings, *American diplomacy*, pp. 263–64.

8 A. Dobrynin, *In confidence. Moscow's ambassador to America's six Cold War presidents*, New York, 1995, pp. 596–615; Oberdorfer, *Cold War to new era*, pp. 127–57, 186–206, 266–68; also H. Adomeit, *Imperial overstretch: Germany in Soviet policy from Stalin to Gorbachev: an analysis based on new archival evidence, memoirs and interviews*, Baden-Baden, 1998, pp. 226–27; and M. S. Gorbachev, *Memoirs*, London, 1995, ch. 18.

9 Shultz, *Turmoil and triumph*, pp. 586–87. 891–93, describes a 'classroom in the Kremlin'. R. Gates, *From the shadows: the ultimate insider's story of five presidents and how they won the Cold War*, New York, 1996, pp. 184–90, 289–92.

10 T. Garton Ash, *In Europe's name: Germany and the divided continent*, London, 1994, pp. 156 ff; Adomeit, *Imperial overstretch*, pp. 220–31, 237–38, 539–58; and Zelikow and Rice, *Germany unified*, pp. 6–7.

11 Oberdorfer, *Cold War to new era*, p. 310.

12 A. Chernyaev, *My six years with Gorbachev*, tr. and ed. R. English and E. Tucker, University Park, Pa., 2000, pp. 26, 90.

13 Chernyaev, *My six years*, pp. 44–45 and *passim*; see also Dobrynin, *In confidence*, p. 581, who dates the new political thinking to Gromyko's departure.

14 S. Mendelson, *Changing course: ideas, politics and the Soviet withdrawal from Afghanistan*, Princeton, 1998, pp. 73–87.

15 Chernyaev, *My six years*, p. 59.

16 Oberdorfer, *Cold War to new era*, pp. 158–65. See also Dobrynin, *In confidence*, pp. 606–08, 621–33.

17 Chernyaev, *My six years*, pp. 148–50.

18 This account draws heavily on Mendelson, *Changing course*.

19 D. Paszyn, *The Soviet attitude to social and political change in Latin America, 1979–1990*, London, 2000, pp. 71–72.

20 Mendelson, *Changing course*, pp. 113–23.

21 Oberdorfer, *Cold War to new era*, pp. 289–90, 405–10, 454–58; Beschloss and Talbott, *At the highest levels*, pp. 112–19, 144–47, 402–07.

22 Hutchings, *American diplomacy*, p. 36.

23 F. Fejtö, *La fin des démocraties populaires*, Paris, 1997, stresses the national issue.

24 T. Garton Ash, 'Refolution in Hungary and Poland', *New York Review of Books*, 18 August 1989, coined the phrase to describe rapid change that was more than reform, but too orderly to be revolution.

25 I. P Aboimov's diary, 25 December 1989: conversation with US Ambassador J. Matlock, 24 December 1989, *CWIHP Bulletin*, no. 10 (1998), pp. 189–91.

26 Zelikow and Rice, *Germany unified*, pp. 206–12.

27 Especially during a meeting with President Von Weizsäcker of the FRG, see Chernyaev, *My six years*, pp. 114–16.

28 Zelikow and Rice, *Germany unified*, pp. 245, 145.

29 Zelikow and Rice, *Germany unified*, p. ix, 1997 edn. The references to the other dates in this paragraph are all from this book.

30 Best accounts are Garton Ash, *In Europe's name*, and Zelikow and Rice, *Germany unified*.

31 The image of the clock was used to symbolise the world's proximity to nuclear disaster, with midnight as Armageddon. It had first appeared on the *Bulletin*'s cover in 1947 set at 7 minutes to midnight, reached 2 minutes to midnight in 1953 and 3 minutes to in 1984. It was changed to 17 minutes to in 1991. See http://www.bullatomsci.org/clock/doomsdayclock.html

Conclusion

The Cold War was a confrontation like none before it. From it major powers derived lessons that continue to affect their behaviour. US deployments overseas continue to be shaped by a 'Vietnam syndrome' that insists on limited objectives, massive use of air power and the use of ground forces only for a brief time or when victory is assured. Russian nationalism continues to produce governments wary of NATO and resistant to the idea of the Baltic states joining that organisation. One lesson of 1919 and 1945 – that defeated enemies should be treated gently and brought into the fold of an interdependent, democratic community of nations – was reinforced. In strikingly Wilsonian tones, President Bush labelled the post Cold War world a 'New World Order'.

There are, however, still places where remnants of the Cold War can be found and where confrontation continues. In the 1990s relations between the USA and Cuba worsened, thanks in part to US politics, in part to Castro's recalcitrance despite being deprived of his backers, and in part to the fact that the confrontation had never been solely the result of the Cold War. Cold War legacies can also be seen in the continued stand-off with Saddam Hussein and intervention in the wars of the former Yugoslavia. On the Asian Pacific Rim crises over Taiwan and tensions in Korea have served as reminders that not all Cold War flashpoints disappeared with the Berlin Wall. Local nationalisms, alliance politics, the internal politics of great and small powers and economic pressures have all contributed to the eventful international relations of the post Cold War world.

This tells us something about the Cold War. Those who predict clashes of cultures in which the West will go marching on together against the rest of the world appear at times to approach nostalgia for the Cold War. They are missing the point that power rivalries alone have not resulted in a new Cold War with new configurations.

The Cold War was an agglomeration of circumstances that will not be easily repeated. It can only be partly explained by geopolitics. Ideology underlay Cold War rivalry and the key geopolitical truth of the Cold War was that the two superpowers were competing for global influence as well as power. Added to this was the fact that the economic competition between the two systems ran along the same lines as their military and ideological fault lines. Since 1990 the rivalries of the world do not fit so neatly into patterns. The confrontation in eastern-central Europe, the nuclear arms race, proxy wars in the developing world and diplomatic rivalry that made up the Cold War did.

In addition, the Cold War was characterised by two connected forces that operated from the mid 1940s to the late 1980s. The first was the interaction of domestic politics and foreign affairs. Choices of friends and enemies were profoundly affected by, and affected, domestic political preferences. This was more than bureaucratic politics and partisan or factional fighting. De-Stalinisation, détente, leanings to one side or the other and choices about weapons systems or foreign aid were all issues that had both domestic and foreign repercussions. The Cold War principle that one's enemy's enemy was necessarily a friend (or their friend one's enemy) spilled into domestic politics of subversion and countersubversion. The fact of such an ideological/economic/political matrix of interaction between foreign and domestic politics was not what made the Cold War unique – the particular ways in which interaction took place did.

The second characteristic derived from a lack of knowledge that shaped Cold War mentalities and convinced leaders on all sides that worst-case scenarios were safest. The Cold War developed in circumstances where knowledge of the other side was either almost non-existent or where it was filtered through ideological and personal preconceptions that held past conduct as the seemingly best guide to future behaviour. Memories of the last war shaped leaders' efforts to avoid the next one. The nuclear warfare of August 1945 and subsequent testing of bigger weapons reinforced that tendency. The problem was that, on all sides, the memory of how the last war came about was strongly coloured by the perceived lesson that weakness had encouraged aggressors. When these combined with older memories (such as Chinese resentment of imperialism, Soviet isolation and civil war, Versailles, Rapallo or American isolationism) the product was the prescription of toughness if new disasters were to be avoided.

The end of the Cold War has taught new lessons and displaced some old ones. Shevardnadze and Chernyaev, like Bush and Kohl, belonged to the 'post-Churchill' world. Munich still holds terrors for democratic statesmen, but Rapallo does not.[1] New paradigms, based on Afghanistan or NATO's Cold War success or the more positive re-evaluation of the Helsinki Accords after the events of 1988–91, have emerged. Dominoes did fall in a spectacular row. They did so in eastern Europe and carried a reflux all the way to the collapse of a superpower. This occurred once the will to prevent the fall of the whole line was no longer present.

It is in this historical and experiential locus of decision making that the uniqueness of the Cold War as a phase in international history lies. The rivals sought to control history because history itself was such a potent force in moulding their behaviour. It is, perhaps, unlikely that future confrontations will be quite so shaped by the forces of the past.

As to the significance of the Cold War, much depends upon perspective. It was the first confrontation in which the major powers had the ability to destroy life on earth. The arms race lends the confrontation a significance greater than any other long-running power struggle. It could be said that it is not yet over and will not be until communist rule ends in Cuba, North Korea and China. From such an ideological viewpoint, the confrontation began in 1917 and survives the USSR. Alternatively, the advent of a single superpower world around 1990–91 may have marked the end of the Cold War, whose roots should then be sought in the geopolitical circumstances of the end of the Second World War. The alignment of Bush and Kohl against Mitterand, Thatcher, Mazowiecki and Gorbachev over German affairs in 1990 supports this view. So does Gorbachev's acknowledgement that Germany reunified and in NATO might be better for Russia than Germany reunified and neutral. It could also be argued that the Cold War was a European confrontation that became globalised. Once the threat to self-determination that Britain and the USA saw in Soviet domination of eastern Europe collapsed in 1989, the Cold War ended. If the Cold War was essentially a contest of rival economies, then it ended when the Soviet system bankrupted itself and became dependent on trade, loans and, later, aid from its rivals.

Any or none of these explanations may be satisfactory. The long-term significance of the Cold War will surely be derived from the circumstances of the observer's day. As new archival material emerges we may come to agree on its course and causes. What we select as important, however, will be influenced by the times in which we write. It may be better to offer possible scenarios than to try to produce a single, definitive answer about the Cold War's significance.

If the globalisation of Western capitalist democratic values continues to gain ground, Russia becomes part of it, and China and the communist remnants succumb to it, the Cold War may come to be seen as a significant stage in a long struggle of these values with successive ideological rivals. By 1900 (or soon after) mercantilism and absolutism had largely succumbed, militarism and fascism did so in the first half of the twentieth century and Soviet communism's challenge was seen off between 1945 and 1991. If, on the other hand, a nominally communist China and/or a resurgent nationalist Russia challenge these values and US hegemony, the Cold War may come to be seen as the first Cold War and part of an ongoing struggle lasting into the twenty-first century.

The fate of the movement for European union and the economic relations between the USA and its Cold War allies will also colour judgements on what was most important about the period. Continued warfare in Europe will strengthen the views of those who argue that the Cold War was actually a 'long peace' and a period of unique stability and absence of conflict between the great powers. A US retreat into isolationism might breed perspectives on the Cold War that stress elements of US unilateralism, its efforts to dominate Europe and Japan, and downplay the solidity and solidarity of NATO or its other commitments or the harshness of the post-1991 settlement.

Zhou Enlai's comment on the significance of the French Revolution – that it was too early to tell – also applies to the Cold War. This is not, however, to despair of understanding it better or of discerning the main patterns and turning points that shaped the Cold War as they, in turn, shaped the world in which we live.

Notes and references

1 Rapallo briefly re-entered French thinking during debates over German reunification; see W. R. Smyser, *From Yalta to Berlin: the Cold War struggle over Germany*, New York, 1999, pp. 355, 394, 405.

Select bibliography

The literature on the Cold War is enormous and constantly growing. This bibliography, therefore, only skims the surface of what is available. Some work defies easy categorisation. For example, C. M. Andrew's work covers the intelligence communities of the USSR, Britain and the USA as well as reproducing material from Soviet sources.

General works

The best of the wide range of international histories and overviews include R. Crockatt, *The fifty years war*, London, 1995; and M. Walker, *The Cold War*, London, 1993. W. Lafeber, *America, Russia and the Cold War*, 8th edn, London, 1997, places the bipolar relationship in a broad context. Recent scholarship is assessed in O. A. Westad, 'The new international history of the Cold War', *Diplomatic History*, vol. 24 (2000). D. Reynolds, *One world divisible: a global history since 1945*, London, 1999; and P. Calvocoressi, *World politics since 1945*, 7th edn, London, 1996, cover much wider topics than the Cold War. J. Isaacs and T. Downing, *Cold War*, London, 1998, accompanied the BBC/Turner television series and has superb images. The website http://www.cnn.com/SPECIALS/cold.war/ has much good material.

Sources

The Cold War International History Project makes massive amounts of material available in English through a website (http://www.cwihp.si.edu), bulletins and working papers. The US official record, the *Foreign Relations of the USA* series, has now reached the Johnson years and is an invaluable resource. Recent volumes are available on the web at http://www.state.gov/www/about_state/history/frusonline.html.

M. Hunt (ed.), *Crises in U.S. foreign policy: an international history reader*, New Haven, 1996, contains material from various countries. There are excellent collections on the Cuban Missile Crisis (P. Kornbluh and L. Chang (eds.), *The Cuban Missile Crisis, 1962: a National Security Archive documents reader*, New York, 1992) and the Prague Spring (J. Navratil et al (eds.), *The Prague Spring of 1968*, Budapest, 1998).

Memoirs are abundant. Some noteworthy examples in English include those by Dean Acheson, Georgi Arbatov, George Ball, Zbigniew Brzezinski, McGeorge Bundy, Anatoly Chernyaev, Anatoly Dobrynin, Alexander Dubček, Robert Gates, Mikhail Gorbachev, Andrei Gromyko, Nikita Khrushchev, Henry Kissinger, Robert McNamara and George Shultz.

Origins and the early Cold War

A number of works synthesise material from all sides on the period before 1960. Among the best are: J. L. Gaddis, *We now know. Rethinking Cold War history*, Oxford, 1997; V. Zubok and C. Pleshakov, *Inside the Kremlin's Cold War. From Stalin to Khrushchev*, Cambridge, Mass., 1996; and V. Mastny, *The Cold War and Soviet insecurity. The Stalin years*, Oxford, 1996; F. Gori and S. Pons (eds.), *The Soviet Union and Europe in the Cold War, 1943–53*, London, 1996; and D. S. Painter and M. Leffler (eds.), *Origins of the Cold War. An international history*, London, 1994, cast light on a wide range of issues. A good synthesis and provocative interpretation is M. Trachtenberg, *A constructed peace. The making of a European settlement, 1945–1963*, Princeton, 1999. The Chinese dimension, especially the relationship with the USSR, is well covered by O. E. Westad (ed.), *Brothers in arms: the rise and fall of the Sino-Soviet Alliance, 1945–1963*, Stanford, 1998. W. Stueck, *The Korean War: an international history*, Princeton, 1995, pp. 44–50; and S. Goncharov, J. W. Lewis and Xue Litai, *Uncertain partners: Stalin, Mao, and the Korean War*, Stanford, 1993, deal with the Korean War. R. H. Immerman (ed.), *John Foster Dulles and the diplomacy of the Cold War*, Princeton, 1990, is good on US diplomacy of the 1950s.

Détente and confrontation

The best treatment of the superpowers in the early 1960s is M. Beschloss, *The crisis years: Kennedy and Khrushchev, 1960–1963*, New York, 1991. L. Freedman, *Kennedy's Wars. Berlin, Cuba, Laos and Vietnam*, London, 2000, is now definitive. On the Cuban Missile Crisis, T. Naftali and A. Fursenko, *'One hell of a gamble': the secret history of the Cuban Missile Crisis*, London, 1997, is the best recent synthesis. R. Ned Lebow and J. G. Stein, *We all lost the Cold War*, Princeton, 1994, is stimulating on that episode and on the Yom Kippur War of 1973. G. H. Chang, *Friends and enemies. The United States, China and the Soviet Union, 1948–1972*, Stanford, 1990, remains the standard work on its topic. P. Lowe (ed.), *The Vietnam War*, Manchester, 1998, gives access to a larger literature and serves as a good introduction. R. L. Garthoff, *Détente and confrontation: American–Soviet relations from Nixon to Reagan*, Washington, DC, revised edn, 1994, is the standard, and compendious, work on détente.

The end of the Cold War

R. Garthoff, *The great transition: American–Soviet relations and the end of the Cold War*, Washington, DC, 1994, carries on the story where his previous volume left off. There are some excellent treatments of recent events that give good access to the final years of the Cold War, most notably D. Oberdorfer, *From the Cold War to a new era: the United States and the Soviet Union, 1983–1991*, Baltimore, 1998. M. R. Beschloss and S. Talbott, *At the highest levels: the inside story of the end of the Cold War*, London, 1993, is also full and well informed. I. Clark, *The post-Cold War order. The spoils of peace*, Oxford, 2001, treats the end of the Cold War as a starting point for its story. Noteworthy participant accounts not mentioned above are G. Bush and B. Scowcroft, *A world transformed*, New York, 1998; C. Rice and P. Zelikow, *Germany unified and Europe transformed: a study in statecraft*, Cambridge, Mass., 1997; and R. Hutchings, *American diplomacy and the end of the Cold War*, Baltimore, 1997. M. Hogan (ed.), *The end of the Cold War. Its meaning and implications*, Cambridge, 1992, ranges more widely than the title might suggest. A. Chernyaev, *My six years with Gorbachev*, tr. and ed. R. English and E. Tucker, University Park, Pa., 2000, is an excellent insider's account of the Gorbachev period.

Single countries or relationships

The list in this section could cover a massive number of titles, but there are some especially useful books on a particular country or relationship over a long period. J. Mann, *Saving face: a history of America's curious relationship with China, from Nixon to Clinton*, New York, 2000; and R. Foot, *The practice of power, U.S. relations with China since 1949*, Oxford, 1995, cover China's relations with the USA. R. Craig Nation, *Black earth, Red star. A history of Soviet security policy, 1917–1991*, London, 1992; and W. I. Cohen, *America in the age of Soviet power*, Cambridge, 1993, deal with the superpowers in an accessible way. The crucial issue of Germany's fate is widely discussed. See W. R. Smyser, *From Yalta to Berlin: the Cold War struggle over Germany*, New York, 1999; T. Garton Ash, *In Europe's name: Germany and the divided continent*, London, 1993; and H. Adomeit, *Imperial overstretch: Germany in Soviet policy from Stalin to Gorbachev*, Baden-Baden, 1998. S. Greenwood, *Britain and the Cold War, 1945–1991*, London, 2000, is especially strong on the 1940s and 1950s. W. I. Hitchcock, *France restored: Cold War diplomacy and the quest for leadership in Europe, 1944–1954*, Chapel Hill, 1998; and M. Vaïsse, P. Mélandri and F. Bozo (eds.), *La France et L'Otan, 1949–1996*, Paris, 1996, deal with different aspects of French policy. The latter contains a number of essays in English. The relationship between the superpowers and the developing world is covered in a large literature. The best single volume on the USSR is M. Light (ed.), *Troubled friendships. Moscow's third world ventures*, London, 1993. S. Mendelson, *Changing course: ideas, politics and the Soviet withdrawal from Afghanistan*, Princeton, 1998, covers 1979 to 1989. Various books cover US policies. Z. Karabell, *Architects of intervention, the United States, the third world and the Cold War, 1946–1962*, Baton Rouge, La., 1999, demonstrates a pattern of US-local interactions in many regions, On what some Americans termed their 'backyard', S. Rabe, *The most dangerous area in the world*, Chapel Hill, 1999, covers the Kennedy years, and W. L. Leogrande, *Our own backyard: the United States in Central America, 1977–1992*, Chapel Hill, 1998, deals with more recent times. A. Shlaim and Y. Sayigh (eds.), *The Cold War and the Middle East*, Oxford, Clarendon, 1997, is excellent on that region.

Index

SOLIHULL SIXTH FORM COLLEGE
THE LEARNING CENTRE